PURITAN PROTAGONIST

President Thomas Clap
of Yale College

The Institute of Early American History and Culture is sponsored jointly by the College of William and Mary and Colonial Williamsburg, Incorporated. Publication of this book has been assisted by a grant from the Lilly Endowment, Inc.

A Front VIEW of YALE-COLLEGE, and the COLLEGE CHAPEL, in New-Haven.

The descriptive text accompanying this print explains that "the present College Edifice, which is of brick, was built during the Presidency of the Rev. THOMAS CLAP, 1750, being 100 feet long, and 40 feet wide, three stories high, containing 32 chambers and 64 studies convenient for the reception of 100 students. The College-Chapel also built of brick, was erected 1761, being 50 feet and 40, with a steeple 125 feet high." Print by Daniel Bowen, June 1785. Courtesy of the Yale University Library.

Puritan Protagonist

President Thomas Clap
of Yale College

by Louis Leonard Tucker

PUBLISHED FOR THE

*Institute of Early American History and
Culture at Williamsburg, Virginia*

BY THE

University of North Carolina Press

CHAPEL HILL

Manufactured in the United States of America
VAN REES PRESS • NEW YORK

To my wife,
and to the memory of my mother.

PREFACE

IN the summer of 1955, while conducting research on Thomas Clap in the Sterling Memorial Library of Yale University, I succumbed to an impulse commonly felt by those who write biography—I decided to visit the gravesite of my subject. Clap's remains, like those of a large number of Yale divines of the eighteenth century, are now interred in the Grove Street Cemetery, adjoining the University; they were transferred there in 1797 from the New Haven Green. To assist visitors, the cemetery officials maintain a detailed wall map which locates the gravesites of the eminent men and provides a brief biographical sketch of each. Taking my bearings from this map, I walked to the designated point and discovered to my surprise that Clap's gravestone was nowhere to be seen. Upon checking with the visibly flustered officials, I learned that the map was in error, that Clap was actually buried in another part of the cemetery.

I was immediately struck by the symbolic propriety of the mistaken location. In the pantheon of American history, Thomas Clap rests with the Mathers, John Winthrop, John Cotton, and other stern heroes of Calvinism. In truth, he would have felt uncomfortable in their presence. He was of New England, he was Congregational, but he was not of the seventeenth century, either chronologically or ideologically.

While Clap's whitened bones lie in isolation in Grove Street Cemetery, memory of him has passed into limbo on the Yale campus. No visual reminder of him, in the form of a plaque or inscription on building, passageway, or portal, is to be found. Overtly, at least, the deeply rooted Yale tradition has no place for Thomas Clap, rector and first president of the college. Even more surprising and more curious is the fact that Clap's anonymity should extend beyond the limits of the Yale campus. Despite his transcendent importance in the cultural and religious life of colonial America, he is almost a total stranger to American history.

It is my hope that in disinterring Thomas Clap, I have not merely reburied him or put him to rest again with the wrong intellectual company. Both hazards exist because the paucity of Clap material scarcely allows his biographer to evoke his life in its full dimensions or to probe very far behind the dogmatic positions upon which he based his official career. There is, for example, no single massive body of Clap manuscripts. During the Revolutionary War, a troop of British soldiers sacked his daughter's home in New Haven and removed two large trunks, one of which contained Clap's scientific writings and correspondence. Later, they dumped the contents of the trunks into Long Island Sound. For that reason alone there will never be a definitive biography of Thomas Clap, for whom interest in science was an essential aspect of mind, but Clap's historical importance fully warrants a personal study so far as the material for it survives.

I have tried to illuminate the range of Clap's interests and the diversity of his career: minister, college administrator, Newtonian scientist, religious leader, and religious and political disputant. Because his life was indissolubly linked with Yale College after 1739, a considerable portion of this study deals with the history of that institution. It was not my intention, however, to write a genetic history of Yale College for the period 1740-66, although such a study is sorely needed. The fortunes of Yale are followed only insofar as they impinge upon the activities of Clap.

I owe thanks to many people for the opportunity here presented of examining Thomas Clap's career. Not all, of course, can be mentioned, but all who helped and who are here unnamed will know my debts to them for many courtesies and will, I hope, accept my gratitude. I cannot escape, however, and would not if I could, giving my thanks to:

My wife and son, Mark, for allowing me to slight my responsibilities as husband and father in order that this study could be brought to completion.

Professor Max Savelle of the University of Washington, my *pater academicus* and Friend, for developing in me an appreciation for history; for teaching me the difference between the good life and the Good Life.

The staff members of the following libraries and institutions for the many courtesies they extended to me in the course of my research: University of Washington Library; Dartmouth College Library; Essex Institute; Harvard University Library; Massachusetts Historical Society; Boston Public Library; Boston Athenaeum; American Antiquarian Society; Connecticut State Library; Connecticut Historical Society; Case Theological Institute; Yale University Library; New Haven Colony Historical Society; New York Public Library; New-York Historical Society; Historical Society of Pennsylvania; Haverford College Library; Library of Congress; College of William and Mary Library; Royal Society of London; Royal Society of Arts, London; Library of the Society for the Propagation of the Gospel in Foreign Parts, London; Congregational Library, London.

The staff of the Institute of Early American History and Culture, especially editors Frederick A. Hetzel (now with the University of Pittsburgh Press) and E. James Ferguson, both of whom understood the distinction between "midwife" and "meddler." I also acknowledge with gratitude the critical suggestions offered by my former colleagues at the Institute, Lawrence W. Towner and James M. Smith, and the typing assistance rendered by Mrs. Patricia Blatt. To the director of the Institute, Lester J. Cappon, I am deeply grateful for his perceptive editorial comments and for many additional favors, all of which contributed to hastening the completion of this study.

The American Philosophical Society for providing a grant which permitted me to conduct research in Great Britain in the summer of 1959.

The editors of *The Historian, The Yale University Library Gazette, The William and Mary Quarterly,* and *ISIS* for permission to reprint materials which had been published earlier in article form.

Frank Geissler of Willimantic (Connecticut) State College for the opportunity to learn.

TABLE OF CONTENTS

INTRODUCTION

INSTALLING a rector at Yale College was from the beginning not an occasion to inspire festivity. And since the calamitous event of 1722, when Rector Timothy Cutler unceremoniously cut his moorings from the established Congregational Church and sailed off to London to take Holy Orders in the Church of England,[1] the ceremony of installation had become funereal. From its establishment in 1701 Yale had been a citadel of Congregationalism.[2] It had been inspired by Congregationalists, founded by Congregationalists, instructed by Congregationalists, and administered by Congregationalists. Now, on the second day of April 1740, in the library of the old wooden structure known as "Yale College," the school's ten trustees were assembled, all Congregational ministers, and as grave in countenance as a consistory of cardinals about to select a pope. Their collective gaze was fixed upon a short, barrel-chested Congregational minister of thirty-six years. He was the man they had selected for the rectorship following the resignation of Elisha Williams in October 1739.[3] It was now their job to con-

1. In addition to Cutler, Daniel Brown (sometimes "Browne"), who was the sole tutor at Yale, and five prominent Congregational ministers were also involved in the "Great Apostasy." The events may be followed in the documents contained in Francis L. Hawks and William S. Perry, eds., *Documentary History of the Protestant Episcopal Church in the United States of America Containing Numerous Hitherto Unpublished Documents Concerning The Church in Connecticut* (New York, 1863), I, 62-80 (hereafter cited as Hawks and Perry, eds., *Documentary History of Episcopal Church*).

2. On the early history of Yale, see Edwin Oviatt, *The Beginnings of Yale, 1701-1726* (New Haven, 1916).

3. Yale Corporation Records, I, 65, typed copy in Secretary's Office, Yale University.

firm the orthodoxy of the candidate prior to his formal induction into office. They entered upon their task with the knowledge that Yale College—and Connecticut Congregationalism—could ill afford another Cutler debacle. Their mood was fiercely sober.

The examination was preceded by the traditional act (since the Cutler defection) of having the candidate give his consent to the accepted Confession of Faith, which was patterned closely upon the Westminster Confession of Faith, and to the rules of church discipline outlined in the Saybrook Platform, the ecclesiastical constitution of Connecticut.[4] Following this affirmation, the trustees directed searching questions to the candidate on key doctrinal issues.[5] Finally, the ordeal was at an end. The examination seemed to confirm what the vigilant trustees had been led to believe by the candidate's record and by the supporting statements of those who had recommended him for the position: he was a man of irreproachable orthodoxy. Under his rectorship there was little question that Yale College would remain "a fountain of orthodoxy." The formal ceremony of installation could now take place.

Leaving the library, which was located on the second floor, the trustees and candidate slowly descended the stairs and made their processional entry into the large meeting hall. In this well-worn room, which served as classroom, dining hall, and auditorium, the Yale student body was seated on hard benches. Some eighty strong, these were the young representatives of the social elite (and near-

4. The significance of the Saybrook Platform lay in its wide departure from the polity of the Cambridge Platform (1648). The polity of the Saybrook Platform was closely modeled after the polity provisions of the Matherian Massachusetts Proposals of 1705, which stressed group authority. The power to regulate individual churches was vested in "consociations," which were organized on a county-by-county basis. The power to police ministers was granted to "associations" of ministers organized in a similar fashion. A General Association, composed of delegates from the county associations, was at the apex of the structure and exercised an advisory superintendency over churches and ministers alike. The new system of polity evidenced the infiltration of Presbyterian ideas into the traditional system of Barrowe, Browne, Ames, Preston, *et al.* The Saybrook Platform is printed in Benjamin Trumbull, *A Complete History of Connecticut, Civil and Ecclesiastical, From the Emigration of Its First Planters, From England, in the Year 1630, to the Year 1764; and to the Close of the Indian Wars* (New London, 1898), I, 410-14 (hereafter cited as Trumbull, *History of Connecticut*).

5. Thomas Clap, *The Annals or History of Yale College ... 1700-1766* (New Haven, 1766), 40-41 (hereafter cited as Clap, *Annals of Yale*). Unfortunately, there is no evidence as to the exact questions that were asked.

elite) of Connecticut and neighboring provinces of New England.[6]
Also in attendance was the usual cluster of dignitaries, including
alumni of the college and prominent magistrates and ministers.
The proceedings began with a prayer by the Reverend Samuel
Whitman, a trustee and the moderator for the ceremony of installation. A congratulatory student oration followed. The high point
of the day was now at hand. With the rectorial candidate standing
in full view of the assemblage, the Reverend Mr. Whitman solemnly
intoned the Latin phrases which committed the instruction of the
college to him. The newly appointed rector, the fourth to hold
the position, concluded the ceremony with a Latin oration appropriate for the occasion. As reported in the *Boston Weekly News-
Letter*, the installation was "performed with much Decency and
good Order, and to the universal Satisfaction of the Students, as
well as to the Joy of all By-Standers." [7]

It would be revealing to know what thoughts passed through the
minds of the students as they listened to the first address of the man
who would direct their education and order their personal lives. As
for the trustees, if they were imbued with optimism about the
future of the college, it was an optimism based upon the knowledge
that Rector Thomas Clap, past minister of the Windham (Connecticut) First Church, had already demonstrated his competence in the
vital areas of discipline and learning; and, equally important, he
had established his orthodoxy beyond a measure of doubt. The
students would have to await the future in order to draw an estimate of the stranger who stood before them. The trustees needed
only to look to the past. They knew the minister's record. They
could draw comfort and assurance from it.

6. This is not to say that colonial Yale was a "rich man's" school. For the most
part, the boys represented the Standing Order of the colony. But there is a sharp
distinction to be made between the "First Gentlemen" of Connecticut and the
"First Gentlemen" of, for example, Virginia.

7. Apr. 24, 1740.

PURITAN PROTAGONIST

*President Thomas Clap
of Yale College*

Chapter One

CAST IN THE PURITAN MOLD

W HAT was once said of the elder Pitt could rightfully be said of Thomas Clap: "He never grew—he was cast." The boy was the man in miniature. Born on June 26, 1703,[1] in the rustic fishing village of Scituate, Massachusetts, near the very heart of Puritan New England, Clap was molded in the same cultural crucible that produced such doctrinaires as Cotton Mather, Thomas Prince, and Mather Byles. His was not a dissenting tradition. If he thought, acted, and lived by rule, as was later said of him by a close friend, it was because he had been thoroughly conditioned to conformity. "Amend thy Hand by diligence and Praise shall be your Recompense," Clap wrote in later years in the margin of one of his manuscripts. It was an obvious bit of doodling. But the little record that remains of his early life strongly suggests that this Biblical maxim was indelibly stamped upon his mind from infancy. Owe obedience to God. Be diligent in your duties. Learn what you are told to learn. Deviate not one whit from the course laid out for you. And praise, meaning praise of God, meaning salvation in the ultimate sense, would be the eternal reward. It was a familiar

1. *Vital Records of Scituate Massachusetts to the Year 1850*, 1 (Boston, 1909), 75, lists Clap's birthdate as June 20, 1703. Clap's records designate June 26. See also Franklin Dexter, ed., *Extracts From the Itineraries and Other Miscellanies of Ezra Stiles* (New Haven, 1916), 283 (hereafter cited as Dexter, ed., *Stiles's Itineraries*).

story in New Zion, and Clap's character was a showpiece of sound
New England breeding. From birth he walked the common way.
Potent family and environmental influences steered him in the
direction of the ministry, into a lifetime of service as an agent of
Puritanism.

His future profession was determined even before his birth, not
an unusual state of affairs for the time. As tradition has it, Clap's
father decreed that should the unborn child be male, the lad would
be tithed to the ministry, the highest of all "callings" by Puritan
standards.[2] The father would thereby make a great contribution to
the church; the child, in turn, would perpetuate the family tradition of dedicated service to the cause of Puritanism.[3] Since the
arrival of Thomas Clap's great-grandfather and namesake in the
New World, three generations of the family had stood high among
the saints. The first Thomas Clap had left Dorchester, England, in
1633 to join the migration to Massachusetts and, after shuttling
between settlements of the Bay area for seven years, decided to
plant ancestral roots in Scituate. Here, he soon earned a stature
in the community which merited his selection as a deacon in the
Congregational Church. The deacon's official function was primarily that of an assistant to the minister. He received the offerings
and gifts to the church, maintained church records, and assisted
the minister in other administrative functions. Like the minister,
he had to be beyond reproach in his personal behavior, a model of
moral purity, and, as expressed in the words of the Cambridge
Platform, "grave, not double tongued, not given to[o] much to
wine, not given to filthy lucre." [4] How well Clap performed his

2. Clap himself wrote in later years that he "chose the work of the Ministry (which
I was designed for by my Parents) for this End because I apprehended that in it I
should have the best Opportunity of enjoying Communion with God and promoting
the Salvation of my own Soul." Memoirs of Some Remarkable Occurrances of Divine
Providence Towards Me in the Course of my Life, Together With Some Reflections
and Observations Upon Them, 2, Yale Manuscripts, Sterling Memorial Library, Yale
University (hereafter cited as Clap, Memoirs, Yale MS. Some of Clap's entries are
undated; in these instances the page citation will be given).

3. For Clap's ancestral background, see: Ebenezer Clapp, *The Clapp Memorial.
Record of the Clapp Family in America, Containing Sketches of the Original Six
Emigrants, and a Genealogy of Their Descendants Bearing the Name* (Boston, 1876),
105-6; Harvey Pratt, *The Early Planters of Scituate* (Scituate, 1929), 109-10, 126,
128, 137.

4. Williston Walker, ed., *The Creeds and Platforms of Congregationalism*
(N. Y., 1893), 213.

duties is not known, but he was sufficiently at home in the situation to indulge in the old New England propensity to accuse the local minister of deviation from accepted practice.

In this case the accusation was well founded. The Reverend Charles Chauncy, already noted for his independence of thought in matters ecclesiastical, had concluded that the true scriptural form of baptism called for total immersion. Some of his parishioners, including Deacon Clap, complained that "dipping," while lawful, was "in this could countrie not so conveniente." [5] Chauncy drove the wedge of dissension more deeply into the congregation by announcing his intention to administer the Lord's Supper at a different time than in the past. It was more the fact that change was proposed rather than any cavil on religious grounds that prompted the First Church parishioners to oppose this plan. Chauncy, a congenital nonconformist who had left England after crossing theological swords with Archbishop Laud, the *bête noire* of Puritanism, was determined to have his way. Discord was the inevitable outcome. Deacon Clap's "conservatives" stood against the Reverend Mr. Chauncy's "liberals," and, in the tradition of the time, the whole town became obsessed with the struggle. The verbal battle raged throughout Chauncy's thirteen-year ministry, during which Scituate was a "scene of constant agitation." The upshot was a division of the church, the Clap group separating and establishing a Second Church.[6] Chauncy subsequently left Scituate to occupy the presidency of Harvard. Offered the position on the condition that he keep his innovating thoughts on baptism to himself, Chauncy no doubt reflected, as Samuel Eliot Morison writes, "that college presidents had no occasion to administer baptismal rites, and [therefore] accepted." [7]

Left in possession of the ground, Thomas Clap prevailed at Scituate, and passed on the status he had earned to his descendants. His son and grandson did not make a heavy mark on New England

5. William T. Davis, ed., *Bradford's History of Plymouth Plantation, 1606-1646* (N. Y., 1908), 362-63.

6. The dispute is discussed in Samuel Deane, *The History of Scituate* (Boston, 1831), 59-89; *Document of the Pilgrim Conference of Churches Containing an Historical Sketch of the First Trinitarian Congregational Church of Christ in Scituate, Massachusetts* (Boston, 1853), 26-28.

7. Morison, *Three Centuries of Harvard, 1636-1936* (Cambridge, Mass., 1937), 37.

religious history, but they performed yeoman service to church
and state, becoming weighty and influential figures in the town.
Men of stringent piety, they served as deacons in the church and
held various civil offices from constable to selectman. Stephen Clap,
the father of the future president of Yale, was especially active in
local political and religious affairs and achieved some prominence
in the colony. By serving as a representative to the General Court
and as a lieutenant in the Bay militia forces, he enhanced the
social prestige of the family. Because of his solid record as a religious and secular leader, this durable Puritan, who lived to the
ripe old age of eighty-six, has been called "the most distinguished
of his father's family." [8]

It was Stephen Clap's deep-seated desire that his son render high
service to the Puritan cause, and having marked him for the ministry, he began laying the groundwork for Thomas's future. The
first step was baptism, which would admit his son to Christian
membership and signify that he had achieved divinely appointed
fellowship in a covenanted church. At the age of thirteen months,
Thomas was baptized in the Second Church,[9] the church that his
great-grandfather had helped to establish, and from the time he
was old enough to listen, the boy was indoctrinated in the moral
precepts of Calvinistic Puritanism. He recalled in later years that
"my Honoured Parents Stephen and Temperance Clap began early
to instruct me in the Principles of Religion and to exhort me to
the practice of it," adding piously, "which . . . I hope had a good
Effect upon me." [10] The parents' efforts to impress him with the
transcendent importance of religion proved eminently successful.
Before he was "7 or 8 years old," he had developed the Puritan
trait of introspection and, on occasion, prayed to God "in Secret." [11]
This intensive indoctrination was the source of his later zeal in
propounding and defending Westminster Calvinism. When as a
mature man he expounded on the power of God or the depravity
of man, he spoke with all the assurance derived from the sanction

8. Clapp, *Record of Clapp Family in America*, 114.

9. "Records of Second Church of Scituate," *New England Historical and Gene-
alogical Register*, 58 (1904), 85. Clap's parents were admitted to full communion in
this church in 1706. *Ibid.*, 57 (1903), 324.

10. Clap, Memoirs, 1, Yale MS.

11. *Ibid.*

of parental authority. Doctrines concerning the divinity of Christ, Christ's atonement and satisfaction, the necessity of divine grace for salvation, and the eternity of future punishments were the gruel upon which he had been reared.

Clap's parents doubtless accepted the current belief that children entered the world in a condition of ignorance and sinfulness. Anne Bradstreet, Puritan poetess of the seventeenth century, grimly expressed the contemporary concept of the inherent depravity of youth:

> Stained from birth with Adams
>   sinful fact,
> Thence I began to sin as soon as act:
> A perverse will, a love to what's
>   forbid,
> A serpent's sting in pleasing force
>   lay hid:
> A lying tongue as soon as it
>   could speak,
> And fifth commandments do
>   daily break.[12]

The situation was not altogether hopeless—there were, of course, means by which the inherently evil nature of a Puritan youth could be ameliorated. If parents were diligent in the application of religious instruction and discipline, and if they provided for a conventional education, there was every hope that a child could be trained to master the earthly passions that darkened his vision.[13]

In the case of a boy destined for the ministry, education had a double function: a Puritan minister had to be learned as well as pious. Grace alone did not make a preacher. To the Puritans, religion was a subtle, highly intellectualized body of thought. There was to be no preaching "out of the head," as was practiced by the Quakers. Theological interpretation required the exercise of "right reason" and a genuine understanding of the principles of logic. A minister must be trained in scriptures from the original Hebrew and be able to read the basic writings of Christianity, including those of the early church fathers, the scholastic philoso-

12. John Ellis, ed., *The Works of Anne Bradstreet*... (Charlestown, 1867), 151.
13. Edmund S. Morgan, *The Puritan Family* (Boston, 1956), 51. Chap. 3 has an excellent discussion of Puritan educational theories.

phers, and the Reformation leaders; he must therefore have an exacting knowledge of Greek and Latin, the vehicles of classical culture. The ideal, as described by one influential commentator, was a "Linguist, a Grammarian, a Critick, an Orator, a Philosopher, an Historian, a Casuist, a Disputant, and whatever Speaks Skill and Knowledge in any Learned Science . . . . He is to speak to all Subjects, and therefore must be made up of all Knowledge and learning." [14] If few ministers achieved the ideal, many made a serious effort to do so.

The process began with parental instruction of both a religious and a secular nature. Massachusetts law required Clap's father to provide catechistical instruction to his children at least once a week.[15] Beyond spiritual tutoring, it is certain that the parents imparted the rudiments of the "two R's," arithmetic not yet having achieved respectability as a course of study.

Formal education began in the local grammar school. Although there is no direct evidence, the presence of a school in Scituate,[16] coupled with the intention of the parents to train the lad for the ministry, strongly suggests that Clap received the traditional New England education.[17] Such an education was an arduous discipline—the school day began shortly after dawn and ended in the late afternoon. Since man's soul was at stake, religion was the alpha and omega of all instruction.[18] Each school day opened and closed with prayer. The precepts of Christianity, both moral and theological, were emphasized at every turn. To impress the

14. John Edwards, *The Preacher,* 3 pts. (London, 1705-7), I, 268-69, quoted in Mary L. Gambrell, *Ministerial Training in Eighteenth-Century New England* (N. Y., 1937), 16.

15. Nathaniel B. Shurtleff, ed., *Records of the Governor and Company of the Massachusetts Bay in New England* (Boston, 1853), II, 8-9.

16. Deane, *History of Scituate,* 94; Walter Small, *Early New England Schools* (Boston, 1914), 37; Pratt, *Early Planters of Scituate,* 146-48.

17. Naphtali Daggett stated in his sermon preached at Clap's funeral that the president had attended grammar school. *The Faithful Serving of God and Our Generation, the Only Way to a Peaceful and Happy Death. A Sermon Occasioned by the Death of the Reverend Thomas Clap . . .* (New Haven, 1767), 30 (hereafter cited as Daggett, *Faithful Serving of God*).

18. The subject matter and underlying theory of education of the grammar school curriculum are discussed in depth by Colyer Meriwether, *Our Colonial Curriculum, 1607-1776* (Washington, D. C., 1907); see also, Paul L. Ford, ed., *The New England Primer, a Reprint of the Earliest Known Edition, with Many Facsimiles and Reproductions and an Historical Introduction* (N. Y., 1899), introduction.

beginner with the proper ends of learning, the so-called Hornbook was employed as the principal educational tool in teaching the alphabet. Shaped in the form of a paddle (and sometimes used as such), the Hornbook set forth the letters of the alphabet, the Lord's Prayer, the Commandments, and additional moral and scriptural verses. It joined the ABC's, theology, and Biblical history in a single context.

At the age of about eight the student moved on to a more advanced text, the *New England Primer*. This work was the principal school book used in Puritan New England.[19] Eighty-eight pages in length and 3¼ by 4¼ inches in size, the *Primer* was a perfect handbook of Christian morality. Included in its pages were proverbs relating to filial duty and service to God, religious poetry, moral injunctions, "Instructive" Biblical questions and answers, hymns, the Lord's Prayer, the Apostle's Creed, and the Westminster Shorter Catechism. Small wonder that it acquired the title, "the Little Bible of New England." The *Primer*'s expressed aims were to inculcate the first principles of Puritanism and turn the youthful mind to sentiments of piety and virtue.

> Time cuts down all,
> Both great and small.
>
> Xerxes must die,
> And so must you and I.
>
> In Adams Fall
> We sinned all.
>
> The Idle Fool
> Is whipt at School.

Proceeding from moral aphorisms, the *Primer* dwelt on fundamental religious tenets:

> Who was the first Man? Adam.
> Who was the first woman? Eve.
> Who was the first Murderer? Cain.
> Who was the first martyr? Abel.[20]

19. Ellwood Cubberley, *Readings in the History of Education* (Boston, Mass., 1920), 311-15.

20. *The New England Primer Improved; or, An Easy and Pleasant Guide To the Art of Reading. To Which is Added, The Assembly's Catechism* (Boston, 1811); I have also used a 1777 edition to which is appended John Cotton's Catechism (see below).

In elucidating first principles, the catechism instructed youth
in the Puritan concept of human existence. Whether the abridged
Westminster version or the catechisms of John Cotton or Samuel
Stone [21] were used, the essential message was that man was conceived in sin and born in iniquity; that his corrupt nature bent
him in the direction of sin and enticed him to commit transgressions of God's commandments; that the wages of sin were
death and eternal damnation in the holocaust of hell. "What is
sin?" Samuel Stone's *Catechism* asked, answering its own question:
"The transgression of the Law, or any swerving from the Law of
God." If, as a lad, Thomas wondered what he was to believe
concerning man's apostasy or fall from obedience to God's government, he needed only to consult his catechism to learn that
"All men by nature being condemned through Adam's transgression, are wholly infected with sin, and under the dominion of
death." Like the *Primer,* the catechism helped establish in the
youngster a solid Christian foundation upon which the more
elaborate Puritan superstructure could later be laid.

"Spiritual Milk" was also dispensed by Thomas's teacher, who
was more than likely a Harvard graduate marking time before
embarking on a ministerial career, and by his parish minister,
the Reverend Nathaniel Eells,[22] the town's supervisor of morals
and education. It was customary for the schoolmaster to pray with
his students, catechize them, and question them on the sermon
delivered by the minister on the Sabbath. The child was expected
to be able to summarize the sermon and even quote some of the
more moving passages. On some fearsome occasions, the Reverend
Mr. Eells visited the school and examined the students himself.

While the grammar school aimed to prepare all youths for
salvation, it also sought to ready a select group for higher education at Harvard. This process did not call for any alteration of the
curriculum; it merely meant a greater emphasis upon the

21. John Cotton, *Spiritual Milk For Boston's Babes in Either England. Drawn
Out of the Breasts of Both Testaments For Their Souls Nourishment. But May Be
of Like Use to Any Children* (Cambridge, Mass., 1656); Samuel Stone, *A Short
Catechism Drawn Out of the Word of God* (Boston, 1684).

22. For Eells's biographical sketch, see Clifford K. Shipton, *Biographical Sketches
of Those Who Attended Harvard College in the Classes 1690-1700 With Bibliographical and Other Notes* (Cambridge, Mass., 1933――), IV, 468-71 (hereafter cited as
Shipton, *Harvard Graduates*).

"tongues." The Harvard entrance requirements specified that a candidate must be able to read and understand Cicero, Virgil, or a comparable classical author, write a Latin essay, compose Latin verse, and be well enough prepared in Greek "to Construe and Grammatically to resolve ordinary Greeke in the Greek Testament, Isocrates, and the minor poets." [23] Since these requirements were a formidable barrier, at least as presented, it was a prime responsibility of the grammar master to prescribe and direct a course of study which, if mastered, would enable a "Lattine Boye" (college-bound scholar) to journey to Cambridge with some assurance that his trip would be more than a sightseeing excursion. Having gone through the process himself, Clap's schoolmaster knew that the requirements were more bark than bite, and that the compassion of the tutors and president frequently counterbalanced a candidate's inability to present a fluid reading of the ancient authors. We may be certain, however, that he maintained the schoolmaster's tradition of keeping the boys ignorant of the realities of the examining process.

Although the Harvard entrance requirements specified a knowledge of Greek, the examination actually hinged almost entirely on Latin; the requirement for Greek was superficial, involving simply the declination and conjugation of paradigmatic nouns and verbs. Latin, therefore, became the principal curricular study for Thomas. His first formal instruction was probably based on Ezekial Cheever's *Accidence,* the "wonder of the age." [24] Providing lucid English explanations for the dark mysteries of Latin grammar, Cheever's text was admirably suited for the young Puritan. With the additional aid of a copybook, the youngster received a thorough grounding in the fundamental rules of Latin grammar. Having mastered first principles, he turned to William Lily's *A Shorte Introduction of Grammar,* which meticulously listed the twenty-five classes of nouns and contained a seemingly impenetrable labyrinth of additional rules of grammar. Young Clap memorized rule upon rule, construed and parsed until the mysteries were dissolved. He increased his vocabulary daily, and by the

---

23. "College Laws and Customs," Colonial Society of Massachusetts, *Publications,* 31 (1935), 329.

24. Elizabeth Gould, *Ezekial Cheever—Schoolmaster* (Boston, 1904), 14.

age of twelve he was probably capable of "making Latin," that is, writing essays, and of limited verbalizations in Greek.

The final years of Clap's pre-college study of the "tongues" were doubtless a period when, as the satiric John Trumbull observed, a "Lattine Boye" spent many uncomfortable hours digesting "husks of Lily," "murd'ring Virgil's verse," "construing Tully into farce," and blundering over a chapter in Greek.[25] At this stage of his siege of Harvard's ramparts, Clap's most effective weapons were Latin and Greek grammars and dictionaries, and a "five-foot shelf," as it were, consisting of such favorites as Aesop, Socrates, Homer, Virgil, Cicero, Terence, Ovid, and Corderius. Since Scituate did not maintain a public library, he probably borrowed his books from the Reverend Mr. Eells. With his head crammed full of the vagaries of the ablative case, subjunctive mood, and other rules of grammar and syntax, the fifteen-year-old scholar was prepared for the thirty-mile ride to Cambridge.[26]

Accompanied by his father and his minister, who by tradition maintained a paternal interest in the educational preparation of the college-bound youth of his parish, Clap journeyed to Harvard in early July of 1718. The brief oral examination was held shortly after the commencement exercises. The tutors conducted the examination, candidate by candidate, in the presence of President John Leverett, whose attendance gave an air of importance to the proceedings. Apparently acquitting himself honorably, Clap was directed to prepare and submit a Latin theme within a week's time. He satisfactorily completed this assignment, and was notified of his acceptance. There remained only the routine of paying a quarter's expenses in advance, filing a bond against the evasion of bills in the future, and making a duplicate copy of the "College

25. *The Poetical Works of John Trumbull* (Hartford, 1820), II, 13. Taken from "The Progress of Dulness."

26. In later years, James McSparran, an Anglican missionary, mistakenly claimed that he had had a hand in Clap's education. He actually tutored Clap's cousin of Taunton. Franklin Dexter, *Biographical Sketches of the Graduates of Yale College with Annals of the College History*, 2d Ser. (N. Y., 1885-1912), I, 636 (hereafter cited as Dexter, *Yale Graduates*); William D. Miller, "The Narragansett Planters," American Antiquarian Society, *Proceedings*, New Ser., 43 (1934), 96-97; Franklin Dexter, ed., *The Literary Diary of Ezra Stiles* (N. Y., 1901), I, 358 (hereafter cited as Dexter, ed., *Literary Diary of Stiles*); Shipton, *Harvard Graduates*, VII, 27.

Laws" and having it signed by President Leverett and the tutors.[27] He would be expected to know the contents when he began his collegiate career. The prospective freshman returned home for a six-week period to await the opening of fall term in mid-August.

The next four years would be the critical period in the life of Thomas Clap. The sedate, provincial atmosphere of Scituate would become a memory. Gone would be the stern parental discipline and the many forms of restraint imposed by village respectability. He was about to enter the magical world of Cambridge and Boston, the former the intellectual center of colonial America, the latter one of its principal commercial centers. Both were windows on a larger world. Both held dangers for the rustic. The atmosphere of Cambridge was charged with the restless, splenetic spirit of youth. Order could, and frequently did, give way to riot. College life had a subversive effect upon piety. Boston was cosmopolitan, worldly, rife with opportunity for moral lapse —the growing sinfulness and materialism of its inhabitants were fast becoming the main stock of the jeremiads. Harvard's history was strewn with accounts of would-be saints who had sallied forth confidently from the villages and townships of Massachusetts, only to flounder on the rocks of Boston immorality.

27. For a discussion of the Harvard examining routine and attendant administrative detail with respect to the process of enrollment, see Morison, *Three Centuries of Harvard*, 26-27, 103-4.

Chapter Two

A HARVARD FINISH

THE waters of the lazy Charles drifting by Harvard College and Cambridge village in the early years of the eighteenth century mirrored a view of pastoral serenity. While the scene did not compare with the wistful beauty of the Cam threading its way through the "backs" of the colleges at old Cambridge, it was nonetheless a respectable colonial imitation, pleasing to the eye and suggestive of a pervasive calm—a proper physical setting for the contemplative life.

But it was a deceptive calm. During the administration of John Leverett, who assumed the presidency in 1707, the little academic community was jarred by a series of disputes so intense that some in authority feared the noble experiment was doomed to extinction.[1] One serious contention was caused by a change in the method of filling vacancies in the Harvard Corporation, one of the two governing bodies of the college. (The other was the Board of Overseers, composed of prominent ministers and magistrates.)

---

1. An instructive, entertaining account of Leverett's administration is to be found in Morison, *Three Centuries of Harvard*, chap. 4. See also Josiah Quincy, *The History of Harvard University* (Cambridge, Mass., 1840), I, chaps. 13, 14; Shipton, *Harvard Graduates*, V, 92-93, VI, 154-55. The Mather-Leverett feud is discussed in Perry Miller, *The New England Mind, From Colony to Province* (Cambridge, Mass., 1953), 455-59.

The members of the Corporation, who were called Fellows of Harvard College, traditionally consisted of the president, the treasurer, and the tutors, and eventually two ministers were added. After a brief period of probation, new tutors were normally elevated to the status of fellows by the Corporation, which was a self-perpetuating body. In 1716, however, the Corporation changed its policy toward tutors. They were no longer, as formerly, to be appointed on permanent tenure, but for three-year terms; also, apparently, they were no longer automatically to become fellows. Very shortly, three vacancies on the Corporation were created by the death of existing members, and the Corporation bypassed two eligible tutors, selecting three Boston clergymen instead. The two tutors, who held short-term appointments, thought they were rightfully entitled to fellowship. They raised a vehement protest, and a rousing administrative quarrel ensued.

While the clouds of this controversy swirled over the college, another furor arose when the Corporation denied a second degree to a student for "contemning, reproaching and insulting the Government of the College." The trouble began when Tutor Nicholas Sever, who was a principal figure in the aforementioned dispute, judged the student, one Ebenezer Pierpont, incompetent. The basis for Sever's judgment was the poor quality of the students Pierpont was sending to Harvard while serving as a schoolmaster in Roxbury. Chafed by the accusation, and inflexibly bent upon receiving his degree, Pierpont broke all precedent by bringing legal proceedings against Sever. The case was ultimately thrown out of court, but its gravity was underscored by Leverett, who recorded that it "threatened the dissolution of the College." [2]

Besides having to cope with these disputes, both of which commanded the attention of the General Court and prominent lay and clerical leaders of the colony, Leverett had to defend his administration against the accusations of the Mathers, whose influence at the college had dwindled with the change of administrations in 1707. Led by the proud and pompous Cotton Mather, who was obsessed with the notion that he was the rightful man for the presidency, a conservative faction launched an attack against

2. Leverett, Diary, 178, typewritten copy in the Harvard University Archives.

Leverett and his supporters, charging them with a nefarious design
to overthrow orthodoxy at Harvard. The dispute was essentially
a renewal of the celebrated Brattle Street Church Controversy of
an earlier day, a struggle between the conservative and liberal
elements of Boston Puritanism. The ideological issues and dramatis
personae were the same; there was merely a change of battlefield.
As incontrovertible proof of their charges, the Mather element
pointed to the election to the Corporation of the Reverend Benjamin Colman, minister of the Brattle Street Church and an
avowed liberal in religious matters. They also asserted that
Leverett had abandoned the time-honored custom of making a
weekly exposition of Scripture to the students. And, horror of
horrors, he leaned heavily upon the works of liberal Anglican
divines in his divinity instruction, not upon those of the orthodox,
seventeenth-century Puritans!

While the prevailing administrative dissension and the protracted liberal-conservative dispute were serious matters, student
waywardness was an even more acute problem.[3] For some years
there had been a perceptible increase in disorderly actions by the
students. Harvard was fast acquiring the reputation of being a
mecca for delinquent saints, a notion that received popular expression in the stinging journalistic shafts of "Silence Dogood,"
the pseudonym of sixteen-year-old Benjamin Franklin. Disputes
at the administrative level may have fostered the mounting student
restlessness. It would perhaps be more accurate, however, to
ascribe the increase in "sinful actions" to the fiery, fun-loving
spirit of youth. Certainly, natural ebullience was manifest in the
popular sport of badgering the tutors, which consisted of hiding
tutorial wigs, raiding cellar lockers for food and drink, placing
live snakes in the tutors' chambers, shattering their windows with
rocks and brickbats, and committing "horrid abuse" to their
horses. The spirit of youth was also behind such common infractions as "cutting class," slipping off to Boston to attend pirate

3. For student life at Harvard, see Morison's delightful chap. 6 in *Three Centuries
of Harvard*. Leverett's Diary, Harvard Univ. Archives, provides insight into the
various types of student transgressions; see 202, 217, 256. Richer primary sources
are the Harvard Faculty Records, which unfortunately date from 1725 (photostat in
Harvard Univ. Archives); and "Benjamin Wadsworth's Book, 1725-1736," Col. Soc. of
Mass., *Publications*, 31 (1935), 452-58.

hangings and horse races, playing cards, thrashing freshmen, frequenting taverns, staging a "great Debauch" in the college hall at "unreasonable" times of the night, and stealing fowl from neighboring farmers for a hen roast behind locked doors in the college hall. The latter indiscretion, it seems, was often inspired by mere hunger, for the quality of college fare approximated Dickens's celebrated "three meals of thin gruel a day, with an onion twice a week, and half a roll on Sunday." Some offenses had a more serious character. One boy, more precocious in his mischief, found himself arraigned before the Corporation on the black charge of fornication, and another splenetic youngster took after a tutor with a pistol in hand. In general, however, the wayward behavior of the students could be regarded as scarcely more than the customary antics of high-spirited boys free from the restraints of parental discipline.[4]

What the young Puritan, Thomas Clap, thought about the Corporation-tutor hassle and Leverett-Mather feud cannot be ascertained. In the realm of discipline, the few facts that are known indicate that he conducted himself circumspectly and with profound piety during his years at Harvard. Although his collegiate career unfolded in an atmosphere of swirling controversy and extraordinary student unrest, Clap was one would-be saint who refused to set foot on the broad road to moral destruction. The fact that he did not reside in the college living quarters, where the temptations to wayward behavior were greater, may partly account for his abstention from mischief.

As a sophomore he did apply for a room in the college hall,[5] but for some undetermined reason did not get it, and he remained an extern, taking bed and board in the village.[6] In submitting his

4. The disciplinary problem came to a head in 1723, the year after Clap's graduation, with an investigation of the college by a committee appointed by the Overseers. The report of the committee cited these prevailing "immoralities": stealing, lying, swearing, idleness, picking of locks, drinking, and nonattendance at prayers. Quincy, *History of Harvard*, I, 319-21.

5. Leverett, Diary, 5-6, Harvard Univ. Archives.

6. Clap's continued residence in Cambridge village may be explained by the fact that in 1718, when he entered Harvard, there were housing accommodations for only 75 students. Some 50 others were compelled to seek lodgings in private homes. The construction of Massachusetts Hall in 1720 greatly alleviated the congestion, but Clap continued to reside in private quarters.

application, Clap had asked to share a room with Thomas Lee, a "quiet and pious" young scholar from Salem.[7] The impeccable Lee was one of a small segment of the student body, dubbed the "praying students," who disapproved of the general hell-raising. This group organized a "Society of Young Students" in 1719, in Clap's sophomore year, and conducted religious meetings on Saturday and Sunday evenings. Of a total membership of twenty-six, fifteen of this society later entered the ministry.[8] Although Clap was not listed as an active member, his association with Lee suggests that his interests were spiritual, rather than hedonistic.

This supposition is strengthened, if not totally verified, by the knowledge that Clap experienced conversion during his sophomore year. The profound significance of this act of regeneration cannot be overstressed. To the devout Puritan, conversion signified a spiritual communion with God and a resurrection from a state of sinfulness. It indicated redemption from evil and corruption, and a restoration of the faculties that enabled the convert to acquire at least a partial comprehension of the immutable beauty of God's will. In an experience in which man played a passive role, the Holy Spirit, through some supernatural process beyond the ken of man, entered the soul, cleansed it of its impurities and evil tendencies, and endowed it with powers of faith which enabled the convert to link his soul with the Deity. Conversion was the highest religious experience for the Puritan.[9]

Spiritual regeneration had preoccupied Clap since his childhood days in Scituate. Life at Harvard now sharpened his religious anxiety and renewed his desire for religious affirmation; he began to read treatises on the subject. Perusal of a work by the Reverend Solomon Stoddard, Jonathan Edwards's grandfather and the leading Puritan Brahmin of western Massachusetts, brought the seventeen-year-old youth to a frightening awareness of his state of sinfulness. He was haunted by a consciousness of sin, and for the next two months he experienced "much concern and Distress of Mind." Following this tempestuous struggle came the dramatic

---

7. For Lee's biographical sketch, see Shipton, *Harvard Graduates*, VII, 86-87.

8. William C. Lane, "A Religious Society at Harvard College, 1719," Col. Soc. of Mass., *Publications*, 24 (1923), 309-12; Morison, *Three Centuries of Harvard*, 62-63.

9. The experience of conversion is treated at length in Perry Miller, *The New England Mind; the Seventeenth Century* (N. Y., 1939), 25-29 and *passim*.

experience of conversion. It was the greatest moment of his religious life, the most memorable event of his college years. He was ravished by the spirit of God. Divine life flowed through him, as he said, cleansing his soul of moral impurity, depositing in its place a love of the good, a love of God. The spiritual pilgrimage was now at an end, and in Clap's words, "I thought I was enabled by the Spirit of God to lay hold upon Christ, and to trust and rely wholly upon his merits, and receive Him as my Savior and Redeemer; and accordingly did seriously and solemnly give up myself to Him; promising by the help and assistance of Divine Grace, to forsake all Sin, and to live a life of holiness and obedience to God's commands." [10] Clap was now constrained by his consciousness of the gift of grace to adopt an attitude of humility and contrition. Soon after his spiritual rebirth, he joined in covenant with the church in Cambridge village, where he "found at times great delight and satisfaction in the ways of religion." [11] Satanic Boston was not to number him among its victims.

Clap was extremely lucky to secure as his tutor the competent and lovable Henry Flynt,[12] who, by the 1720's, was something of an institution at Harvard. "Father" Flynt, as he was affectionately called by the students, began tutoring at Harvard in 1699, and he remained in this capacity until 1754, the fourteenth year of Clap's presidency at Yale. Flynt, Professor Morison writes, "was the great college character of the century. Presidents came and went, but Henry Flynt was always on hand when the first bell rang for prayers at the end of summer vacation." [13]

It was the crusty,[14] but pious, Flynt who guided Clap through his four-year course of study—Harvard employed the Cambridge system of having one tutor instruct a class from its entrance to graduation. He was an uncommonly hard-working, conscientious teacher. Unlike the great majority of eighteenth-century tutors,

10. Clap, Memoirs, 1, Yale MS.
11. *Ibid.*, 1-2; *Records of the Church of Christ at Cambridge in New England, 1632-1830* (Boston, 1906), 86.
12. For Flynt's biographical sketch, see Shipton, *Harvard Graduates*, IV, 162-67.
13. *Three Centuries of Harvard*, 108.
14. During the Great Awakening, George Whitefield, the English revivalist, commented in Boston that Tillotson, known as a freethinker, "is now in hell for his heresy"; to which Flynt quipped: "It is my opinion, that you will not meet him there." Massachusetts Historical Society, *Collections*, 2d Ser., 3 (1815), 211*n*.

who were usually recent graduates preparing to enter other professions, chiefly the ministry, Flynt had dedicated his life to the
profession. His conspicuous competence as an educator and disciplinarian led the Yale trustees to offer him the rectorship in
1718. Flynt, however, declined the offer, probably because of the
unsettled condition of the Connecticut college, and chose to remain at Harvard. Yale's loss proved to be Clap's gain. The proficiency he later displayed in a wide spectrum of scholarly activity
is ample testimony of the thorough educational training he received from this seasoned schoolmaster during these four years of
unremitting mental and spiritual discipline.[15]

The general curriculum under which Clap was trained by Flynt
was a composite of three core areas and was closely patterned upon
the course of study in effect at old Cambridge.[16] One area consisted
of six of the seven traditional liberal arts of the trivium and
quadrivium (music was excluded), and the three philosophies—
mental (metaphysics), natural (science), and moral (ethics). This
portion of the curriculum represented the standard intellectual
regimen of medieval universities. The two remaining areas,
classical belles-lettres (*bonae litterae*) and the "learned tongues"
(especially Hebrew), first became fixed in the curricula of European universities during the Renaissance. Like the Cambridge
course of study, the Harvard curriculum applied to all students,
those who prepared for the ministry as well as those who planned
careers as lawyers or governmental officials. The elective process
was unheard of in colonial America.

As a freshman, Clap devoted the greater portion of his academic
week to recitations in Latin, Greek, and Hebrew. A mastery of
Latin, the "queen of languages" and the great vehicle of classical
thought, was especially important. Many of the texts, including
those on Hebrew and Greek, were written in Latin, and a great
proportion of the scholastic exercises (disputations, declamations,

15. See Ezra Stiles's delineation of Clap's "literary character" in his letter to
Naphtali Daggett, July 28, 1767, Yale MS.
16. The following discussion of the Harvard curriculum is largely based on
Samuel Eliot Morison's magnificent 2-volume study, *Harvard College in the Seventeenth Century* (Cambridge, Mass., 1937), especially I, chaps. 7-13. "Benjamin Wadsworth's Book," Col. Soc. of Mass., *Publications*, 31 (1935), 455-56, lists the subjects
of the curriculum of 1725/6 as prepared by the three tutors.

and many recitations) were conducted in this language. Following a refresher course in basic Latin grammar (the Harvard freshmen were found to be weak in the area notwithstanding their "cramming" for entrance examinations), Clap undertook the writing of Latin compositions. At the same time, he studied the works of the standard Roman authorities, especially Virgil and Cicero. Four to five times a week he had instruction in Greek, a knowledge of which was necessary for the study of the New Testament. In addition, he received instruction in Hebrew, the language of the Renaissance "gentleman" and a vital tongue for the prospective Congregational minister who would be expected to read and make critical analyses of the Old Testament. (Later, he would revive the language at Yale.) On Friday morning of each week he focused upon rhetoric and composition, which also were staple subjects for a ministerial student. After poring over the classical models of Cicero, Demosthenes, and Isocrates, Clap exhibited the techniques and knowledge he had amassed in a Latin oration, written by himself. His study of grammar was designed to teach him to write and speak with clarity, correctness, and felicity of expression, while rhetoric was purposed to train him to speak in an eloquent manner. As his later life indicates, he concentrated his efforts upon clarity and correctness in both his writing and speaking.

Toward the latter part of the school year, on Monday and Tuesday mornings, the young scholar received his first taste of disputations, with the propositions usually taken from Petrus Ramus's popular *Definitions*. Conducted under the rules of formal logic, the disputation, that "quibbling machine," as one critic of scholasticism has labeled it,[17] was regarded as a central exercise in the curriculum. It was an academic device for gauging the intellectual abilities of a student. In the manner of medieval disputations, one student undertook the defense of a stated thesis while a second sought to present a refutation. At the conclusion of the forensic duel, Tutor Flynt made a "determination" and drew a synthesis, citing instances of weak or fallacious reasoning and offering suggestions on techniques of reasoning. At the close of the week, Saturday morning was set apart as "Divinity Day," during which

17. Meriwether, *Colonial Curriculum*, 46.

all classes applied themselves to some phase of religious study.
Clap's assignment during his freshman year was to master a catechism in Greek, which he duly recited to Tutor Flynt.

The sophomore year found Clap traversing much of the same
academic ground but on a more elevated level. He continued his
study of the classical authors, branching out from Virgil and
Cicero to other venerable Romans. He also began a formal study
of logic, traditionally defined on the commencement theses as
"Ars investigandi et communicandi Veritatem" (the art of investi-
gating and communicating truth). Although the texts on logic
used at Harvard were either by disciples or popularizers of
Aristotle, the system of reasoning was not entirely based upon the
syllogism. Actually, three distinct systems of logic were stressed—
Ramean, Cartesian, and Aristotelian. Logic, however, was not
conceived of as an intellectual entity in itself, but in the medieval
tradition of the hierarchy of the arts. The Puritan system of education as a whole was based on the Ramean doctrine that all
knowledge could be systematically arranged in a rational pattern
and thereby could be comprehended; on the commencement
sheets, this doctrine was listed as *technologicae.* Disputations, the
exercise closely allied to logic, continued with propositions becoming increasingly abstruse, the students becoming more polished
in the dialectic method. The young scholar was also introduced
to natural philosophy, or general science. While this study en-
compassed the entire realm of science, from geology to medicine,
the Harvard curriculum concentrated largely upon physics and
astronomy. The student also received instruction in mathematics,
a vital appurtenance to natural philosophy. The religious treatises
of the venerable Johann Wollebius, and principally his *Abridge-
ment of Christian Divinity,* highlighted the catechistical instruction on Saturday morning.

The junior year stressed mathematical subjects (including algebra, trigonometry, and algebraic conics and fluxions) and natural
philosophy. In the latter course, the basic text was Charles Morton's *Compendium Physicae,* a work which represented a fusion of
Aristotelian and "new Science" theories. While its presentation
was largely Cartesian and in terms of scholastic "categories," it did
have a modern orientation. It was this book that bridged the gap

between Aristotle and Newton and prepared the way for the scientific thought of the Enlightenment.[18] Clap began ethics, geography, and metaphysics, in addition to continuing disputations and declamations. "Divinity Day" was reserved for the continued study of Wollebius's religious writings.

The three philosophies were the principal subjects of his senior year. Disputations and declamations were less frequent. On Saturday mornings he pored over William Ames's *Medulla Theologica* (*The Marrow of Sacred Divinity*) and *De Conscientia et ejus Iure, ve Casibus* (*The Cases of Conscience*), additional repositories of the orthodox formulation. Toward the latter part of the year he began a general review in preparation for the two-week period in June when the senior sophisters would gather in the college hall and await questioning. While the college officials, M.A. candidates, and other gentlemen of liberal education were empowered to question the youth, or to ask him to engage in extemporaneous disputation with one of his fellows, the customary interrogators were members of the Board of Overseers. "Sitting solstices," as it was called, was the only formal examination; promotion or failure of a student was contingent upon the report of the boy's tutor.

In analyzing the possible effects of the Harvard curriculum on Clap, it is important to note the amount of religious instruction the college gave him. Samuel Eliot Morison has conclusively shown that Harvard was not intended, and did not function, as a seminary for the Congregational Church. But even Morison admits that a religious spirit permeated the institution; [19] although the professional study of theology technically began only in the post-B.A. period, the curriculum itself rested upon a religious base. Harvard certainly strengthened Clap's ancestral bias. The young Puritan studied the Bible in its Hebrew, Greek, and Latin texts; read and recited on the works of the prominent Protestant divines; and attended sermons and morning and evening prayers. In the

18. Adopted in 1687, Morton's manuscript textbook remained in use for at least the next 40 years. The work has been published (in English) in the Col. Soc. of Mass., *Publications*, 33 (1940). The volume is enhanced by a biographical sketch of Morton by Samuel E. Morison, and an introduction by Theodore Hornberger. See also, Morison, *Harvard College in the Seventeenth Century*, I, 236-49.

19. *Three Centuries of Harvard*, 22-25; S. E. Morison, *The Intellectual Life of Colonial New England* (N. Y., 1956), 32.

morning prayer period he translated the Old Testament from
Hebrew into Greek; in the evening session he translated the New
Testament from Latin into Greek. Disputations were often based
on theological propositions.

Flynt's influence was vitally important. The boy was impressionable, and for four years he listened almost daily to his tutor expound the eternal verities of Christianity. Like many divines of his
age, Flynt pressed his powers of literary invention into service on
the subject of human self-delusion. "The world," he told his students, "is miserably deluded from Age to Age; one Generation
goes blind and deceived into another world, and another comes
and carries on the Cheat, and train up their posterity in it, teaching them . . . that it is their supreme Interest, to suck out all the
Sweetness and Satisfaction they can from carnal and worldly En-
joyments, to Eat and Drink and divert themselves; because their
Time is short, and to morrow they must dye." If this be so, if
men deceived themselves with their vaulting self-delusions, what
was the remedy? Flynt had a ready answer: Man should "lay to
Heart the evil Nature and tendency of a carnal Life, and the great
Advantage we shall reap by turning our Feet into the Ways of
God's Commands."

Clap heard Flynt flay away at the multitudinous sins of man,
warn against gratification of the senses, and preach that if man is
to live for eternity, not for time, he must concern himself with the
welfare of his soul. His exhortation to the Harvard youth to cul-
tivate virtuous habits and maintain a godly behavior was starkly
plain: Paint Boston red if you wish, but expect to spend the days
of the hereafter in the land of the devil. Frequently, Flynt took
Clap and his classmates on a verbal field trip to the edge of the
pit. From this vantage they could witness the agonies of the
damned: "Hell is the Blackness of Darkness and Desperation;
there is no Light nor Joy there; nothing but Weeping, Wailing,
and Sorrow, it rings with bitter Groans and doleful Accents of lost
Creatures, that have for the Sake of their Lusts cast themselves out
of the Favour of God, and involved themselves in Guilt and
Misery, beyond Hope or Possibility of Retrieve." [20] Flynt left
little to the imagination.

20. Henry Flynt, Twenty Sermons, MS. in Harvard Univ. Archives.

Young Clap remembered well Flynt's words. Later, at Yale, when he gazed across the rostrum into the faces of a similar band of high-spirited, potential hellions, he would stress these same themes of restraint. Perhaps he was a harder man than Flynt, perhaps only a better stylist; in any case, he outdid his master in grisly explicitness. One of his themes for student sermons was entitled, "The Importance of Realizing Death and the Grave." "Let us check . . . inordinate Desires," he pleaded, "by a realising Sense of Death." He reminded the young men of Yale of the destiny of the flesh: "These delicate Bodies will become pale and loathsome Corpses, the Food and Repasts of Worms." When death comes, "he that is then found holy will be fixedly holy still; and he that is then filthy will be filthy still. There will be no more Offers, or Overtures of Mercy: the Door will be shut. We must then appear in our true Character before the Bar of God, the Judge of all, and receive the impartial Sentence from his Mouth, that will fix our State either in consummate Happiness, or inutterable Misery."[21] The speaker was Clap, but the message was Flynt's, or perhaps that of Flynt's teacher, or of his before him. No one can say for certain when this spool of Christian thought was first wound. But with Thomas Clap the thread extended through another generation.

If the aura of religion at Harvard helped form Clap, so he was also molded by concepts of Newtonian science which prevailed at the institution. Remarkably significant changes in the teaching of science had taken place in the early eighteenth century.[22] In the early decades of the school's history, a period that saw the dawning of modern science, the curriculum had emphasized the scientific concepts of Aristotle, Ptolemy, and the Peripatetic school of the Middle Ages. Harvard students were still being taught the geocentric cosmology of Ptolemy, the theory of nine transparent and concentric orbs revolving around a fixed earth, the center of crea-

21. MS. sermon in the Congregational Memorial Library, London.
22. For a discussion of scientific developments in colonial Harvard, see I. Bernard Cohen, *Some Early Tools of American Science: An Account of the Early Scientific Instruments and Mineralogical and Biological Collections in Harvard University* (Cambridge, Mass., 1950) (hereafter cited as Cohen, *Early Tools of Science*); Samuel E. Morison, "The Harvard School of Astronomy in the Seventeenth Century," *New England Quarterly*, 7 (1934), 3-24; Theodore Hornberger, *Scientific Thought in the American Colleges, 1638-1800* (Austin, Texas, 1945), *passim*.

tion. Likewise, the teaching of physics continued to be bound by the Aristotelian beliefs of a universe composed of the four antagonistic elements of earth, air, fire, and water, each with its distinctive qualities. Then the winds of the Enlightenment swept across the Atlantic and whipped against the medieval walls that had been erected around the curriculum by the founding fathers of Harvard.

Gradually the new philosophy began to take hold, and Harvard began to move with the tide of intellectual change. Aristotle and Ptolemy slowly gave way before the advance of Copernicus, Galileo, Kepler, Descartes, Bacon, Locke, and Newton. Ancient and scholastic scientific concepts were replaced by new theories—the heliocentric planetary system of Copernicus, the three Keplerian laws of planetary motion, Galileo's laws of falling bodies, Gilbert's principle of magnetic force. By 1659, Ptolemy had been swept aside by Copernicus; and by the second decade of the eighteenth century, even before Clap entered Harvard, Newtonian concepts were seeping into the curriculum. Similar modifications occurred in mathematics, the companion study to natural philosophy. Newtonian fluxions, comparable to present-day calculus, was being taught as early as 1719,[23] Clap's sophomore year.

The process by which mathematical and scientific subjects engendered a new philosophical outlook was visibly accelerated during the period of Thomas Robie's tutorship.[24] During his twelve-year span of service, Robie made the experimental philosophy of Newton and his fellow scientists standard intellectual fare for the students. It is safe to assume that Robie was the "accident we cannot now discover" in the scientific training of Clap; [25] the strong filiation of their scientific points of view is more than coincidence. The internal evidence strongly suggests that Robie, who

23. Lao G. Simons, "The Adoption of the Method of Fluxions in American Schools," *Scripta Mathematica,* 4 (1936), 209.
24. For accounts of Robie and his multifarious scientific activities, see: Frederick Kilgour, "Thomas Robie (1689-1729) Colonial Scientist and Physician," *ISIS,* 30 (1939), 473-90; Kilgour, "The Rise of Scientific Activity in Colonial New England," *Yale Journal of Biology and Medicine,* 22 (1949), 133-37; Raymond P. Stearns, "Colonial Fellows of the Royal Society of London," *William and Mary Quarterly,* 3d Ser., 3 (1946), 232.
25. Louis McKeehan, *Yale Science, the First Hundred Years, 1701-1801* (N. Y., 1947), 17 (hereafter cited as McKeehan, *Yale Science*).

"specialized in Science," [26] indoctrinated Clap in Newtonian theory and aroused his interest in mathematics, physics, and astronomy.

Clap's baptism in science raises a question as to whether the juxtaposition of Newtonian science and Calvinistic Puritanism posed a dilemma for him. Samuel Johnson and Charles Chauncy had been brought up in much the same rigid Puritan environment. In accepting the implications of Newtonian thought, they modified their religious outlook, shaking off the more styptic elements of the old faith. For Clap, also, could not the Supreme Being who appeared to govern the universe through a marvelous and intricate system of natural law be a reasonable and benevolent God whose primary concern was with man's salvation and happiness, not a Deity of vengeance who condemned men to eternal damnation? And could a God who created such a seemingly perfect universe create an imperfect man?

The biographer can only speculate on the existence of such an inner conflict by examining the manner in which science was presented to the Harvard youth and evaluating Clap's convictions as an adult. It seems clear that along with a scientific baptism Harvard provided Clap with a philosophical accommodation of science and religion. Robie was a modernist, but he was also a devout Puritan. He was well aware that the road of science was a two-way road, one direction leading to Christian truth, the other to skepticism and, possibly, atheism. He took care to place his scholars on the well-marked Puritan route by linking all phenomena to the activities of the Deity. He did not conceive, nor did he teach, science as an independent course of study. He regarded it more as a method than as a philosophy, as a technique of investigation and not as an account of being. Scientific knowledge remained tightly bound with moral and theological precepts, and in such a frame of reference, science and religion, natural causation and divine determination, became mutually compatible. Science stood as a bulwark to religion, buttressing and fortifying the truths of Christianity. If Newton's celestial mechanics enlarged

26. Morison, *Three Centuries of Harvard*, 58-59. Robie was also responsible for the accumulation of scientific instruments. So many pieces were acquired that a special room had to be set aside for housing the equipment.

man's conception of the universe, such increment cast greater glory, not doubt, upon the Creator. Observe the universe through a telescope and you will see planets, stars, comets, nebulae—a spectacle that proclaims the glory of God. In this spirit Robie instructed his students.

Science, then, provided man with a matchless opportunity to acquire an insight into the wondrous design of the Creation. Through the knowledge derived, man could better determine his position in God's intended scheme and live in closer accord with the Divine Plan. With such an outlook, a reconciliation of the two apparently antagonistic systems of thought was easy to achieve. Cotton Mather spoke for all Puritans with a Newtonian bent when he stated, "Philosophy [Science] is no Enemy, but a mighty and wondrous Incentive to Religion." [27] Clap later exhibited surprising rationalistic tendencies in his scientific writings, and occasionally committed to paper thoughts that would have seemed scandalous to the most liberal Puritan devotee of Newtonian science; but in his more reflective religious treatises, he reaffirmed the traditional Puritan tenet that divine revelation provided a more accurate, a more spiritually satisfying, form of truth than could be acquired by the application of human reason. In the last analysis, God-consciousness remained at the center of his vision. In his scientific thought Clap was made in the image of Robie; but between Robie, the scholar of science, and Flynt, the theologian, there was no philosophical gap.

Upon his graduation in 1722 Clap departed from Cambridge, but where he took up residence cannot be determined.[28] More than likely, he was in financial straits at this juncture.[29] Many a

27. Kenneth Murdock, ed., *Selections From Cotton Mather* (N. Y., 1926), 286.

28. Franklin Dexter has written that Clap remained in Cambridge in the period 1722-25 studying theology. Dexter, "Thomas Clap and His Writings," New Haven Colony Historical Society, *Papers,* 5 (1894), 248-49. Clifford Shipton has found no reference to Clap in the college financial accounts or in other documents pertraining to Harvard's history for this period. It would therefore appear that Clap did not remain in Cambridge.

29. Trumbull's satiric shaft (*Poetical Works,* II, 25),
> Few months now past, he sees with pain
> His purse as empty as his brain;

accurately depicts the indigence of a sizable number of college graduates in the eighteenth century. The practice of resuming residence within the ancestral home was a standard custom during the colonial period.

Harvard graduate rode out of Cambridge with little more than a slab of cheese and a degree in his pocket. An expedient and customary course of action for a Harvard B.A., long on ministerial ambition but short on funds, was to return home, secure an appointment as schoolmaster,[30] and apprentice himself to the local minister for theological instruction.

This kind of apprenticeship offered many advantages to a ministerial candidate.[31] The tutorial minister would direct the neophyte to write research papers on religious themes ranging from the primary problem of proving the existence of God to equally abstruse and unanswerable questions relating to the will and the soul. The student had free rein in the minister's library, usually the only one in town. While the minister might not believe that his student was likely to find definitive answers to these questions rummaging through the books of his library, he was intent upon having him study the standard works of Christianity. The value of the exercise lay in the search. The candidate was also expected to perform additional free-lance inquiries into age-honored religious problems and draw up treatises incorporating the findings of his investigations.

The greatest value of this training was its practicality. By working directly with an experienced minister and aiding him in the performance of his everyday duties, the student underwent an intensely practical apprenticeship. He looked on while infants were baptized, couples were married, and the dead were buried. He sat through the two Sunday sermons, special prayer meetings, and the mid-week lecture-sermon. He was assisted in the exercise of preparing his own sermons, the minister offering advice on the canons of form, content, organization, and exposition. On occasion, he would preach a sermon before the congregation. There could be no better training ground for an aspiring minister. While definite evidence is lacking, it is reasonable to suppose that Clap was trained for the ministry in Scituate by the Reverend Mr. Eells.

30. According to Pratt, Clap served as a schoolmaster in Scituate. *Early Planters of Scituate*, 184.

31. An excellent and comprehensive study of this subject is Gambrell, *Ministerial Training in New England*. An important contemporary work is Samuel Willard, *Brief Directions to a Young Scholar Designing the Ministry for the Study of the Divinity* (Boston, 1735). Willard outlined a course of study for the post-B.A. candidate for the ministry.

As the spring of 1725 broke across New England, Clap thought himself sufficiently prepared to begin his ministerial career. Hearing of an opening in Hull, Massachusetts, a nearby community, he decided to try for the post. The standard procedure was for a candidate to preach to the congregation for a period of time, usually from two to six months, in competition with other candidates. In June the Hull congregation made its selection: Ezra Carpenter (Harvard B.A., 1720).[32]

The following month Clap journeyed to Cambridge to take his second degree. As a rule, only ministerial candidates took the master's degree. It required no special course of preparation. A candidate needed only to satisfy these requirements: wait a three-year period after receipt of the B.A.; pay a specified fee; present a written synopsis of some art; make a syllogistic exposition of three philosophical problems; "declaym" twice; and take part in disputations. As a prospective minister, Clap was further required to deliver a brief sermon in the college hall. These requirements for the M.A. were sufficiently easy to meet, but they had not as yet dropped to the nadir of the nineteenth century when the degree was achieved by little more than the effort "to pay five dollars and stay out of jail." [33]

Commencement time was always festive, and in 1725 it was an especially gay (and wet) affair. For on this day Harvard was installing a new president, Benjamin Wadsworth. In the custom of the times, ministers, magistrates, medicine men, cheap-jacks, sailors, and acrobats converged upon Cambridge. But only such respectable figures as ministers and magistrates were to be seen in the meetinghouse during the formal installation of Wadsworth, the opening event of the day's activities. Then came the stately and colorful procession to the college hall, the bachelor's candidates leading the way, followed by the bareheaded master's candidates, President Wadsworth, the Corporation and tutors, Lieutenant Governor Dummer, the Council, and the "rest of the gentlemen." The morning exercises were reserved for candidates for the baccalaureate.[34]

32. Shipton, *Harvard Graduates*, VI, 373; *Boston News-Letter*, Dec. 2, 1725.
33. Morison, *Three Centuries of Harvard*, 35.
34. "Benjamin Wadsworth's Book," Col. Soc. of Mass., *Publications*, 31 (1935), 445-46.

The "inceptors," or candidates for the M.A., held the spotlight in the afternoon meeting. Following the presentation of degrees, they entertained the assemblage of dignitaries by disputing some *quaestiones;* the theses actually represented the synopses of subjects that the candidates had been studying. One question was: "An Remissio Peccati Ratione, Naturali, Investigari possit?" [35] (Is it possible to secure remission of sins through natural reason?) To a New England that was feeling for the first time the powerful effects of a surging rationalism, such a question had a pressing import. Clap responded in the negative, delighting the huge audience with his conservative argument. As the perceptive Clifford Shipton has observed: "Probably few of his hearers realized the effect that this attitude of mind in him was going to have on New England." [36] Clap's exposition was not merely an exercise in dialectics, as was usually the case; it was an argument that drew inspiration and forcefulness from a deep-seated conviction. In matters of faith, he was not one to assume a pose.

After receiving his second degree, Clap returned to Scituate before embarking in earnest on his ministerial career. His visit home was lengthened when he suddenly fell ill. For a month he remained bedridden, suffering the effects of "fever and Ague." Upon his recovery he saddled his horse and set out for Norwich, Connecticut, to compete for a vacant pulpit.[37] While in Norwich, he learned of the death of the Reverend Samuel Whiting, minister of the First Church in the nearby town of Windham.[38] He remained in Norwich for another three months and then traveled to Windham to try for that pulpit.[39]

With the sudden passing of the Reverend Mr. Whiting, the elders of the First Church had set the ecclesiastical machinery in motion for the selection of a replacement. Following the custom of the day, the Windham parishioners called a council of neighboring ministers to keep with them "a day of humiliation, witnessed

35. *Harvard Commencement Sheet for the Year 1725,* Harvard Univ. Lib.
36. *Harvard Graduates,* VII, 28.
37. Thomas Clap to Rev. Nathaniel Clap, Sept. 23, 1725, *New Eng. Hist. and Geneal. Reg.,* 14 (1860), 275.
38. On Whiting, see Ellen Larned, *History of Windham County* (Worcester, Mass., 1874), I, 82-83, 103.
39. Clap, Memoirs, 2, Yale MS.

by solemn fasting and earnest prayer to God for his guidance and
direction in the weighty affair of calling and settling a minister
among us to supply the place now vacant." The council suggested
three candidates, all of whom were respected clerical figures.
Should these men refuse, the First Church was advised to consult
with President Wadsworth for additional candidates.[40] While preparations were being made to act on this advice, Clap made his appearance in Windham and announced his candidacy for the pulpit.
He began to preach as a probationer on December 31, 1725, and
after a trial period was pronounced acceptable.[41]

On August 3, 1726, eight months after his arrival in Windham,
Clap was formally ordained. The weather was hot and muggy.[42]
The guest speaker, the Reverend Eliphalet Adams, a neighboring
clergyman, was dull and dry. It was traditional for ministers de-
livering ordination sermons to belabor the theme of application to
religious duty, and Mr. Adams was no exception. Warning the
neophyte not to "flubber" over his work nor attend it "only by
Halves," he adjured him to "admonish and discipline" those who
walked in the paths of sin. And he instructed him to hold fast to
the theological propositions in the accepted creed. In the summer's
heat, Adams droned on to a finish: "Take heed to the Ministry
that you are now about to receive from the Lord, that you fulfil it.
That you may be made an able Minister of the New Testament,
not meerly of the Letter, but of the Spirit, whose Praise is not of
Men, but of God." [43]

The Reverend Mr. Clap was soon to demonstrate that he was not
one to "flubber" over his work or do it "by Halves," and that he
would tolerate neither sinfulness among his parishioners nor
innovation in religion. Trained from birth for the ministry, he

40. Larned, *History of Windham*, I, 104; Elijah Waterman, *A Century Sermon
Preached Before the First Church in Windham, December 10, A.D. 1800* (Windham,
1801), 26.

41. Connecticut Archives: Ecclesiastical Affairs, IV, 109, Connecticut State Library,
Hartford.

42. "Diary of Joshua Hempstead," New London County Historical Society,
Collections, 1 (1901), 172-73.

43. *Ministers Must Take Heed to Their Ministry to Fulfil It. A Discourse Delivered
at Windham, at the Ordination of the Reverend Mr. Thomas Clap, August 3rd, 1726*
(New London, 1726).

entered upon his duties with the inflamed zeal of a first-generation Puritan cleric. The earnest entreaties of the Reverend Mr. Adams were soon to be carried out to the letter, possibly beyond his expectations. Never in its history had Windham seen the likes of Thomas Clap.

Salaries upon annuities with the balances and of other generation. For first year. The earlier carefulness of the Reverend Mr. Joslus were some to period out in the 1770's, possible beyond the provincial. Power in its hiring had rebellious seen the "fleet" of Thomas Clap.

Chapter Three

SAVING SOULS AND
CHASTISING SINNERS

THE ministerial career of Thomas Clap seems to confirm the principle that opportunity makes the man. Had he secured the position in Hull, his stature as a religious leader would probably not have transcended that of a country parson. Rural Hull lay in the shadows of Boston, the center of New England Puritanism and the home of clerical giants. While the religious history of the Bay Colony does record the rise of a John Wise, such examples are rare indeed. To a minister thirsting for prestige and prominence (and the statements of contemporaries strongly suggest that Clap was ambitious), Hull was a cul-de-sac.

As it happened, the young Harvard graduate staked his future in a primitive, back-country community where eminent clerics were as scarce as rocks were abundant. The county itself was a distinct cultural entity—isolated, rural, and provincial. Boston lay a mere eighty miles to the northeast, but it was more spoken of than visited. For residents of the area, Windham village was the substitute for Boston; for many, the town boundaries were the boundaries of life. The town owed its rise to the relative absence of wolves and hostile Indians, a liberal policy of selling land, and its accessibility to Norwich and New London, which served as markets for local produce and centers of supply. By 1715 Windham could boast of a meetinghouse, two schools, an ordinary, and various shops. As Windham was the political and economic hub of the county, so was its First Church the pivotal religious institution of the county, and its minister the leading divine.[1]

For more than a quarter of a century, Clap's predecessor, Samuel Whiting, had been the guiding spirit of county religious affairs, and had acquired a strong personal following. Among the people of his charge, Whiting had walked with the authority and dignity of a combined prophet and feudal lord. For the ministers of the county, he was the chief spokesman. He had served as minister of the First Church from its establishment in 1700. Local tradition has it that he preached his first sermon "on the first day of the week, and the first day of the year, from the first chapter of the Bible, and the first verse." [2]

Clap had only to step into the place that Whiting had established. Even without benefit of this legacy, however, he was certain to become the spiritual, moral, and intellectual leader of Windham village. As a minister of the established Congregational Church, Clap held a position of vested authority and prestige. As the earthly symbol of divine majesty, he commanded veneration and he could exact obedience; his will was law in his parish. While the power of the clergy may not have been as pervasive as in earlier times, it was still a mighty force in the community. New England remained under the sway of the attitude of mind expressed by Melville's Father Mapple: "The pulpit is ever this Earth's foremost part." It was so in Windham, and fortunately for Clap the town was not only his spiritual estate but a regional center. Within a few years of his ordination, he enjoyed a distinctive reputation among the clergy of the county.

After gaining his pulpit, this imperious young man of twenty-

---

1. On Windham, see Larned, *History of Windham*, I, 76-77, 91-94, 267, 269-70; Clap to Thomas Prince, Mar. 29, 1729, "Extracts of Letters to Rev. Thomas Prince," Connecticut Historical Society, *Collections*, 3 (1895), 294-95. There were 12 ecclesiastical societies in the county.

2. The Rev. Samuel Whiting, *A Sermon Preached at Windham* (New London, 1721), 3-5; *A Memorial Volume of the Bi-Centennial Celebration of the Town of Windham, Connecticut* (Hartford, 1893), 24 (hereafter cited as *Windham Bi-Centennial*).

three deemed it proper to consummate a bit of exigent personal business: "Sometime After I Had Concluded to Settel att Windham Having Left the Conversation of all my old friends and Aquaintance, I thought I Wanted one Near friend and Companion, one that Should be another Self and Help meet for me." [3] In short, the Reverend Mr. Clap wished a wife. Aside from personal promptings, social convention obliged him to marry; Puritan parishioners did not expect their minister to be celibate. The annals of Puritan religious history, like the annals of the Greek Church, rarely record a case of clerical bachelorhood. Finding a "Near friend and Companion," however, was not a simple task because a Puritan clergyman was severely restricted in his choices. As a representative of the Standing Order, he was socially eminent and was expected to marry within his class. Whatever the virtues possessed by the daughter of an innkeeper, she would not be considered as proper for a Puritan spiritual leader. Of equal importance was the spiritual state of the bride-to-be. A minister's wife must be of uncommon piety, a paragon of moral virtue, pure in soul and free of moral taint.[4]

In his thoughts on marriage and the relationship of wife and husband, the fledgling minister indicated the extent to which he had absorbed Puritan conventions. His ideas and attitudes were as typically Puritan as the mid-week sermon. Marriage he regarded as a divinely ordered institution, a spiritual union instituted by God and designed wholly to further His glory. Its purpose was not gratification of emotional and physical appetites; like all Puritans, Clap sought eternal bliss, and he was certain that it could not be discovered in the arms of earthly passion. In outlining the qualities of his ideal wife, he placed primary value upon "a Steady Serene Natural temper, and true Piety." Meekness must also be evident, and his mate must be of "good Understanding and great Prudence in the Conduct of herself." Her functions were to educate the children to the ways of God, manage domestic

3. Clap, "Memoirs of a College President, Womanhood in Early America," *Journal of American History*, 2 (1908), 474. This document is a charming monument of husbandly devotion, revealing a side of Clap's personality rarely uncovered.
4. On the Puritan attitude toward love and marriage, see Morgan, *Puritan Family*, 9-27; and William Haller, *The Rise of Puritanism* (N. Y., 1938), 120-23.

affairs, and serve as a "Spiritual Friend and Companion to converse with upon Heavenly and Divine Things." [5]

Since his arrival in Windham, the young minister had lodged in the Whiting household, and in this very house lived a girl who measured up to his exacting specifications. She was Mary Whiting, one of the late minister's thirteen children. Piety was her "first mark of Beauty and amiableness," Clap later wrote, and he chose her for marriage because "I thot She Had Long before chose Christ for Her Husband And I always Esteemed my Self Hapy in Having one So near and Dear to me that I thot was so Near and Dear to god." [6]

But Mary Whiting possessed yet another virtue—one that Clap never committed to paper. Coming from a moderately wealthy family, she represented for him the difference between near-abject poverty and a comfortable living. His contractual arrangements with the parish assured him of little but sufficient firewood during the cold winter months. The salary was so small as to be almost negligible, and often it was not forthcoming. Samuel Whiting had been able to accumulate extensive land holdings in the Windham area through the years, and although his property was not comparable in value with the rich farm lands of the Connecticut River valley, it was a comfortable source of wealth. When Clap chose Mary for his wife, he increased his income as well as his happiness.[7] After a brief courtship, they were married on November 23, 1727. He was then twenty-four; the bride, one day shy of fifteen. Neither the disparity in ages nor the youthfulness of the girl was uncommon by Puritan standards.

Despite her youth, Mary Clap capably discharged the manifold duties of a minister's wife and, in a short time, as a mother. She was no novice in parish affairs, for she had the model of her mother, and in every way she fulfilled Clap's high expectations.

5. See Clap, Memoirs, May 9, 1737, Yale MS., and "Memoirs of a College President, Womanhood in Early America," *Jour. of Amer. Hist.*, 2 (1908), 474-75.

6. *Ibid.*, 475.

7. There is evidence to indicate that Clap did acquire something more than a "Near friend and Companion." A Yale MS., dated Apr. 22, 1747, denotes that he owned 15 acres in Windham. His will also listed property holdings in Windham. Surely, this land was not purchased by savings from Clap's niggardly salary. For Whiting's holdings, see Larned, *History of Windham*, I, 83.

His later description makes it evident that he could have asked
for nothing more:

She was a woman of Such great Prudence and Discretion in the
Conduct of Her Self and Affairs, that She Was Scarce ever taxed
with taking a wry Step. She was Diligent neat and Saving, and always endeavoured to make the Best of what She had. The Heart
of Her Husband Could Safely trust in her So that he feered no
Spoil. She Endeavoured to treat Her friends and Al that Came in
as Handsome and Decent tho not Costly a mannar, as She Could:
and was very Kind and Compasionate to the Poor and all In
Distress. She was Adorned with great Humility and meekness, and
Never Affected anything above Her Degree, or to Apear fine or
gay. but Rather Like the Holy women of old who Trusted in god
She Put on the ornament of a meek and quiet Spirit which is in
the Sight of god a Pearl of great Price. She did not affect to Put
Herself forward In Conversation And Chose to Speak Discree[t]ly
Rather than much Yet was Always free Pleasant and Chearfull in
her Conversation with every one. She ex[c]eeded a[ll] Parsons
that ever I Saw in a most Serene Pleasant and Excellent Natural
temper. I Lived In the House with Her near Eleven years, and
She was my wife Almost nine: And Never once Saw Her in any
unpleasant temper neither did one unpleasant word, or So much
as shor[t] Ever Pass between us upon any ocasion whatsoever.[8]

Of all her virtues, it was her lofty piety that most impressed
Clap. Morning and evening, in times of sickness and tragedy, she
maintained the practice of "Private Retirement," that is, isolating
herself and praying. Occasionally, during periods of grief, she
requested her husband to join her in prayerful meditation. One
of their frequent prayers was, "that If it was the will of god, He
would Continue our Lives together near to the End of both of
them." When parishioners came to their home to discuss "Spiritual
Concerns" with Clap, the young wife herself sometimes acquired
gnawing doubts about her spiritual condition. Frequently, she
directed her husband to discourse with her and judge as to the
sincerity of her convictions.[9] Religion was her life and it occupied
every conscious moment.

8. "Memoirs of a College President, Womanhood in Early America," *Jour. of
Amer. Hist.*, 2 (1908), 474.
    9. *Ibid.*, 475-76,

In some of her qualities, the wife stood as a counterpoise to the husband. While he was stern and obdurate, she was merciful and submissive. She probably interceded with her husband on behalf of those weak mortals who were about to feel his appalling wrath for some moral or religious violation.[10] But she was not one to question at length her husband's judgments. When, on occasion, she found herself on the left side of an issue she tactfully crossed the line and fell in with him. In the testimony of Clap, "She did not Chuse to Debate long upon any Such thing but was Always free and Ready Enough to Acquiesce in the opinion or inclination of Her Husband." [11] As Mrs. Clap evidently knew, it could be no other way.

Although Clap was blessed with an excellent and submissive wife, much of his personal life in Windham was pervaded with inconsolable grief. Tragedy struck hard—and often. Six children were born of the marriage, and four of them did not outlive their first year.[12] The death of the first child was especially grievous. It was born prematurely after the mother had suffered an injury. Further intensifying the tragedy, the infant lived for a few moments before death mercifully intervened. It was a shocking experience for the couple, but their religious faith never wavered in this moment of heart-rending sorrow, and they looked upon their "grevious Loss" as an act conversant with the plan of Providence. Reproving themselves for holding "Hopes and Expectations" for their unborn child, they pledged in the future "to give up our Children to God by Faith and Prayer before they were born." [13] With the death of another premature child, a girl, on July 25, 1736, Clap's sorrowful personal life inexorably moved to the climax. Two weeks later, the twenty-three-year-old mother, who often confessed to her husband that "Bearing tending and Burying

10. Shipton, *Harvard Graduates,* VII, 29.
11. "Memoirs of a College President, Womanhood in Early America," *Jour. of Amer. Hist.,* 2 (1908), 474.
12. Clap, Memoirs, 3, Yale MS. Mary (b. 1729) and Temperance (b. 1732) were the only children to reach adulthood. Both married prominent figures. Mary married David Wooster of Revolutionary War fame; the New Haven chapter of the D. A. R. was named after her. Temperance married Timothy Pitkin, son of a Connecticut governor.
13. *Ibid.,* 2. The child was four and one-half months premature.

Children, was Hard work," [14] joined her four children beneath the
sod of the village cemetery.

The death of his wife had a devastating effect upon Clap. The
young minister was too thoroughly indoctrinated in Puritan social
theory to admit the thought on paper, but he passionately loved
his wife. He would marry again in due course, but he would never
again experience what he felt for Mary Whiting. Her death
smashed through his protective Puritan mental cast and exposed
him as universal man suffering overwhelming grief. He continued
to hold the vision of Christian prophecy before him, but nothing
availed against his anguish. While under the "smarting Rod of
Affliction," he engaged in "lonely and melancholly mourning."
Three months after the death of his wife, he poured out his grief
in his Memoirs: "All the Afflictions which I have ever met with
in my whole Life put together are small in Comparison to this.
My spirits have been much sunk and my Body Emaciated by it."
Bereavement became an intense personal fact.

Then the black mood passed; self became submerged. He became suffused with a sense of the vanity of worldly things, of personal desire. "In my greatest Distress under my most heavy Loss,"
he wrote six months after her death, "I think I have grieved and
mourned more for Sin, and the workings of Corruption in my own
Heart, than for my outward Affliction and Bereavement." He was
now prepared to concede that mortification of the spirit was not
only to be accepted but was to be welcomed; sorrow and pain were
the badges of Christian discipleship. If the premature deaths of
his wife and children proved anything, they confirmed the truth
of his religious creed. Could one deny that mortal existence was
a period of trial, filled with lamentations and woe? Could one
deny that grief was an indisputable fact of human experience? To
suffer is man's fate. Clap recognized the "need and necessity of
this Tryal and of being in Heaviness for a Season." He assumed a
perfect resignation to the Divine will: "The Lord is Good, he is
my Rock and there is no Unrighteousness in him." The spiritual
struggle was at an end.

It is a revealing fact about Clap's mind and character that al-

14. "Memoirs of a College President, Womanhood in Early America," *Jour. of
Amer. Hist.*, 2 (1908), 476.

though family tragedies cut deeply into his heart, they had no observable negative effect on his professional life. Throughout the periods of personal misfortune he applied himself diligently to the work of the church, never breaking ministerial routine. Energized and held to his purpose by a sense of mission, he strove to elevate the spiritual state of his parishioners, to educate, discipline, and guide them. He regarded himself as the faithful steward of a Master who might return at any moment and who would require to find everything ready for his convenience. The enormous energy he expended in matters ecclesiastical, coupled with his singular sense of duty and dedication, fortifies Clifford Shipton's observation that "his real bride was the church and his great love, her law." [15]

One trait, in particular, set Clap apart from the generality of contemporary ministers: a deep-seated reverence for detail, a meticulous concern for minutiae. Unlike Jonathan Edwards, who did not make periodic pastoral visits,[16] Clap tried to visit every family in his parish once a year and familiarize himself with their personal problems. During one such tour, conducted a few months after his wife's death, he catechized all the children and took down the names and ages of all his parishioners so that, as he explained, "I might have a more full knoledge and clear Remembrance of every Soul committed to my care and charge, and the Circumstances and Condition of each Perticular Person." On this tour, he inscribed 722 names in his notebook! [17]

Clap's entrance into office signified the beginning of a new level of administrative order in the First Church. One of his initial acts was to insist upon written records. Prior to his ministry, ecclesiastical decisions and business transactions had not been recorded.[18]

Another of his measures clarified the status of an appreciable number of Windham residents who were not in full communion

15. *Harvard Graduates*, VII, 29.
16. Ola Winslow, *Jonathan Edwards, 1703-1758; A Biography* (N. Y., 1940), 124-25. Edwards is reputed to have once said that he refused to make pastoral visits because he had no talent for entertaining his parishioners, and received no profit by their entertainment. Perry Miller, *Jonathan Edwards* (N. Y., 1949), 128.
17. Clap, Memoirs, Jan. 1, 1737, Yale MS.
18. Dexter, ed., *Stiles's Itineraries*, 280.

with the church. Most of them were newcomers to the area, and having failed to acquire letters of identification from their previous church, they were legally barred from entering into full communion. To remedy this situation, Clap established a policy whereby all residents of Windham were admitted to full membership, provided they had resided in the town for at least three years, in which time they had shown "constant attendance" upon the church ordinances and lived "sober" lives. Those who had not lived in Windham for three years were ordered to procure letters of identification within three months. Future residents were also to be given a three-month period of grace. Failure to comply with this edict was to be construed as either "utter negligence," or as evidence that the person was "under some scandal"—the penalty for such failure was suspension from the First Church. Clap also tried to secure the membership of a number of longtime Windham residents who had not affiliated with the church.[19]

An interesting feature of Clap's efforts to increase church membership is that they were liberal in character. They indicate the extent to which the traditional concept of "owning the covenant" had declined in New England religious life—full church membership was no longer contingent upon the experience of conversion. Like many of his colleagues, Clap recognized that it was necessary to lower the requirements in order to fill the pews, and extant statistics show that he was far more successful than his predecessor or successor in bringing Windham residents into the orbit of the church.[20] When he left Windham in 1740, every head of a household within the limits of his parish was associated with the church, either by profession of faith or by "owning the covenant." [21]

While Clap displayed special abilities as a recruiter of parishioners and as a clerical administrator, his main talent was in en-

19. Windham First Congregational Church Records, I, 23, Conn. State Lib.

20. During his 13-year ministry, Clap baptized 475; for a 9-year period, 1760-68, his successor baptized 208. Dexter, ed., *Stiles's Itineraries*, 283; Windham First Congregational Church Records, I, 22, Conn. State Lib. Whiting admitted 375 to full communion in a 25-year period; Clap, 219 in 13 years. Notwithstanding the breakoff of two societies, Clap's church had a membership of 287 when he left Windham, 23 more than when he had assumed office. Waterman, *Century Sermon*, 88.

21. Larned, *History of Windham*, I, 285-86. See also, the Rev. John Tyler, *Historical Discourse Delivered on the One Hundred and Fiftieth Anniversary of the Formation of the First Church in Windham* (Hartford, 1851), 17.

forcing discipline. Very soon after taking office, he called for the organization of a committee of four deacons and three laymen, whose function it was to assist him in regulating the sinners in his parish. He justified this action on the ground that his extensive duties did not permit him sufficient time to inquire into, or keep abreast of, public scandals.[22] To these "Seven Pillars" was delegated the authority to investigate any First Church parishioner who was as much as suspected of committing a "public sin" or "scandalous evil." The information they gathered was to be submitted to Clap, who would act in counsel with the committee.[23] The establishment of the "Seven Pillars" did not mean that Clap was excluded from conducting personal inquiries into disciplinary cases. He was careful to insert a clause granting to himself ex officio powers.

So frequently did Clap exercise his ex officio powers in the business of striking down sin that he soon acquired the reputation of being a "terror to evil doers." [24] Public confessions delivered by delinquent parishioners became a frequent occurrence.[25] So as to provide assurance that the offender's misdeeds were brought to full public attention, Clap decreed that confessions be delivered only on Sabbath days or in special meetings, at which times all the baptized parishioners were obliged to attend.[26]

Clap's success in disciplining his congregation owed much to his authoritative personality, which had a distinctly Old Testament quality. He never found himself in the position of the Reverend William Billings, minister of the recently organized Second Church of Windham, whose disciplinary problems got out of hand. Excessive drinking was especially prevalent among his parishioners. So serious did the situation become that Billings was finally forced to concede defeat in his personal efforts at reformation and issue a humiliating call for assistance from the County Association of Ministers. Underlying Billings's failure to

22. Windham First Congregational Church Records, I, 23-24, Conn. State Lib.
23. This group fell into desuetude after Clap's removal. Dexter, ed., *Stiles's Itineraries*, 281-82. These pages contain extracts from the Windham First Church records.
24. Waterman, *Century Sermon*, 28.
25. Larned, *History of Windham*, I, 271.
26. Windham First Congregational Church Records, I, 23, Conn. State Lib.

administer discipline was his inability to command the respect of his parishioners: "I had rather hear my dog bark than Mr. Billings preach," [27] publicly commented one of his flock. It is unthinkable that any member of the First Church would have dared to speak of Clap in these terms. Indeed, had Clap been asked by a stranger if he was the parson who "served" the First Church, he could have rightfully answered as did Parson Phillips of Andover when a similar question was put to him: "I am, Sir, the parson who rules here." [28]

The few who refused to comply with Clap's edicts had little choice but to leave the town. On one occasion, Israel and "Goody" Fulsome were summoned before Clap and the "Seven Pillars" and judged guilty of "scandalous talk and reviling." Their real crime, not cited in the indictment, was a warm sympathy toward the doctrines of the Church of England. The Fulsomes were ordered to draw up a confession and present it before the congregation. They balked at this directive and appealed the First Church's decision to a council representing all of the churches in the county—but to no avail. Again they were censured. Clap "waited" upon them but was unable to persuade them to confess. Then, in a dramatic gesture of defiance of Clap's authority, they invited into their home an S.P.G. missionary from New London, who began conducting special services for the Fulsomes and select friends.[29] Significantly, these were the first formal Anglican meetings to be held in Windham. Clap was enraged. He and his fellow Congregationalists brought pressure to bear against those involved, and the meetings were soon terminated; as one Windham Congregationalist later wrote, "like the pleasures of sin they [meetings] were only for a season." [30] After being expelled from the First

27. Larned, *History of Windham*, I, 280-81.
28. Quoted in Charles M. Andrews, *Colonial Folkways; a Chronicle of American Life in the Reign of the Georges* (New Haven, 1916), 166.
29. Hawks and Perry, eds., *Documentary History of Episcopal Church*, I, 160-61.
30. Waterman, *Century Sermon*, 28. It was common talk in Windham that "old Goody Fullsom" was a witch (shades of "Goody" Proctor!), a report to which Clap himself gave credulity in conversation with Eleazar Wheelock. Clap informed Wheelock that an old woman in his parish who was ill and sometimes became delirious was tormented by the troublesome Mrs. Fulsome. On one occasion, an "Ill Looken Dog" entered the sick woman's room whereupon her brother took up a broom and gave it a blow, causing the dog to go away in a lame condition. At that very instant, so Clap asserted, Mrs. Fulsome, who was in a church meeting, roared out that she

Church, the Fulsomes found it expedient to move on to New London where they joined in communion with the Church of England.

Clap saw the Fulsome incident as evidence of the growing threat of ecclesiastical disunity provoked by the rise of Anglicanism. The Church of England threatened to breach, if not shatter, the erstwhile homogeneous Congregational system of Connecticut. Clap had previously abominated the Anglicans for ideological reasons. Now he was consumed by anger at their disruptive influence on his disciplined parish. He realized that he could not enforce discipline when the Church of England stood in the background like an "ark of safety," beckoning with open arms to those Congregationalists who had been condemned for scandalous behavior and threatened with expulsion. How was it possible to enforce discipline and deal with the faults of men, he once inquired of the patriarchal Benjamin Colman of Boston, if these men could evade authority and responsibility for their misdeeds by merely repudiating their covenanted churches and taking communion in the Church of England? "It is a Disorderly and Scandalous thing," he added, "for one Church or Community of Christians, to receive the Members of another Church while they are under Censure for Scandalous Immoralties in the Church where they belong." [31] And what of the "Principles of Universal Liberty by some pleaded," which held that a man could willfully withdraw from the church to which he was covenanted and join another church? To Clap, this liberal principle was rank sophistry. The duties of man and rights of authority took precedence over liberty and the rights of man. In this particular ecclesiastical issue Clap agreed with the Cambridge Platform, which explicitly stated that covenants were not to be broken without good cause, for "such departure tends to the dissolution and ruine of the body: as the pulling of stones, and peeces of timber from the building, and of members from the naturall body, tend to the destruction of the

---

had a sharp pain in her shoulder. When "Sherriff Huntington the Bone Setter Came to feal of it the Next Day he found the Bones much Broken in so much that he co[uld] hear them Rattle in her Skin." Wheelock to Stephen Williams, Aug. 18, 1737, Dartmouth College MS.

31. Clap to Colman, Dec. 8, 1735, Mass. Hist. Soc. MS., Boston.

whole." [32] The key to social peace and progress was religious unity. Destroy this unity and the floodgates of anarchy would be opened.

In the area of church polity as well, Clap would have no truck with libertarian notions; to allow the generality of church members a free rein in the management of parish affairs was unthinkable. Man was too much inclined to heed his dark blood, as the doctrine of original sin clearly indicated. Clap thus considered the consociated form of polity set forth in the Saybrook Platform as the "true Medium between the unscriptural Encroachments of Prelacy on the one hand, and the Confusions of Independency on the other." [33] He embraced the principle which one authority has aptly designated as "Presbyterianized Congregationalism." [34] The important powers of decision were to be vested in a central board, not in the general body of the church membership as in pure Congregationalism. In Clap's own church, this theory took the form of a power-wielding group consisting of the "Seven Pillars" and himself. In other areas of polity, as in his acceptance of the consociated church and ministerial association arrangements, Clap also revealed Presbyterian tendencies. His position on church government was halfway between the decentralized autonomous structure of seventeenth-century Congregationalism and the highly centralized synodical organization of nineteenth-century Presbyterianism.

Clap's efforts to impose strict discipline extended beyond his parish to the county at large. By nature prone to seek power, he soon became the commanding figure of the county ministerial association, a high tribunal on intra- and inter-church disputes. This group could render a final judgment on any matter remotely associated with church affairs, from people jostling for seats before the service to lofty matters of moral principle.[35] So vigorous did the Association become in the prosecution of its duties with Clap at

32. Walker, ed., *Creeds of Congregationalism*, 224-29.

33. Daggett, *Faithful Serving of God*, 31-32. Clap's Presbyterian tendencies are revealed in his sermon, *The Greatness and Difficulty of the Work of the Ministry. A Sermon Preached at the Ordination of the Reverend Mr. Ephraim Little at Colchester, September 20, 1732* (Boston, 1732), and in his MS., Thots on the Present State of Religion Occasionally Minuted Down, date unknown, Yale MS.

34. Henry M. Dexter, *The Congregationalism of the Last Three Hundred Years, as Seen in its Literature...* (N. Y., 1880), 463.

35. Larned, *History of Windham*, I, 390-92.

its helm that the Windham residents came to refer to its members as the "County Watchdogs."

Nor was the Association's authority exercised exclusively upon parishioners. Some of the county ministers also felt the sharp sting of ecclesiastical rebuke. In accordance with the Saybrook Platform, the Association could inquire into the character and fitness of any established minister within the county; it could judge—and challenge—the qualifications of ministerial candidates. The Association suspended one minister for "indecent jesting," and another for threatening violence to his brother.[36] Clap's own brother-in-law, also a minister, was brought before the tribunal for immoderate drinking.[37]

In a case in which Clap personally took a conspicuous hand, a minister from Pomfret, Connecticut, was ordered to appear before the "County Watchdogs" and render an account of his religious doctrines, as well as to explain some "irregular procedures" in his practice. The minister, the Reverend Mr. Blossom, was not to be muzzled easily. Displaying uncommon courage, he refused to comply with the directive. His suspension from the ministerial guild followed as a matter of course. At a subsequent meeting, in which the accused was tried *in absentia,* the Association formally moved for his expulsion after testimony revealed contradictions and inconsistencies in his doctrinal presentation. A more damning indictment rendered by the ecclesiastical court was that the minister had assumed the authorship of a sermon "which we have very good grounds to believe was not of his own composing." For a minister, plagiarism was an unpardonable breach of conduct. Blossom was ordered to desist from preaching, and, should he refuse to comply with the decree, his parishioners were warned against attending his services.[38]

Clap's special talents as a disciplinarian compensated for his only average ability as a sermonizer. The orator's gift, the gift of evocation, was not his. He lacked the eloquence and pulpit majesty of a John Wise, he was not capable of the exegetical finesse of a

36. *Ibid.;* Dexter, *Yale Graduates,* I, 334.

37. Dexter, *Yale Graduates,* I, 253. Another of Clap's brothers-in-law was summoned before the Association in 1727 for preaching without a license. *Ibid.,* I, 342.

38. Connecticut Archives: Ecclesiastical Affairs, A-G, 1658-1789, III, 235b, Conn. State Lib.

Jonathan Edwards, nor was he a "soul-melting preacher." In a
standard Puritan fashion, he spoke as a prophet who persuaded by
logic and reason, not by eloquence. Clap's extant religious writings
are conspicuous for the absence of parables, exempla, homely
similes, and the numerous other literary devices employed by more
successful preachers. Avoiding pretentiousness, he strove for plain-
ness, perspicuity, and gravity—like Increase Mather, pursuing
"that one Art of Being Intelligible." [39] In later years, one of his
close friends described his pulpit performance: "As a preacher, he
was not of the florid, showey sort: but solid, grave and powerful,
more by the weightiness of the matter, than by the flowers of
Rhetoric, or any very superior Talent in the Art of Speaking. . . .
He was plain and impressive, solid in his matter, but not eloquent
in his manner; neither did he adorn his ideas with the ornaments
of language. Having a confidence in the truth he left it to speak for
itself." [40]

Lack of evidence prevents a critical appraisal of the theology
expounded by Clap. There is little reason to doubt, however, that
he espoused the doctrines of moderate or Westminster Calvinism.[41] Central to this theological system were beliefs in the all-
controlling Providence of God and the depravity of man (original
sin). Also included were the doctrines of Christ's divinity and
atonement, the trinity, and salvation through unremitting faith
in Christ. Calvinism began with the proposition that man originally had been pure and perfect, but in consequence of Adam's
sin became destitute of his native propensity to holiness and was
now corrupt and disordered. It was beyond man's power to recover his former holiness or make an atonement through his own
efforts. A believer's total acceptance of Christ's atonement provided the foundation for his ultimate salvation, but this in itself
did not assure salvation. Regeneration, or conversion, was a contingent necessity. Through the influence and operation of the
Holy Spirit, God brought about a transformation of personality,
a spiritual ablution, by which sinful tendencies were eradicated.

39. Cotton Mather, *Parentator* (Boston, 1724), 215.
40. Daggett, *Faithful Serving of God,* 30.
41. In his letter of July 28, 1767, to Daggett, Yale MS., Ezra Stiles wrote that
"Westminster Calvinism was his [Clap's] theology, and he was a perfect master of it."

Although a believer was then committed to a life of purity, holiness, and virtue, salvation was still the prerogative of God. This was essentially the theological exegesis Clap presented while serving as president of Yale,[42] and there is no evidence to suggest that he deviated from it in the slightest degree from his student days at Harvard to his later adult life.

In 1733, in the eighth year of his ministry, the Reverend Mr. Clap enjoyed a wide measure of local fame. He held a central position in Windham County. His future, however, offered no promise of greater success. Because Puritan ministers commonly settled for life with one congregation, Clap seemed destined to serve out his career as the patriarch of northeastern Connecticut, much as Whiting had done before him. Clap's ambition, however, was not to be shackled to a long pastorate. On a cold December day, Robert Breck, a young Harvard ministerial candidate, rode into Windham and announced his intention to try out for the vacant pulpit of the town's Third Church, a parish organized and endowed with the privileges of a society in 1732.[43] His arrival set in motion a train of events ultimately resulting in Clap's elevation to the rectorship of Yale College.

Robert Breck was a would-be Puritan divine who went astray at Harvard College. The son of an eminent minister and Hebraist, and a boy of unusually high native intelligence, Breck was more distinguished at Harvard for dissipation and loose living than for classroom performance. He was frequently admonished for drinking and gambling. Finally, suspected of stealing, he was on the verge of expulsion, and only the intrusion of his father saved him. He completed his undergraduate program under parental supervision, and, after confessing to his former misdeeds, the resurrected young divine was permitted to graduate with his assigned class in 1730. Three years later he took his second degree.[44]

As a ministerial candidate Breck created a stir by preaching doctrines which, however orthodox they may have seemed in Cam-

42. See chap. 7 and *passim.*
43. Larned, *History of Windham,* I, 273-80.
44. Breck's biographical sketch can be seen in Shipton, *Harvard Graduates,* VIII, 661-79.

bridge, were in Windham branded as Arminianism. He asserted that salvation could be achieved without the traditional and traumatic experience of conversion. Moreover, he insisted that faith in Christ was in its own nature not essential for salvation. All that was really necessary was to forsake sin and lead a moral life. One of his favorite themes for a sermon was "That the Heathen that liv'd up to the Light of Nature Should be Saved." He also played hard on the idea that God would magnanimously forgive sin without exacting punishment or atonement. Finally, he questioned the divine inspiration of select portions of the Bible.[45]

The doctrinal notions of the young Harvard graduate were a stench in the orthodox nostrils of the Reverend Mr. Clap. Clap became further incensed when Breck preached his brand of rationalistic theology from the pulpit of the First Church while substituting for Clap in his absence. Rumors of Breck's profligate scholastic career had also come to his attention, and to determine the validity of the reports he had sent letters of inquiry to authorities in the Boston area.[46]

It seemed to Clap that the situation called for his intervention. The Scotland District was technically subject to his authority, since it had not as yet ordained a minister. In any case, the legality of his intervention was a secondary consideration. Breck was skating on the thin ice of heterodoxy, and who else but the spiritual leader of the county had the right or authority to inquire into the matter? He met with Breck "several times." On long winter evenings, they discussed theological questions before an open fire. Clap's initial purpose was to point out to the headstrong youth the errors in his theological opinions and persuade him to make the necessary modifications. Breck reacted sharply to Clap's interference. In the course of one conversation, he brashly asserted "that he would preach People out of those false and stingy Notions

45. *A Narrative of the Proceedings of Those Ministers of the County Hampshire, That Have Disapproved of the Late Measures Taken in Order To the Settlement of Mr. Robert Breck, in the Pastoral Office in the First Church in Springfield* (Boston, 1736), 4-12 (hereafter cited as *A Narrative of the Proceedings*).

46. *An Examination of and Some Answer To a Pamphlet, Intitled 'A Narrative and Defence of the Proceedings of the Ministers of Hampshire, Who Disapproved of Mr. Breck's Settlement at Springfield: With a Vindication of Those Ministers and Churches, That Disapproved of, and Acted in the Settlement of said Mr. Breck'* (Boston, 1736), 16-17 (hereafter cited as *Answer to a Pamphlet*).

which they have been taught in; that the common People out of Pride, and Self-conceit, confin'd Salvation only to themselves; but I will have them to know, that the Heathen may be Saved as well as they can."

"You are but a young Man," Clap cautioned, "and I would not have you set up to Reform the World too soon; least instead of Reforming of it, you should happen to corrupt it." This sally irritated Breck intensely. "I suppose you wou'd have it here, as in Scotland," he exploded in blustering anger. "There the young Ministers cannot think freely for themselves; but they must think as the old Ministers do, or else they will not ordain them."

Clap was chafed by the "indecent Talk" of the petulant young minister-to-be. He inquired of the youth if he had been involved in acts of thievery at Harvard, and if he had been expelled for this and other "scandalous Immoralities." Breck vehemently denied involvement in theft and insisted that his removal had been prompted by a smallpox threat, not by expulsion.[47] Later, Clap received reports to the contrary from his Boston correspondents. Breck's character was confirmed in Clap's estimation. A rough tongue could be excused, but not stealing and lying. From his own collegiate experience, Clap knew the type well. There was no doubt in his mind that Robert Breck was not fit to preach the gospel.

Clap made it clear that he would oppose Breck's ordination, despite a vote of confidence and call to settlement by the Third Church parishioners. To these parishioners, Clap laid down his dictum: They were not to ordain Breck. He then told the young Harvard graduate to seek out a pulpit elsewhere. Realizing the hopelessness of overcoming Clap's opposition, and recognizing that he was *persona non grata* to a large body of Windham believers, Breck rode out of Windham in the spring of 1734 toward Massachusetts. Clap's will had prevailed and the incident appeared at an end.

Upon leaving Windham, Breck moved on to Springfield, Massachusetts, some forty miles to the northwest in the Connecticut River valley. He began preaching in the Springfield First Church with a view toward staying there. Having learned that a ministerial

47. *A Narrative of the Proceedings*, 4-6, 56.

candidate should contain within himself whatever liberal doctrinal ideas he held—at least until after his ordination—he displayed greater restraint in his sermonizing and was judged
acceptable by a majority of the parishioners. He was on the verge
of ordination in May 1734 when his immediate past in Windham
came to light as a result of a letter sent by the Reverend Eleazar
Williams of the Windham area to his brother, also a minister, in
Springfield.[48] Williams recounted Breck's experience in Windham—just as he had heard it from Clap.

The Springfield minister promptly sounded the warning bell.
He circulated the letter among the members of the Hampshire
Association of Ministers, an organization composed of ministers
from thirteen churches in the Springfield area, whose function it
was to preserve ecclesiastical harmony within the district. The
Hampshire Association, which was under the leadership of Jonathan Edwards of Northampton, questioned Breck about his Windham experience and finally advised him to return there, clear up
his disagreement with Clap, and secure a letter from him confirming
his orthodoxy. Should he refuse to comply with this advice, the
Association would then be inclined to oppose his ordination.

Breck doubtless knew that satisfying such a request would be
highly difficult under ordinary circumstances, but recent events
had made it virtually impossible. Previous to his appearance before the Hampshire Association, Breck had dispatched a sharp
letter of reproof to Clap, whom he suspected of spreading the
word about his purported heterodoxy. He had no doubt that Clap
was responsible for a rumor circulating throughout Springfield
that he had expressed Arian beliefs in Windham. To be accused of
latitudinarian tendencies was one matter, but to be stigmatized
as a non-believer in the divinity of Christ was more serious. "Is
this the part of a Christian Gentleman—is this the part of a
Gentleman and a Christian?" Breck demanded of Clap. He upbraided his adversary for the "Barbarious treatment . . . and Un-
speakable and Irreparable Injury" he had suffered.[49] Clap was not
one to forget such comments.

48. *Ibid.*, 2-3.
49. The letter is printed in Mason Green, *Springfield, 1636-1886, History of Town
and City* (Springfield, Mass., 1888), 230-31. The Breck affair is discussed on pp. 228-52.

Nevertheless, shortly after sending this letter, in late September 1734, Breck journeyed to Windham to mend his relations with Clap and secure the necessary letter of orthodoxy. In conference with the Windham minister, he shifted his theological position slightly, but continued to insist on the principle that the good heathen might be saved without a conversion experience. As for his prior testimony about his thievery and subsequent expulsion, Breck casuistically maintained that his answers to Clap had been consistent with the truth and "that he was neither expelled, nor sent away privately." [50] But his effort was in vain. He rode out of Windham without a letter of clearance.

As the year 1734 progressed, Breck's hopes in Springfield faded. He could not agree with the First Church on salary, and finally the young candidate returned to Cambridge. In November, however, the First Church again offered him the pulpit. Breck accepted, but the Hampshire Association refused to sanction his appointment. It became apparent to Breck that his ordination was contingent upon his exculpation by Clap. He again swallowed his pride and directed a conciliatory, almost apologetic, letter to his nemesis in which he appealed for consideration and asked for "Christian Forgiveness" for his "indecent Talk" and impulsive accusations— among which was the assertion that Clap was a downright liar! He admitted having been "inconsiderate and incautious" in expressing his religious doctrines, and attributed his dogmatism on some points to a compulsive desire to argue controversial points of divinity. Despite this sudden humility, Clap refused to draw up the letter of clearance.

The flames of controversy were now fanned by the First Church of Springfield. Ignoring the edict of the Hampshire Association, its parishioners laid plans for Breck's ordination, with or without a statement of orthodoxy from Clap. They were not unanimous in supporting him; there was a hard core of anti-Breck parishioners. A majority, however, resented the Hampshire Association's attempt to dictate and was determined to install Breck. By statute the authority of the Association was carefully limited; it did not have legal sanction to impose discipline, as was the case in Con-

50. *A Narrative of the Proceedings*, 7-9.

necticut. But by customary right the Association, which had been organized by the autocratic Solomon Stoddard, maintained a vigilant watch over the churches in the area. It was opposed in many quarters, even by the Mathers, who thought that Stoddard had carried authority to excess. The Springfield group that favored Breck disapproved of its practice of setting public standards of heresy and of interfering in affairs over which it had no legal jurisdiction. In the case of Breck, they believed it had overstepped the bounds of its authority.

What had originated as a local tiff over the orthodoxy of one young ministerial candidate suddenly mushroomed into a theological *cause célèbre*. The issues involved the fundamental structure of the Congregational System in Massachusetts. These questions were not being raised for the first time. Debate on them had persisted since the late decades of the seventeenth century and had been intensified after 1705 when the Mathers failed in their attempt to ram down the throats of the clergy their "Proposals" to centralize authority in Massachusetts. Here in Springfield, the great theological battle of the age was being waged in miniature: whether or not final authority in ecclesiastical affairs resided in the individual church or with the ministerial association. The pro-Breck element contended, as did John Wise in an earlier day, that the individual church held the sole authority to regulate its internal affairs:

But if such associated Pastors, whose Original [authority?] as an Association is only from themselves, come at length to look upon themselves as sort of Body Corporate, and assume the Exercise of Government; if they claim a Right to take the sole or the first Cognizance of Ecclesiastical Cases within those Bounds which they have drawn for themselves, or to direct and limit Churches in the Election of Officers, and the Calling of Councils; if they declare it irregular and unwarrantable in a particular Church to chuse and ordain a Pastor, without first consulting them, and having their Consent thereto; such an Association of Pastors, wherever it is found, is an Usurpation upon the Liberties of Congregational Churches, and those Churches are servile indeed that tamely submit to them therein.[51]

51. *Answer to a Pamphlet,* 5.

One immediate consequence of the theological wrangling was a split in the Hampshire Association. Six of the thirteen ministers who formerly had opposed Breck's ordination now turned their support to him.[52] The remaining seven, led by Jonathan Edwards, relentlessly pursued their efforts to block the ordination.

A local issue at the outset, the controversy gradually widened in scope. Before long, the winds of ecclesiastical dispute were whipping against Boston to the east and New Haven to the south. Some of the most prominent religious figures of New England were soon to be involved in the proceedings. Breck himself implicated some leading ministers of Boston in the dispute: in a final attempt to mollify the Hampshire Association, the young candidate, on his return to Springfield from Cambridge, stopped off in Boston and asked some of the more eminent ministers of that city to sign a certificate proclaiming his orthodoxy. He took care not to inform them of his past difficulties in Windham and his present plight in Springfield; viewing Breck's request as routine, they did not investigate his recent activities. When they subsequently learned the facts, they were deeply angered by his apparent duplicity. As one of the ministers later wrote, "Breck had delt Fallaciously and Imperiously with them in that Affair."[53] These ministers, among whom were such pre-eminent figures as Benjamin Colman, William Checkley, Thomas Foxcroft, and Mather Byles, now entered the fray. Rector Elisha Williams of Yale College also kept a close watch on events in Springfield, as did Clap and his clerical confreres in the Windham area.

The controversy raged during the spring and summer months of 1735. Both sides indulged in abuse. In the finest traditions of eighteenth-century theological dispute, scurrilous criminations and equally scurrilous recriminations were hurled recklessly in an effort to discredit the opposition. To the Breck adherents, Clap became the focus of vilification, for the Hampshire Association's case rested squarely on the "main Foundation" of his testimony. They turned their wrath upon him, charging, for example, that he had dictated testimonials from Windham residents relative to Breck's heterodoxy that had been sent to the Hampshire Associa-

52. *Ibid.*, 26.
53. *A Narrative of the Proceedings,* 31.

tion. Some of these depositions, they affirmed, were drawn up
against the will of the signers. They cited the testimony of one
Windhamite who had refused to draw up a deposition because "he
[Clap] would have had it run in such Terms as he could not in
Conscience subscribe to." [54] They also assailed Clap for probing
into Breck's past and publicizing the unsavory aspects of his
undergraduate career, especially his thievery. The incident, they
argued, had occurred when Breck was a boy of thirteen, and therefore should be regarded as an indiscretion of youth. It did not
prove conclusively, as Clap was insisting, that Breck was a moral
delinquent.[55]

While the argument continued, the First Church laid plans
for Breck's ordination. By custom, lay and clerical representatives
from churches of the immediate area were chosen as members of
ordaining councils. It was also customary to permit the minister-
elect to designate the churches he wished to be represented. Breck
departed from convention by selecting four ministers from Boston,
all of whom held pronounced liberal theological views. By pack-
ing the council with liberals, Breck assured his ordination.

The breaking point was reached with the arrival of the "foreign" delegation in October 1735. The anti-Breck ministers of the
Hampshire Association branded their clerical brethren from Boston as interlopers. They lodged a protest with the council, declaring that it was without jurisdiction to ordain Breck, that some of
its members were "fetch'd from very remote Parts of the Country,"
and that "they meddled with an Affair that did not belong to
them." The Cambridge Platform, they railed, "is an utter stranger
to any such way of authorizing a Council to act." [56] These sentiments were echoed in another statement ostensibly drawn up by
the minority party of the First Church.[57]

By this time the issues had become hopelessly tangled, and both
sides were keenly anxious for a resolution of their difficulties and
a return to normalcy. After much unseemly wrangling and behind-
the-scenes maneuvering, the contesting parties ultimately decided

54. *Answer to a Pamphlet*, 83.
55. *Ibid.*, 14-16.
56. *A Narrative of the Proceedings*, 77-89.
57. *Answer to a Pamphlet*, 59.

that the ordaining council, "foreign" representatives and all, should hold a meeting closed to everyone but the principal agents of both factions. Breck and Clap, the central protagonists, were to present their arguments in a face-to-face encounter. The Hampshire Association gave its assent to this general ventilation of the controversy, but secretly laid plans with the civil magistrates to make certain that the council would not be in a position to render a final judgment on the matter.

The day of the hearing, October 7, 1735, found Springfield in a mood of febrile excitement. Public interest had been whipped to a high pitch during the nine-month dispute and a large, unruly crowd milled through the street in front of the Town House. Religious personages from neighboring communities and from Connecticut were in attendance. Rector Williams had ridden up from New Haven to assist the anti-Breck forces in formulating their strategy.[58] Clap made the journey from Windham, his saddlebag filled with affidavits and assorted documentary evidence. A contingent of witnesses from Windham, some for Breck, some against, further swelled the attendance.

The hearing opened with Clap's testimony. Breck instantly took umbrage at Clap's initial statements but was warned against further interruption; he would be permitted to state his case when the Windham minister concluded his report. With characteristic thoroughness, Clap first produced a batch of letters attesting to his high standing in the Windham area and his acknowledged orthodoxy. Next he read affidavits establishing the reputable character of Windhamites who had pointed the finger of heresy at Breck. While he testified, however, a curious incident took place. A man on horseback, obviously a messenger, raced through the street to the council room, pushed through the pressing mob, and, after gaining entrance into the inner chamber, exchanged some hurried whispers with Clap. He then quickly left the room, mounted his horse, and rode off in haste. It was a most unusual intrusion. What the two discussed has never been determined, but the pro-Breck group had good reason to believe that the interruption related to a plot concocted by Clap and his friends to thwart Breck's ordination with one bold stroke. For, just as Clap

58. So the pro-Breck group asserted. *Answer to a Pamphlet*, 75-76.

completed his lengthy testimony, and before Breck could speak, as if by prearrangement the sheriff strode into the room and presented a warrant calling for Breck's arrest.[59] This action threw the meeting into consternation.

It was evident that Clap and his Hampshire allies were equally startled by this turn of events, and this fact may have served to dispel momentarily any thought among the Breck forces that there was collusion between the Hampshire group and the civil authorities. At the moment, the sequence of events appeared to be a singular coincidence. Later, however, when all the facts were pieced together, it became perfectly clear to the Breck group why their opponents had been visibly shaken. Actually, what had occurred was not according to plan: the original scheme of the Hampshire element had called for the arrest of the Boston ministers of the ordaining council, not Breck! [60] The design had gone awry when one of the higher officers among the civil magistracy, after weighing the possible repercussions of this action and without notifying the Hampshire group, changed the orders at the last moment.[61] Despite the switch of arrest, the anti-Breck faction was pleased. When they later gathered in conclave to recount the day's affairs, one was moved to remark, "Well, Gentlemen, we have had a fine Ordination to Day!" [62]

As the facts became known, the Breck element regarded Clap as the master architect of a nefarious plot—the perfect timing of the arrest and his private conversation with the messenger strongly implicated him. The Boston ministers seethed with rage at the thought of his sitting among them after having conspired to bring about their arrest. That Clap was implicated in the "extraordinary Interruption" seems clear; whether he was its main contriver is open to question, notwithstanding the strident charges of the pro-Breck forces then and the writers of the Harvard-liberal-Unitarian school now.[63]

59. *Ibid.*, 59-64.
60. *Ibid.*, 79-80.
61. *Ibid.*, 78-79.
62. *Answer to a Pamphlet*, 81.
63. For a typical opinion, see Henry Bamford Parkes, *Jonathan Edwards, the Fiery Puritan* (N. Y., 1930), 114-15.

This dramatic and somewhat farcical climax gave the controversy an increased notoriety.[64] The Boston papers kept their readers informed of the "Affair of Springfield," [65] and even the *New-York Weekly Journal* found the dispute newsworthy.[66] Excitement was highest in the Springfield area.[67] In nearby Northampton, Jonathan Edwards saw the religious revival he was carefully conducting wane in intensity as men's thoughts turned from salvation to the polemics of religious strife; Edwards later lamented that the Springfield controversy had contributed to the decline of his revival.[68] Both parties to the dispute eventually published pamphlets in which the documents in the case and the views of its partisans were laid out with uninhibited spleen.[69] The tracts swarmed with insults.

And what of the principal disputants? With his arrest Breck found himself not only in popular favor but well on the road to martyrdom. In the public eye he appeared as a defenseless victim

64. After his arrest, Breck was brought to the Town House where Clap and his associates presented additional testimony against him. He was released that evening in the custody of the ordaining council. On the following morning, the council resumed its hearing, but the justices again intervened. They ordered Breck be returned to their custody, after which they readied him for extradition to Connecticut.

65. *Boston Evening Post*, Dec. 1, 22, 29, 1735; *Boston Weekly News-Letter*, Dec. 18, 1735; *New-England Weekly Journal* (Boston), Dec. 23, 1735, Jan. 6, Feb. 3, Mar. 2, 1736.

66. Jan. 26, 1735.

67. On the day following Breck's arrest, virtually the entire population of Springfield gathered around the Town House and hooted and hollered for his release. Their mobbish tendencies were stimulated when a man on horseback read a confession of faith allegedly written by Breck. Later, the Clap forces sarcastically reported: "A young Gentleman who was present at that Transaction, made this Remark upon it, viz. 'The old Horse stood astonished at what was doing; and if he had the tongue of Balaam's Ass, he would have reproved the madness of the Prophet.'" *A Narrative of the Proceedings*, 66. Breck's confession of faith, which is surprisingly orthodox in doctrine in view of his earlier statements, is printed in *Answer to a Pamphlet*, 88-90.

68. *Narrative of Surprising Conversions* in *The Works of President Edwards*, 4 vols. (N. Y., 1879), III, 271.

69. The principal primary sources for the Breck dispute are the two pamphlets cited above. While entirely partisan in view, they are of inestimable value for the documents they contain. The most accurate secondary account is that of Shipton, *Harvard Graduates*, VIII, 663-79. Useful are: E. Byington, "The Reverend Robert Breck Controversy," Connecticut Valley Historical Society, *Papers and Proceedings*, 2 (1904), 1-19; Mason Green, "The Breck Controversy in the First Parish in Springfield in 1735," *ibid.*, 1 (1881), 8-16.

of ecclesiastical tyranny. He played the part well. A day or two after his arrest, the embarrassed and harassed civil magistrates of Springfield, who were reluctant to invoke court proceedings in the face of strong public reaction and were anxious to wash their hands of the entire affair, ordered that he be returned to Connecticut. There he was to be tried for his earlier alleged indiscretions. Escorted by an informal honor guard of his supporters, Breck was taken to the Connecticut line by the sheriff and placed in the custody of that colony's authorities. While the cortege was winding its way down the Connecticut River valley, Breck's supporters of the First Church held a tearful prayer meeting in his behalf.

Their prayers were seemingly answered, for a few days later the martyr triumphantly returned to Springfield—his case was never tried in Connecticut. The Windham County officials confiscated his surety bond when he failed to appear for trial and happily dropped the matter.[70] Breck was ultimately ordained by the First Church in January 1736,[71] after the Massachusetts General Court issued a declaration legalizing the disputed council; it also reprimanded the three Hampshire justices who had issued the warrant for Breck's arrest.[72]

Although Clap emerged from the affair something less than a public hero, his participation had a happy effect on his career. The obscure country parson was suddenly elevated to a pinnacle of notoriety upon the wings of religious controversy. He became a main topic of conversation in New England. Moreover, he had worked on an intimate basis with some of the most distinguished clerics in New England. Most important to his career was the close relationship he established with Rector Elisha Williams of Yale College. In the parlance of the modern business world, Clap had made a contact.

On October 31, 1739, some four years after the Breck imbroglio, Elisha Williams resigned the rectorship, and the trustees of Yale College promptly appointed Clap as his successor. There can be

70. *New-England Weekly Journal* (Boston), Dec. 23, 1735.
71. *Ibid.*, Feb. 3, 1736.
72. *Journals of the House of Representatives of Massachusetts*, 13 ([Boston, Mass.], 1932), 187.

little doubt that Williams was an important, if not the decisive, factor in Clap's selection.[73] On the other hand, it must have been apparent to the trustees that the strong-willed Windham minister was eminently qualified for the position. At the age of thirty-two he stood out as an inflexible defender of the Congregational way. His ministerial record provided substantial evidence of his capabilities as an administrator and disciplinarian. Moreover, he had exhibited special ability as a clerical scholar; ministers from as far away as Hartford were aware of his interest in astronomical research.[74] His participation with a group of ministers in the establishment of a library in Lebanon, Connecticut, stamped him as a man of wide cultural interests,[75] and despite his lack of sympathy with transgressors he had been a successful teacher. As Naphtali Daggett later wrote, "he was very instructive, uncommonly apt to teach, both in public and private. Instructing seemed to be the natural exercise and diversion of his mind." [76] He had prepared twenty-six Windham boys for entrance into Yale, an astonishingly high number considering the size and social composition of his parish.[77]

The trustees appointed two of its members to extend the formal invitation to Clap and receive his answer. After a short deliberation, he accepted the committee's offer. His decision must have been influenced by a desire to leave the area in which he had suffered so much spiritual anguish. While he had built himself solidly into the traditions of the community, Windham held tormenting memories that must have twisted his heart. On the positive side, there was the attraction of New Haven, much smaller than Boston, Newport, or New York, but a bustling town and a cultural center. Although its harbor would scarcely bristle with masts until the 1760's, when a long wharf was built to compensate

73. The well-informed Franklin Dexter held to this belief. "An Historical Study of the Powers and Duties of the Presidency in Yale College," *Amer. Antiq. Soc., Proceedings,* New Ser., 12 (1899), 33.

74. George Leon Walker, ed., *Daniel Wadsworth's Diary* (Hartford, 1894), 38.

75. Martha W. Hooker, "Booklovers of 1738—One of the First Libraries in America," *Connecticut Magazine,* 10 (1906), 717-18.

76. *Faithful Serving of God,* 30-31.

77. *Windham Bi-Centennial,* 25.

for shallow water,[78] New Haven already was stirring with the rest-less spirit of commercial enterprise. In touch with its hinterland and stimulated by contact with near and distant ports, New Haven was infused with a more active intellectual life than Clap's old parish. And there was the new college which had good prospects of future development. Connecticut's population was expanding rapidly. Settlers from Massachusetts were flocking into the fertile Connecticut River valley, setting up towns on the Long Island Sound shoreline to the south, and pushing into the stony wilds of the west and east. More than likely Yale would keep in step with the increase in population. Above all, the rectorship presented Clap with an opportunity to further the cause of Puritanism. He regarded his appointment as being in accord with the plan of Divine Providence. It was a call from God. On this basis alone, he was obliged to accept.

Having agreed to take the position, Clap had to secure his re-lease from the First Church. As a general rule, parishes were reluc-tant to give up their ministers, since the process of replacement, especially in an isolated rural area, was time-consuming and costly. There is some reason to believe, however, that Windham parish may have been the exception to this rule. Clap unquestionably had the respect of his parishioners, but he was not greatly beloved by them. He exaggerated when he wrote in his *Annals of Yale* that the "Generality of the People [at Windham] could not be satisfied that it was their Duty to part with their Minister, on this Occasion." [79] The indication is that the "Generality" was far from displeased at the prospect of losing their head and censor.

In the custom of the time, an ecclesiastical council composed of representatives of the churches of the county was called to advise the First Society on the proper course of action. With little deliberation, this body reached the decision that Clap be released from his ministry so that he could accept "a post of greater Useful-ness and more Publick Service than the Post he is now in and there-

---

78. Thomas R. Trowbridge, Jr., "History of the Ancient Maritime Interests of New Haven," New Haven Colony Hist. Soc., *Papers*, 3 (1882), 112-14. For a more composite picture of New Haven, see Lawrence H. Gipson, *Jared Ingersoll—A Study of American Loyalism in Relation to British Colonial Government* (New Haven, 1920), chap. 1.

79. P. 40.

fore we think it a Call of Divine Providence." It advised Clap to be "speedy in accepting and undertaking the Business." [80] The matter was settled; Clap was given his release, effective upon his installation as president of Yale, which was planned for April 2, 1740. In mid-December 1739, Clap went to New Haven to have a closer look at his future assignment,[81] then returned to Windham and resumed his ministerial duties.[82] His war against sin in Windham continued without abatement until he took final leave of the town. No one expected anything different.

One month after Clap's installation as rector, the parishioners of the First Church, who on Clap's departure had "acted like boys let out of school," [83] ordained their new minister, the Reverend Stephen White. A recent Yale graduate, the youthful White, like Samuel Whiting, was conspicuous for his "mild and sweet temper." [84] The parishioners had selected for their new spiritual leader a man whose qualities of personality were antithetical to those of Clap. The First Church had come full circle. There was nothing unusual in their vote that White should serve as their

80. Windham First Society Meeting, Nov. 19, 1739, Yale MS.; Clap, *Annals of Yale,* 40; and Report of an Ecclesiastical Council at Windham, Dec. 4, 1739, Yale MS. Upon Clap's appointment as rector, the First Church followed the traditional practice of petitioning the General Assembly for monetary compensation. The Yale trustees also petitioned the Assembly, requesting that body to assume the full burden of the financial loss sustained by the First Church. The Assembly agreed to pay the church £310 for "temporal damages." Connecticut Archives: Colleges and Schools, 1st Ser., Pt. ii, I, 255a, 257-58, Conn. State Lib.; Yale Corporation Records, I, 66, Yale Univ.; James Trumbull and Charles Hoadly, eds., *Public Records of the Colony of Connecticut* (Hartford, 1850-90), VIII, 308 (hereafter cited as Trumbull and Hoadly, eds., *Conn. Recs*).

81. Much has been made of the fact that some of the trustees were conspicuously absent at the reception for Clap when he arrived in New Haven. Shipton and Dexter affirm that certain trustees had opposed Clap because of his pronounced Calvinism. Shipton, *Harvard Graduates,* VII, 31; Dexter, "Clap and Writings," New Haven Colony Hist. Soc., *Papers,* 5 (1894), 253. Clap apparently had been led to believe that he was to be installed at this time. He noted that the absence of a committee to "mount him into office... made some talk in the Country." Windham First Congregational Church Records, I, 26, Conn. State Lib.; Clap, Memoirs, Dec. 19, 1739, Yale MS.; see also Warham Williams to ——— Williams, Mar. 12, 1739/40, Pennsylvania Historical Society MS. In one part of a letter from Eleazar Wheelock to Clap (Sept. 1743, Dartmouth College MS.), there is an intimation that Clap had been advised by certain ministers to reject the offer to become rector.

82. Windham First Congregational Church Records, I, 22, Conn. State Lib.

83. Larned, *History of Windham,* I, 285-86.

84. Dexter, *Yale Graduates,* I, 567-68.

minister "as long as he lives, or is able to preach the Gospel" [85]—
this was a traditional contractual agreement between congregation and minister. However, the words may have held a special
meaning to the Windham parishioners. If they had never had a
minister like Clap before, they were apparently determined never
to have one again.

85. It would seem that White admirably fulfilled these conditions. He married
the daughter of a prominent citizen of Windham, accumulated a sizable estate,
and died in theological harness at the age of 76. White was not an efficient administrator, but this defect never became an issue with his parishioners.

Chapter Four

THE RISE OF YALE COLLEGE

WITH his installation as rector of Yale, Clap acquired greater status and dignity, but little more. Although the rectorship conferred considerable prestige upon its incumbent, it was not an office of strong executive authority or responsibility. The original Charter of 1701 was explicit: The trustees alone "shall have henceforward the Oversight, full and complete Right, Liberty, Power and Privilege, to furnish, direct, manage, order, improve and encourage from Time to Time and in all Times hereafter, the said Collegiate School."[1] The Charter was silent on the duties and responsibilities of the chief officer. Apparently the founding fathers, who were Congregational ministers, shared the conviction that the most effective type of administrative organization was an all-powerful, unicameral governing body. These ministers, of whom all but one had been trained at Harvard, were fully aware of the power struggle taking place at Cambridge between the president and Corporation, and the Board of Overseers. They wished to avoid internecine warfare.

Departing from the English and Harvard precedents, the Yale trustees created a rectorial office of no executive force and denied

1. Clap, *Annals of Yale*, 7. The Charter is printed in entirety on pages 5-8.

the rector a seat on the governing board. His prime responsibility was to ground the students in the principles of the reformed theology. He was to conduct morning and evening prayers, expound on "practical Theology" on the Sabbath, disseminate the religious principles contained in the writings of William Ames and the Westminster Confession of Faith, "and in all other Ways according to his best Discretion, shall at all Times studiously endeavour in the Education of the Students, *to promote the Power and purity of Religion, and the best Edification of these* New-England Churches." [2] The trustees, on the other hand, prescribed the type of divinity to be taught, the curricular content, the mode of instruction, and the course of discipline. Subject to pre-emptory dismissal, with or without cause, by a majority vote of the trustees, the rector was a glorified schoolmaster. Nor was his status appreciably altered in 1723 when the Connecticut General Assembly passed a measure granting him the right to attend trustee meetings and endowing him with ex officio trustee powers. [3] For the ensuing five years the trustees sturdily ignored the Assembly's action and continued to function as they had in the past. Finally, they acquiesced and allowed Rector Williams to sit in on their deliberations. [4]

The early rectors generally observed the letter and spirit of the Charter and left important administrative matters to the trustees. Only Rector Pierson, it would seem, managed to influence the determination of administrative policy. Rectors Cutler and Williams were forceful men, endowed with executive abilities, but they made little effort to impress the stamp of their personalities and ideals upon the trustees and the college.

Clap's appearance on the Yale scene in 1740 brought an abrupt end to the concept of the rector as a mere teacher and hireling of the trustees. Without legal sanction, Clap took up the mace of leadership and became the source of all directive energy. Whereas his predecessor had attended trustee meetings by sufferance, [5] Clap

2. *Ibid.*, 10-11.
3. *Ibid.*, 34.
4. Dexter, "Historical Study of Presidency," Amer. Antiq. Soc., *Proceedings*, New Ser., 12 (1899), 32.
5. *Ibid.*, 33.

took his place with the avowed purpose of molding administrative policy. He became virtual self-appointed chairman of the board.

Clap threw himself into a reorganization of the college. Reform began inauspiciously with a measure designed to eliminate a long-standing habit among freshmen of beginning attendance at New Haven after "half or more of the year is expired." Under Clap's urging, the trustees passed a decree stating that freshmen entering late would be placed in the lowest positions in the class ranking [6]— a policy already in effect at Harvard. At this time, no more severe punishment, unless it were expulsion, could be inflicted upon a student. The ranking of students was established largely on the basis of "family Dignity," [7] and because New England was still acutely sensitive about class distinctions, social degradation was a penalty of telling impact.

Commencement procedure had been upset in the past by student laxness. Many master's candidates arrived on commencement day without warning and announced their intention of taking the degree; others who had planned to take a degree failed to appear on the appointed day. Again Clap reached into the Harvard legal bag. A law was passed requiring master's candidates to notify the authorities at least one month prior to commencement and to participate in the exercises. If they failed to fulfill these two conditions, they would not be given their degrees.[8]

The library was another source of irritation to which Clap directed his reforming energy. Once more drawing upon the Harvard code, he came forth with stringent regulations governing the use of books and the management of the library. Hereafter, if a student put pen to a book, he was to be charged "for every word that he shall write in it." Furthermore, a student might

6. Yale Corporation Records, I, 66, Yale Univ.

7. Clap personally arranged the class lists. For this purpose he kept notebooks in which he listed the occupation and pertinent financial data of each student's father. A student's rank was established midway during the freshman year and remained unchanged for the rest of his collegiate days. This system was finally discarded in 1766. See Franklin Dexter, "On Some Social Distinctions at Harvard and Yale, Before the Revolution," Amer. Antiq. Soc., *Proceedings*, New Ser., 9 (1893), 34-59. Interestingly, the Yale system deviated from that of Harvard which was based, partially at least, on academic ability. The entire question of academic ranking is in need of further study.

8. Yale Corporation Records, I, 67, Yale Univ.

borrow a book only through the keeper (a tutor) who was to keep
an accurate record of the loan.[9]

From these small beginnings Clap's new order developed at
Yale. As he had reconstituted the First Church and First Society
of Windham, so he began to refashion Yale, giving it order and
system. His reforms soon began to widen in scope and came to
affect every area of the college, from the kitchen to the curriculum.
In his *Annals of Yale,* Clap wrote that upon his accession Yale was
"in the main, in a good State; yet not so perfect, but that it would
admit of sundry Emendations." [10] For the next quarter of a century
Clap steadily went about the business of bringing it "forward towards a State of Perfection." It was more than a new administration. It was a new era in Yale's history.

Clap was not long on the job before he concluded that the college desperately needed a comprehensive body of rules and regulations.[11] His principles of administration were grounded on the
premise that government, to be effective, must rest squarely on a
foundation of written law. In a statement that is suggestive of
Edmund Burke, Clap laid down "this general maxim of policy in
Government, that the more perfect state of any [Judiciary or]
Polity is to have large numbers of good general rules to go by;
and to act *pro hic et nunc* only in that case where they have not
had wisdom, time or experience enough to fix upon more particular rules." [12]

9. *Ibid.,* 67-68. The keeper was directed to record the title of the work, its size,
the name of the borrower, the time taken, and the date to be returned.
10. P. 41.
11. He apparently also concluded that he was in dire need of a wife, for he re-
married shortly after taking up residence in New Haven. His social (and financial)
status was now considerably enhanced, for his second wife, Mary Saltonstall, who had
already outlived two husbands, was of John Haynes stock; Haynes, Hooker, and
Ludlow were the leading agents in the original settlement of Connecticut. Clap's
marriage to a wealthy widow ("Affluent were her Circumstances, from her Youth")
was in keeping with Puritan convention. As Edmund Morgan impishly writes: "In
the case of second marriages the bargaining over estates played a more direct part
in the procedure of courtship. Mrs. [Alice M.] Earle remarks that it sometimes seems
difficult to see how the poor virgins ever got a man to marry them." Morgan,
Puritan Family, 21-22. For a biographical sketch of Clap's wife, see Chauncey
Whittelsey, *A Discourse, Occasioned by the Death, and Delivered at the Funeral,
of Mrs. Mary Clap, Relict of the Late Reverend President Clap* (New Haven, 1769).
12. Clap to [unknown], 1764, Yale MS.

Yale had operated largely on an *ad hoc* basis. In the early days of the school, the custom was to turn to the Harvard laws whenever an administrative problem or question of discipline arose which was not covered by existing law. After the settlement of the college in New Haven in 1718, a "short Body of Laws" was compiled, but with the expansion of enrollment and the natural organic development of the school, these were soon outmoded. It was no longer feasible to operate on the basis of tradition and a handful of general rules. In 1735, the trustees assigned to Rector Williams and a committee drawn from its body the task of revising and enlarging the existing code. Nothing came of it, however.[13]

Clap personally applied himself to the job during his first years in office. He compiled a new code, drawing its provisions from the "ancient Laws and Statutes" and past customs of Yale, from the laws of Harvard, and from the statutes of the University of Oxford, but adding regulations of his own. His finished work was submitted to the trustees and approved by them in 1745.[14]

The most noteworthy feature of Clap's "College Laws" was their comprehensiveness.[15] Every conceivable phase of administration was blanketed with rules. There were sections devoted to admission requirements and procedure, to religious responsibilities of the students, to the daily schedule, and to the management of the library. Even the duties of the non-academic personnel were outlined in meticulous detail. The steward, for example, was to render a yearly written report listing the "Platters and Other Utensils" in the kitchen, and he was to make certain that all the utensils were kept "Neat and Sweet." Should any of the kitchen equipment "be Lost or Damnified by Him or those whome he imploys ... he Shall make it Good."

Probably the most significant section of Clap's code was Chapter IV—"Of Penal Laws." Listed in an ascending scale of heinousness were improper actions and their corresponding punishments. The students were hedged in by a phalanx of law. Every imaginable wayward action likely to be conceived in the fertile mind of youth was anticipated: blasphemy, fornication, robbery, forgery,

13. Clap, *Annals of Yale*, 42.
14. Yale Corporation Records, I, 67-77, Yale Univ.
15. The laws are printed in Dexter, *Yale Graduates*, II, 2-18.

heresy, profane use of names, "Disobedient or Contumacious or Refractory Carriage towards his Superiours," fighting, quarreling, stealing, card playing, singing, loud talking during study periods, wearing women's clothes—and many more. Clap even had the foresight to insert a provision giving to himself and the tutors a sanction to "Break open any College Door to Suppress any Disorder." As it turned out, this inclusion proved to be a stroke of genius, for Clap and the tutors were forced to take ax in hand on numerous occasions, especially in the last years of his career.

The "College Laws" as a whole, and especially Chapter IV, embody Clap's theory of discipline which, in the main, was the traditional theory of Puritan New England. He once succinctly summarized his thoughts on discipline as follows:

Some persons have such a strong Propensity to Vice, Vanity and Disorder, as that they will not be influenced by Religion, Reason, Duty, or any just motive of true interest or prospect of real good. Such persons must therefore be influenced or restrained from those things which are plainly detrimental to themselves or the Society by *fear of Punishment* or *Shame*.[16] And perhaps there are few who are so entirely good, without any mixture of the remainder of the corruption, as not to need sometime a mixture of fear, especially in such a company of giddy youth, where there are so many temptations and evil examples.[17]

Although fear was the core of Clap's discipline, he warned that the Yale government should not arbitrarily impose penalties that were disproportionate to the infraction. The "rule of all Legislation," in Clap's words, was "to proportion the greatness of the Punishment to the greatness or the Impetus or Inclination to commit the Crime, in conjunction with the greatness of the Crime itself." [18] And what is the over-all aim of punishment? In a statement that is significant for its social and political implications (and interesting for its semantics), Clap averred: "The End and Design of Punishment is primarily to restrain the offender but principally to deter others. For the good of many is more to be aimed at than the good of one Individual." [19] Clap was certain that admonitions,

16. The underlining was done by Clap.
17. Some Observations Relating to the Government of the College, 4, Yale MS.
18. *Ibid.*, 7.
19. *Ibid.*, 13.

reprimands, and fines were proper penalties for minor infractions, but chronic offenders should be removed from the college community, for these students exerted a "pernicious" influence on the entire student body. "A little leaven," Clap pointed out, "leavens the whole Lump." [20]

In addition to compiling the "College Laws," Clap recorded the "customs" that prevailed at Yale.[21] These were a set of traditions relating to such matters as the stratification of the classes, and the deportment of the students in their relationships with one another and with college officers. A carry-over from medieval days, "customs" had a fourfold purpose in the collegiate system of education: to create and foster a paternalistic attitude among the ruling orders of the college community; to teach the students to respect their "Superiors"; to impress upon them the principle of social gradation; and to develop within them a sense of loyalty to class. It was Clap's belief that with the systematizing of the "customs" the rules "by which the Officers and Students of the College were to conduct themselves, became better fixed and known, and the Government of the College was rendered more steady and uniform, and less arbitrary." [22]

With its system of gradation and rank, Yale was a microcosm of Connecticut society. At the apex of the collegiate hierarchy stood the rector and trustees; next came the tutors, those with longer service lording it over recent appointees; [23] then the resident graduates, the seniors, juniors, sophomores, and finally the lowly freshmen. Among the undergraduates the seniors reigned as temporal lords. One of the special privileges they enjoyed was to utilize freshmen as personal valets, who hauled their wood and water, tended their fires, cleaned their boots, and ran all "reasonable and proper" errands. In theory, the seniors had the responsi-

20. A brief exposition of Clap's theory of discipline is to be found in his *Annals of Yale*, 85-86.

21. The volume was either lost or destroyed when the British ravaged New Haven during the Revolution. Extracts from the customs in effect in 1764 are printed in William Kingsley, "History of Yale College," *American Journal of Education*, 5 (1858), 561. See also, Theodore Woolsey, *Historical Discourse to Graduates of Yale College* (New Haven, 1850), 54-56.

22. Clap, *Annals of Yale*, 42-43. For student life at Yale, see below, chap. 10.

23. Note the controversies that developed over the ranking of the tutors in Dexter, ed., *Literary Diary of Stiles*, II, 513-14.

bility of maintaining a paternal interest in their charges. They were to guide and instruct them, to serve as moral and academic exemplars, and to protect them from the demonic sophomores.

As the lowest element in the social scale, the freshmen were expected to pay every mark of deference to their superiors. In addition to performing menial services, they were required to bare their heads when passing superiors, stand at military attention when spoken to, and pause before entryways and stairways and survey the scene for upperclassmen who would give them permission to proceed. Clap heartily approved of this fagging. It blended perfectly with the conservative social philosophy that underlay both the Yale system of education and Connecticut's social organization. Whatever damage it inflicted upon a freshman's sense of dignity, fagging instilled in him a respect for authority and impressed upon him the principle of social gradation. One harassed freshman who doubted the benefits of this training commented in 1765: "Freshmen have attained almost the happiness of negroes."

The library, which had been one of the first objects of Clap's zeal for reform, felt its further effects. The library laws of 1740 were superseded by the "College Laws" of 1745, one section of which listed in fine detail the rules and regulations governing the use of books and the management of the library. But Clap's most significant library reforms came in 1742 with the rearrangement of the books and the establishment of catalogues. Prior to this time, the books had been arranged in a so-called "press catalogue" system: catalogues were posted on the ends of each section, listing books on its shelves.[24] A student seeking a specific work under this system usually had a long search before finding his book.

With "considerable Labour and Pains," Clap, assisted by a tutor, reorganized the library of 2,500 volumes, book by book. He organized the library into sections, numbered each book, and placed the volumes in a fixed order on the shelves. Next he drew up three catalogues. One listed the books as they stood in their proper order on the shelves. A second listed them alphabetically by author

24. Anna Monrad, "Historical Notes on the Catalogues and Classifications of the Yale University Library," *Papers in Honor of Andrew Keogh* (New Haven, 1938), 251-56. For the early history of the library, see "An Address by Andrew Keogh at the Dedication of Sterling Library," *Yale University Library Gazette,* 5 (1931), 129-32.

or title. A third listed them by subject matter under twenty-five classes [25]—Clap's passion for systematic organization is revealed by the listing of some books under as many as five different headings. In the opinion of one library expert, Clap's method of cataloguing, although technically imperfect by modern standards, could be considered "perfect in that it incorporated the three approaches required by modern library science." [26] Upon the completion of this laborious task, Clap published the third catalogue for use by the students.[27] He was undoubtedly correct in his assumption that the new cataloguing system was "a great Incitement to the Diligence and Industry of the Scholars" in reading.[28]

Clap also worked assiduously to enlarge the collection. The total increase in the library's resources amounted to about fourteen hundred volumes between the years 1743 and 1766.[29] The addition of so many books without benefit of a library fund was no small achievement—the result of his persistent badgering of "Liberal Benefactors" and "Generous Gentlemen." But if Clap was the library's friend, he was also its censor. On one occasion he refused to accept a collection of books because they contained Baptist tracts; at another time he proscribed a book because it presented a point of view contrary to the orthodox formulation.

Among other important reforms effected by Clap were an increase in faculty and readjustment of faculty assignments. For some years prior to 1743 the teaching staff consisted of two tutors plus the rector. The tutors were often placed under the burden

25. Clap, *Annals of Yale*, 43.
26. This is the opinion of Anna Monrad. See *n.* 24.
27. Clap, *A Catalogue of the Library of Yale College in New Haven* (New London, 1743). The remaining two catalogues have survived in manuscript form. Only the printed form of the third catalogue is available. The manuscript was doubtless used as copy by Timothy Green, the New London publisher. See Andrew Keogh, "The Yale Library in 1742," in Harry Lydenberg and Andrew Keogh, eds., *William Warner Bishop, a Tribute* (New Haven, 1941), 76-87. For an analysis of the Library of 1742, see E. P. Morris, "A Library of 1742," *Yale Univ. Lib. Gazette*, 2 (1934), 1-11. For the gifts of one important benefactor, see Anne S. Pratt, *Isaac Watts and his Gifts of Books to Yale College* (New Haven, 1938).
28. Clap, *Annals of Yale*, 43.
29. Clap's *Catalogue of Yale Library* of 1743 listed 2,600 volumes; his *Catalogue of Yale Library* of 1755, 3,000 volumes. In his *Annals of Yale* (p. 86), for the year 1765, he numbered the volumes at "about" 4,000. Andrew Keogh asserts that Clap's first-printed *Catalogue of Yale Library* was in error, in that it listed about 150 more volumes than were owned by the college. "Address," *Yale Univ. Lib. Gazette*, 5 (1931).

of instructing two classes, "and sometimes more," in the course of an academic year. In 1743 Clap prodded the General Assembly into increasing the grant to the college and thereby obtained funds to hire a third tutor. Reserving for himself the instruction of seniors, he assigned a tutor to each of the three lower classes. A tutor now started with the freshman class, carried it through the junior year, then returned to the incoming freshman group to repeat the cycle.[30] In Clap's judgment the students under the new system "studied and recited much more than they had done in Years past." [31]

Ezra Stiles, a later president of Yale, theorized that Clap's "Chief Reason" for readjusting faculty assignments was to give himself more time for transacting college business; the seniors recited but once a day.[32] Stiles's belief seems plausible, for Clap's area of executive responsibility covered a wide spectrum of administrative duty. There was no part of college business to which he did not put a hand, and there was no detail too small for his consideration. In addition to instructing the seniors, he conducted morning and evening prayers; preached on Sundays; gave special evening lectures for the entire student body; maintained business correspondence with other academic administrators; attended ministerial meetings and sessions of the General Assembly; represented Yale at Harvard commencements; transacted all business matters relating to the college; maintained the financial records; imposed discipline; and supervised the tutors.[33] All the various functions carried out by the Hydra-headed administrations of modern colleges and universities were handled by Clap alone. He functioned as dean of men, dean of faculty, registrar, superintendent of buildings and grounds, director of development, public relations officer, head librarian, alumni secretary, and campus police chief. He was "a rare pattern of industry," reflected Naphtali Daggett after Clap's death. "It is almost incredible that he should be able to pay

30. Clap, *Annals of Yale*, 43; Clap to Eleazar Wheelock, Nov. 17, 1743, Boston Public Library MS.; Franklin Dexter, ed., *The Documentary History of Yale College, 1701-1745* (New Haven, 1916), 363-64.

31. Clap, *Annals of Yale*, 43.

32. Dexter, ed., *Literary Diary of Stiles*, II, 515.

33. Partial insight into the enormous scope of Clap's duties can be acquired by examining his College Memoirs and such records as the Land Book (Yale MSS.).

a proper attention to, and go through with such a multiplicity of different and arduous services at the same time." [34]

Clap's immediate reforms were substantial and visibly constructive, but, without a doubt, his greatest single achievement in the reorganization of the college was the Charter of 1745.[35] The question of whether this document was inspired by his seemingly insatiable lust for power, as his critics and enemies later claimed, is subordinate to the fact that it revolutionized Yale's government and laid the foundations for the future university. In this sense the Charter of 1745 is a monumental tribute to the sagacity, foresight, and administrative acumen of its creator.

While Clap never specified what he considered the defects of the existing Charter of 1701, there can be little doubt of his opinion. The trustees who managed the college lacked legal autonomy; they were not a corporate body, and were therefore in a weak legal position in handling important business, such as appointing new trustees, formulating administrative policy, and transacting financial affairs. Under the original charter the trustees functioned merely as caretakers. They were subject to the direct authority of the General Assembly, which had fallen into the habit of intervening in the internal affairs of the college. The Assembly's Act of 1723, which granted ex officio trustee powers to the rector, prescribed the age limit for new trustees, and set the number of trustees needed for a quorum, is but one example of legislative intrusion.

In the early years, when church-state ties were rigid, Assembly interference was not opposed and there was a natural accord between trustees and legislature. Gradually, however, the relationship began to chill. In time, the trustees came to resent legislative encroachments upon their prerogatives. To a strong-minded executive of Clap's mettle, the dependent status of Yale's governing body was intolerable; so, too, was his own dependent and powerless position.

The Charter of 1745, as Clap proclaimed in his *Annals of Yale*

34. *Faithful Serving of God*, 32-33.
35. Yale Corporation Records, II, 73, Yale Univ.; Trumbull and Hoadly, eds., *Conn. Recs.*, IX, 113-18; Connecticut Archives: Colleges and Schools, 1st Ser., Pt. ii, I, 278, Conn. State Lib.; Clap, *Annals of Yale*, 45-52. The Yale Library also has a manuscript copy of the Charter.

with something less than modesty, "set the College in a much more perfect and agreable State, than it was before." [36] The president and the fellows, as the rector and trustees of the college were now titled, became an "Incorporate Society," enjoying all the legal benefits of such an entity. Both were vested with authority to manage and dispose of all the land and other property belonging to the college. To them fell the sole right of appointing future trustees; the Corporation became a self-perpetuating agency. Legislative review and disallowance of Corporation acts were specified in the Charter of 1745, but only the president and fellows held the power to establish "Laws, Rules and Ordinances."

While the Charter had many noteworthy features, the most striking ones were the creation of the office of president and the lodging of executive power in this office. By the new charter, the president and fellows were given joint executive authority; both shared the authority to transact college business; both shared the responsibility for Yale's "Government, Care and Management." By endowing himself with co-ordinate administrative power, Clap had effected a veritable reconstitution of the governmental structure of Yale. The powerless rector of the past was suddenly elevated into a position of authority. And whereas the tenure of the rector had been subject to the discretion of the trustees, now the president could be dismissed only if found guilty of misdemeanors, unfaithfulness, default, or incapacity; and six of the ten fellows had to concur in his dismissal.

Although the Charter of 1745 distributed administrative power between president and fellows, in reality Clap became the controlling executive agent, who unilaterally shaped major policy and made the key decisions. The chief function of the fellows became confirmation, not the formulation, of policy. In later years some of the fellows actively opposed Clap, but they were never able to muster a majority.[37]

The enlargement of Yale's physical facilities was another of Clap's impressive achievements. Until 1752 the college proper consisted of the ungainly three-story wooden structure that had been dedicated to Elihu Yale in 1718. It provided sleeping ac-

36. P. 52*n*.
37. The dissension within the Corporation is discussed in chap. 8.

commodations for a maximum of fifty occupants. In 1747 Yale's enrollment stood at one hundred and twenty, and many students were lodged in private homes [38]—an arrangement which displeased Clap, for it was contrary to his notion of a "collegiate way of life," and it prevented him from maintaining a close vigil over the students' moral behavior. He projected a scheme for building a second college hall. The ever-present stumbling block of financial shortage was partly overcome by holding a lottery—a traditional money-raising device in the eighteenth century. It netted the building fund the fat sum of £500. The General Assembly provided an additional £363, derived from the sale of a French frigate captured by a Connecticut privateer in 1749.[39] Clap acted as surveyor, architect, and construction foreman; it has even been said that he frequently took shovel in hand and participated in the digging of the cellar. In design the new building resembled the old one, although smaller in size. Clap incorporated some architectural ideas passed on by President "Guts" Holyoke of Harvard,[40] who contributed two pieces of executive wisdom: eliminate gutters, "because you will find they will be filled with Ordure, ashes etc.," and have iron rather than lead springs on the sashes—the students were inclined to steal lead.[41] The foundations of the new hall were laid in 1750 and the outside walls finished two years later. The structure was one hundred feet long, forty feet wide, and three stories high. Walled with brick, it contained a cellar, a garret, a kitchen, thirty-two chambers, and sixty-four studies. At the Commencement of 1752, in a lavish ceremony, the building was named "Connecticut Hall" in honor of the General Assembly whose financial munificence was largely responsible for its completion.[42]

Connecticut Hall proved to be only a stopgap, for during the 1750's enrollment swelled to 170. Insufficient classroom space had become a serious problem, and there was also need for a larger library to house the growing book collection and scientific appara-

38. Clap, *Annals of Yale*, 54.
39. *Ibid.*, 55.
40. "The students nicknamed him 'Guts,' of which he certainly had a-plenty." Morison, *Three Centuries of Harvard*, 83.
41. Holyoke to Clap, Aug. 18, 1747, Yale MS.
42. Clap, *Annals of Yale*, 55-56.

tus. Mainly to alleviate these conditions, Clap made plans for a new hall or chapel. By means of a subscription,[43] a grant from the legislature, and surplus college funds, he was able to hurdle the financial obstacle. Construction began in April 1761, and the chapel was opened for use in June 1763. It was to serve as a place of worship until 1824. The brick building, forty by fifty feet in dimensions, contained a "Steeple and Galleries" and had space for the college's books and scientific equipment in a library room on the second floor. As in the case of Connecticut Hall, the chapel was situated with a mind to future expansion. "It is set near the South End of the Brick College," Clap wrote, "with a View that when another College is built, it will be set near the South Side of the Chapel." [44] The president was also actively involved in the planning and construction of a home for the use of Naphtali Daggett, Professor of Divinity. Clap not only arranged for its financing, which was done through subscription, but he also donated a plot of his own land. The house was begun in 1757 and finished the next summer.[45]

Clap's building program is dwarfed by comparison with Yale's later development, yet Connecticut Hall and the chapel were remarkable achievements for their time. The college was in a period of transition, and the president's vigor was matched by the dynamics of Yale's growth. Judged on the basis of enrollment and the number of graduates, Clap's administration represents the period of greatest expansion in Yale's colonial history; indeed, no other colonial college had a comparable rate of growth. During the decade 1753-73, there was an average of 170 undergraduates, more than twice the number enrolled in Yale's strongest year in the past.[46] Equally significant as an index to expansion are the statistics on graduates. More than seven hundred boys received degrees during Clap's reign,[47] a figure almost twice the number of all Yale graduates from 1701 to 1740. And although Yale was founded fifty-five years after Harvard, it began to produce more graduates than

43. Subscription List for a Chapel, Yale MS.; Subscription List for a Chapel Spire and Turret, Yale MS.
44. Clap, *Annals of Yale*, 77.
45. *Ibid.*, 68, 99-100.
46. Dexter, ed., *Literary Diary of Stiles*, II, 226; Clap, *Annals of Yale*, 77.
47. All Yale graduates to the year 1765 are listed in Clap, *Annals of Yale*, 105-24.

its sister college before the end of Clap's administration. From 1753 to 1760 Yale granted 254 degrees to Harvard's 205.[48] For Yale's truly meteoric growth, Clap must be given a considerable measure of credit.[49]

If Clap was zealously intent upon overhauling Yale's government, he was satisfied merely to tinker with the curriculum. He readjusted, rearranged, but did not disassemble and reconstruct. All of the traditional forms and subjects were retained. The scholastic lecture, declamations, and disputations—forms developed in the medieval universities and later instituted at Harvard—remained the central curricular exercises. There was one modification, however, which indicated a modernist tendency. Forensic argumentation was introduced in disputations in the 1750's and came to rank equally with the long-established syllogistic method. Allowing for greater flexibility in presenting arguments and delivered in English, forensic debate was ideally suited for theses of secular content; as Clap put it, forensic form "gives a greater Scope to their Genius." On Mondays the two upper classes disputed in the syllogistic form, and on Tuesdays they disputed in the forensic style.[50] A parallel development is to be noticed at Harvard.

Cut from a Harvard cloth, the Yale curriculum during Clap's span of office was the standard liberal arts course of study, strengthened by the subjects made popular during the Renaissance and shaded with Westminster Calvinism. Featured were such longtime staples of the hallowed trivium and quadrivium as the "tongues" (principally Latin, and, to a far lesser extent, Greek

48. See the comparison by Quincy, *History of Harvard*, II, 462; and by Charles F. Thwing, *A History of Higher Education in America* (N. Y., 1906), 104-5.

49. Attention should be directed to a scheme proposed by Clap whereby all of the colleges in the American colonies were to be united in the "same plan of Education." The plan called for uniform standards for admission and a uniform code of general laws. This important proposal is mentioned by Francis Alison of the College of Philadelphia in a letter to Ezra Stiles (May 27, 1759), Dexter, ed., *Stiles's Itineraries*, 423. It is to be lamented that Clap's papers do not yield further information on the proposal which Alison believed "deserves a serious consideration."

50. Clap, *Annals of Yale*, 82. Clap also introduced English declamations; previously, only Latin declamations had been delivered. See John Bigelow, comp. and ed., *The Works of Benjamin Franklin* ... (New York and New London, 1904), II, 358; Franklin to Jared Eliot, Dec. 24, 1751, Yale MS.

and Hebrew), arithmetic, geometry, and astronomy. The three
philosophies (natural, mental, and moral) capped the undergraduate course of instruction. As at Harvard, all students followed the
same academic regimen. It was, externally at least, very much the
same curriculum under which Clap himself had been trained.
Within the limitations of this general framework, however, Clap
did make significant modifications.

The stress on religion, an indigenous feature of the Yale system,
if not intensified, at least remained constant during Clap's tenure.
It was in the degree to which religion dominated the curriculum
that Harvard and Yale were showing the greatest divergence.
Eighteenth-century Harvard did not strictly adhere to the dictum
of its founding fathers: "Every one shall consider the main end
of his life and studies to know God and Jesus Christ." [51] As a principle of action it had lost its force. Indeed, according to the historian of Harvard, the founding fathers merely cited this
injunction to emphasize the continuity of the school with medieval
universities; they were actually intent on providing a rich and
varied liberal arts education and promoting the diffusion of useful
knowledge.[52] Harvard moved steadily into the mainstream of
secularism, steadily decreasing the emphasis on theology. Yale, on
the other hand, held back and continued to stress a religious orientation toward education.

For the president, religion was the serious business of the human
race. A close friend recalled in later years that Clap frequently
told him that learning was important but religion "is the great
object of my fear and concern." [53] In his *Annals of Yale,* Clap
underscored the place of religion: "Above all, Care is taken to
instil into their [the students'] Minds, the principles of true
Religion, in Doctrine and Practice, by publick and private
Discourses and personal Conversations." [54] It was more from
conviction than force of habit that he described Yale in his official
writings as a "Seminary of Religion and Learning." Nor was the
sequential order of these terms merely accidental.

51. Harvard College Laws, 1642, in Col. Soc. of Mass., *Publications,* 15 (1925), 24-27,
29-31, 187-90.
52. Morison, *Intellectual Life of New England,* 33.
53. Daggett, *Faithful Serving of God,* 33-34.
54. P. 83.

True religion at Yale was Westminster Calvinism, and at every turn the students were exposed to the dogma of the orthodox faith. In many of their regular scholastic exercises, and particularly during the special religious classes on Saturday, the boys examined, debated, and discussed the orthodox doctrines. In declamations and disputations they espoused and defended the principles of such revered Reformation apostles as Wollebius and Ames. Orthodox tenets were also thrust upon them in the daily morning and evening prayers, in special lectures, and in the regular services on Sunday and special holidays.[55] Religion was welded into the curriculum.

Clap's theory of education was rooted in the medieval principle that knowledge should be directed toward moral ends. For Clap, as for Aquinas, the overriding purpose of education was to instill in youth the precepts of Christian morality. The acquisition of secular knowledge was a subordinate consideration, and Clap believed that a curriculum devoid of religious instruction was "worth but little."[56] Intelligence motivated by the ethical principles of Christianity was the educational ideal underlying the Yale system. In 1743, Clap drew up a general curriculum for his students to which he appended this exhortation: "Above all have an Eye to the great End of all your Studies, which is to obtain the Clearest Conceptions of Divine Things and to lead you to a Saving Knowledge of God in his Son JESUS CHRIST."[57]

Because he insistently stressed the unity of religion and education in his writings, and because he overtly sought to perpetuate the religious character of the school, Clap has been singled out by educationists and historians as the prototypal academic reactionary of eighteenth-century America. He is often cast as the polar opposite of Provost William Smith of the College of Philadelphia, a

55. John Cleaveland's Autobiography, Essex Institute MS., provides partial insight into the religious character of the curriculum. For the benefit of ministerial candidates, Clap provided instruction in Hebrew. See Ezra Stiles, Memoir Concerning my Learning Hebrew, May 12, 1768, Yale MS.

56. Observations Relating to Government of College, 1, Yale MS. A similar view is expressed in Clap, *The Religious Constitution of Colleges, Especially of Yale College in New-Haven, in the Colony of Connecticut* (New London, 1754), 13 (hereafter cited as Clap, *Religious Constitution of Colleges*).

57. Clap, *Catalogue of Yale Library* (1743), Advertisement.

modernist and exponent of the utilitarian curriculum.[58] It is commonly held that Yale, under Clap, provided its students with intellectual pabulum that could be digested only by prospective ministers.

Although Clap repeatedly asserted that the one great purpose of Yale was to train ministers for the Congregational Church, cursory examination shows that the Yale curriculum was not a divinity curriculum. Yale was not a seminary; theology was not the exclusive scholarly preoccupation of Clap's students. The president undeniably fortified the intellectual matter of the curriculum with Puritan religious dogma, but he correspondingly broadened and liberalized it and gave to it a secular base. The curriculum, in short, began to reflect a concern for the useful and the practical.

One of the important features of the curriculum was the evening lectures, or "publick Dissertations." Held at stated intervals and directed to the entire student body, they were delivered by Clap after evening prayers. In earlier years, it had been customary for the rector to expound a point of theology that had been touched upon during evening devotions. Clap, however, recognizing, and perhaps lamenting, that a large portion of Yale graduates were entering into "publick and important Stations in civil Life," used this time to present material of a secular character. His lectures traversed a wide field of knowledge, including English law (common, civil, canon, military, and maritime), agriculture, commerce, navigation, anatomy, heraldry, and gunnery. Instruction in surveying and navigation was also provided, on occasion, in the regular academic schedule.[59] In these ways, Clap expanded the curriculum and brought its subject matter more closely in touch with the needs of contemporary life. The annual commencement theses offer the best proof of the growing emphasis on secular education; the number bearing on practical knowledge increased yearly.

The most notable curricular changes came in the areas of mathematics and natural philosophy. In the early history of the college,

58. On Smith, see Albert Gegenheimer, *William Smith: Educator and Churchman, 1727-1803* (Philadelphia, 1943).
59. The curriculum is discussed in Clap, *Annals of Yale,* 80-84.

particularly in the period 1701-16, little heed was paid to these disciplines. They were included in the curriculum, but the conservative-minded trustees who prescribed the subject matter of the curriculum adhered closely to the medieval convention of emphasizing the "tongues," moral philosophy, and divinity. As a result, the curriculum was mired in scholasticism. Even the little mathematical and scientific instruction provided was medieval in theory and content. Aristotle supplied the principles of physics, and Ptolemy, a cosmology. Samuel Johnson, a tutor in the years of 1716-19 who later became the first president of King's College, wrote perhaps with slight exaggeration that the "pre-Enlightenment" curriculum was "nothing but the scholastic cobwebs of a few little English and Dutch systems that would hardly now be taken up on the street." [60]

Science at Yale was on nearly the same level as at Harvard in this early period, except for certain specialties such as astronomy, in which the northern school was more advanced. That Harvard like Yale was on a scientific plane with Dante can be seen in some of the concepts then in vogue along the Charles River. Harvard students were taught that a person killed by lightning while asleep died with his eyes open, but one struck while in the process of waking died with his eyes shut, "because it so amaseth him, that he winketh and dyes before he can open his eyes again." Students were warned against gazing at lightning, which "may dry up or so waste the chrystalline humor of the eyes that it may cause the sight to perish, or it may swell the face, making it to break out with scabs, caused by a kind of poyson in the exalation which the pores of the face and eyes do admit." Harvard science held that sleep was caused by "steames of food, and blood ascending into the Brain, by whose coldness they are said to be condens'd into moisture, which obstructs the passage of the Spirits that they can't freely permeate to the Organs of Senses." [61]

At Yale, Samuel Johnson's appointment as a tutor in 1716

---

60. Herbert and Carol Schneider, eds., *Samuel Johnson — President of King's College — His Career and Writings* (N. Y., 1929), I, 5-7 (hereafter cited as Schneider, eds., *Writings of Johnson*). For a detailed analysis of the curriculum by one trained under it, see Benjamin Lord to Ezra Stiles, May 28, 1779, in Dexter, *Yale Graduates*, I, 115-16.

61. Quoted in Oviatt, *Beginnings of Yale*, 273-76.

marked the first important departure in the teaching of mathematics and science. It was he who shook the college out of its intellectual torpor. During Johnson's senior year as a student (1714), the college had received a collection of books from Jeremiah Dummer,[62] the Massachusetts colonial agent in London, who was a warm supporter of both Harvard and Yale. Among the collection were some of the chief writings of the English scientific galaxy, including Newton's *Principia Mathematica* and *Optics*, and the works of Edmund Halley, William Whiston, Richard Bentley, Robert Boyle, and Francis Bacon. These writings furnished Johnson's famished intellect with a "feast of fat things." His tutors cautioned him against the toxic effects of such rich fare, arguing that "the new philosophy would soon bring in a new divinity and corrupt the pure religion of the country." Johnson cast off these admonitions and plunged ahead into the scientific thought fostered by the Enlightenment. Upon becoming a tutor, he swept out much of the accumulated scholastic rubbish and began to introduce into the curriculum the empiricism of Locke, the inductive method of Bacon, and the cosmology of Kepler, Copernicus, and Newton. He also introduced the vitally necessary adjunctive mathematical studies. He himself was obliged to acquire a teachable knowledge of "Euclid, Algebra and Conic Sections"; such instruction had not been provided during his own undergraduate career.[63] During his three-year tutorial stint, Johnson was eminently successful in establishing an up-to-date scientific tradition,[64] although lack of equipment prevented him from conducting significant experiments.

After Johnson left Yale in 1719, the impulse of his teaching was sustained under Rector Cutler and Tutor Daniel Brown, both of whom also made a surreptitious examination of the books in the Dummer collection, especially the sermons of Anglican divines. But with the religious explosion of 1722 which precipitated the Cutler defection, all the Newtonian-influenced teachers were

62. For analyses of the Dummer Collection, see *ibid.*, 289-303; Thomas G. Wright, *Literary Culture in Early New England, 1620-1730* (New Haven, 1920), 184-87; Louis Shores, *Origins of the American College Library, 1638-1800* (N. Y., 1935), 75-80, 127-35, 218-23.

63. Schneider, eds., *Writings of Johnson*, I, 7-9.

64. McKeehan, *Yale Science*, 9.

eliminated. Science and mathematics continued to be stressed during the tutorship of Jonathan Edwards (1724-28), but with distinctly less secular emphasis. During Williams's rectorship, notable progress was made in the accumulation of scientific apparatus, but since Williams had no deep-seated interest in mathematics and science, these subjects were not stressed in the curriculum.[65]

Clap's era represented the golden age of mathematics and science in Yale's colonial history. The president was responsible for the establishment of a remarkably advanced and comprehensive program. It was during Clap's administration that students came to "woo the skeleton of science," as John Trumbull wrote in his slashing attack upon the Yale curriculum.[66]

Mathematics leaped into prominence. Previously, under Williams, the students had not been taught mathematics until the senior year. From 1742 on, the subject was started in the freshman year. Clap, like Samuel Johnson, thought college education should begin with the "Languages and the Mathematics (which are themselves indeed a kind of language) for these are both of them a necessary Furniture in order to the attainment of any considerable Perfection in the other parts of Learning." [67] Students at Yale got arithmetic and algebra the first year, geometry the second, and advanced mathematics—algebraic conics and fluxions—in the junior year.[68]

A second curriculum drawn up by Clap in 1766 shows a similar emphasis. "Mathematics" was offered to freshmen, trigonometry and algebra to sophomores, and "most Branches of the Mathe-

65. *Ibid.,* 14. It is to be noted that the commencement theses during Williams's rectorship contain a surprisingly large number of propositions on mathematics and physics. Some authorities have affirmed, however, that the quality of instruction could not have been of a high order if these theses are to be taken as an indication of curricular content.

66. *Poetical Works,* II, 17. Trumbull contended that the greatest weakness of the Yale curriculum (under Clap) was its lack of emphasis upon *belles lettres*. While serving as tutors under President Naphtali Daggett in later years, Trumbull, Joseph Howe, and Timothy Dwight took Yale off the beaten paths of mental discipline by introducing "polite literature" and emphasizing the aesthetics of literature.

67. Johnson, *An Introduction to the Study of Philosophy* (New London, 1743), Advertisement.

68. Clap, *Catalogue of Yale Library* (1743), Advertisement.

maticks" to juniors. A parenthetical remark by Clap that "many of them well understand Surveying, Navigation and the Calculation of the Eclipses; and some of them are considerable Proficients in Conic Sections and Fluxions" suggests the prominence of mathematics in the life of the Yale student.[69] The commencement sheets, a sure barometer of the academic climate, list propositions relating to all phases of the discipline, from simple algebra to complex fluxions,[70] and in many sheets the mathematical propositions represent the greatest numerical proportion. Thus, while some clerical leaders, such as John Wesley, inveighed against mathematical instruction, claiming that it set youth straight on the path to atheism, Clap gave his students an abundance of such instruction, never for a moment entertaining the notion that he was misdirecting them into irreligion.

Natural philosophy also became prominent and by the 1750's was the aristocrat of the non-religious section of the curriculum. A number of scientific areas were touched upon, but particular emphasis was placed upon physics and astronomy. The commencement sheet of 1751, for example, listed 125 propositions, of which 38 were placed under the rubric *Theses Physicae*. Of these, at least one-third dealt more properly with astrophysics than with physics. The commencement sheet of 1765 contained forty-seven propositions on physics, more than twice the number of any other category.

A similar stress is to be noticed in the astronomical propositions; astronomy was Clap's personal favorite. Most conspicuous is their variety in range of investigation and their interdependence with mathematics and theology. A few examples, selected at random, lend color to the point. In 1752, a proposition held: "Annis 25,919,

69. Clap, *Annals of Yale*, 81. Clap also adopted more up-to-date texts, such as Willem Jacob Van 's Gravesande's *Mathematical Elements of Natural Philosophy Confirmed by Experiments; or, an Introduction to Sir Isaac Newton's Philosophy*, trans. J. T. Desaguliers (London, 1720-21); William Whiston, *Astronomical Principles of Religion* (London, 1717); William Derham, *Astro-Theology: Or a Demonstration of the Being and Attributes of God, From a Survey of the Heavens* (London, 1715). These books presented scientific knowledge within the traditional Puritan framework. While the Newtonian point of view was emphasized, there was a continued insistence upon divine purpose.

70. Fluxions first appeared in the Commencement Sheet of 1758. Simons, "Adoption of Fluxions in American Schools," *Scripta Mathematica*, 4 (1936), 207-10.

Poli Aequatoris, circà Polos Eclipticae, revolvunt." In 1753: "Cometae in Ellipsibus longè excentricis, maximè appropinquantibus Parabolis, circa Solem revolvunt." In 1754: "Cometae Usui totius hujusce Systematis inserviunt." In 1755: "Si Sol circa Terram quotidiè revolvatur, Velocitate 353,571 Milliarium, uno moveatur minuto." In 1764: "Planetarium a Sole Distantia, et earum Diametri sunt ut sequens exhibit Tabella:

	Distantia	Diameter
Mercurii	37,090,000	3,596
Veneris	69,290,000	9,285
Terrae	95,820,000	7,897
Martis	146,000,000	5,275
Jovis	495,000,000	95,319
Saturnii	913,800,000	79,828" [71]

Student astronomical almanacs,[72] the comments of such qualified contemporaries as Samuel Johnson and Bishop George Berkeley,[73] and student manuscripts and commonplace books [74] further indicate that Clap charged his students, in Cotton Mather's rhetoric, to "soar Upwards, to the Attainments of ASTRONOMY." [75]

The success of a program of experimental science was, of course,

71. Translated, the propositions read: 1752—In 25,919 years the poles of the equator revolve around the poles of the ecliptic; 1753—Comets revolve around the sun in eccentric ellipses at a great distance and in parabolas which approach the sun as closely as possible; 1754—Comets serve the use of the whole system; 1755—If the sun revolves around the earth daily, it would be moved with a velocity of 353,571 miles in a minute; 1764—The distance of the planets from the sun and the diameters of them are as the following tables show.

72. Joseph Huntington, *College Almanack, 1761. An Astronomical Diary* . . . (New Haven, 1761); Huntington, *College Almanack, 1762. An Astronomical Diary* . . . (New Haven, 1762).

73. Berkeley to Clap, July 17, 1750, *Yale Univ. Lib. Gazette,* 8 (1933), 28; Schneider, eds., *Writings of Johnson,* I, 102.

74. Manasseh Cutler, Commonplace Book Kept at Yale From June 10, 1762, typed copy in Library of Congress; Cutler, Book of Astronomical Recreations, Performed at Yale College, New Haven, A.D. 1763, Essex Institute MS.; Trumbull, *Poetical Works,* I, 11; Eleazar May, Commonplace Book, Yale MS. Notice should also be directed to Clap's letter to Cromwell Mortimer (Apr. 1, 1744, Royal Society MS., London), which stated that he had set one of his pupils to the task of tracing the trajectory of a comet he had been observing. This letter suggests that Clap collaborated with students in carrying out his personal research, assuredly in an instructional capacity.

75. Mather, *Manductio ad Ministerium* (Boston, 1726), 53.

contingent upon the amount and quality of available apparatus. This was especially true in the areas of physics and astronomy, which, for proper study, required such basic instruments as globes, thermometers, quadrants, and telescopes. When Clap came to Yale he found only a closet-full of equipment accumulated by Rector Williams and soon set himself to the task of augmenting this meager collection. Since the college did not have sufficient funds, Clap applied to wealthy and influential colonials and Britons known to have an interest in science.

At times, his approach was subtle (or, at least, was intended to be subtle). On May 31, 1743, he began a correspondence with Cromwell Mortimer, secretary of the Royal Society, who was in a strategic position to solicit English aid for Yale. Clap opened his letter with a brief account of a transit of Mercury he had witnessed through the college-owned telescope, an instrument thirty inches in length and four inches in diameter. Next he related his impressions of some sun spots. On October 28, as he was viewing the sun about four o'clock in the afternoon, he detected "three Macula or Spots in a direct Line nearly Horizontal: the eastermost about Half a Digit from the Sun's Limb, and the westermost about a Digit from that." The next morning he observed the spots again —and for the next few mornings viewed their movement across the face of the sun.

After a few more observations designed to stimulate Mortimer's astronomical interests, the president moved to the heart of the matter. "As we are yet but an Infant College, of scarce 40 years Standing in a new Count[r]y, and destitute of mathematical Instruments, particularly an Orrery, an astronomical Quadrant and an Air Pump, It is not as yet to be expected that we should make much Proficiency in Astronomy, and some other Parts of the Mathematicks." Continuing in this apologetic vein, he reported the lack of an instrument "by which I can take the exact Distance of a Planet, or Spot from the Center of Limb of Sun" and complained that he could not see "above Half the Body of the Sun at once in our Telescope, so that what I have said about the Distance is only guess'd." As for books, while the college had a few basic works on astronomy, such as "Whiston's, Gregory's and Keil's Astronomy and the philosophical Transactions abridg'd to the

Year 1720, and at large for the Years 1737, 1738," it owned no planetary tables, which were indispensable for astronomical research. As a final shot, Clap informed Mortimer that the "B[a]rometer Tube is broke." Clap ended his letter by expressing the fervent desire that he would have the opportunity in the future to make astronomical observations "more Accurate and Worthy of Communication. Thus hoping for your Smiles upon our young Nursery of Learning." [76]

The following year, after the dramatic appearance of a comet, Clap renewed his efforts to win Mortimer's assistance. "I suppose," he wrote, "the late Remarkable Comet has engaged the Attention and Critical Observations of all the Astronomers in Europe. We in this Infant College are under no manner of Advantages for such a Purpose having no Astronomical Quadrant, nor any kind of Instrument adapted to take the angular Distance of any of the heavenly Bodies." [77] There could be no mistaking Clap's purpose.

Whether these communications brought "Smiles" from Mortimer is not known. Clap was involved in a highly competitive enterprise, for all of the colonial colleges were vying for "foreign aid," and some of them had agents in England. In January 1762, the trustees of the College of Philadelphia dispatched William Smith to England for the purpose of tapping the pockets of the wealthy. Arriving in London, Smith was both embarrassed and annoyed to encounter James Jay, who was performing the same type of mission for King's College. His annoyance stemmed from the fact that earlier in the year he had told Jay of his proposed trip. It was now obvious that King's College had beaten the College of Philadelphia to the punch. Since it was not possible for the two colonial agents to block out the country into "spheres of influence," as Edward Cheyney writes, they were obliged to join forces and carry out their solicitations in common.[78]

76. Royal Society MS., London.
77. Apr. 1, 1744, Royal Society MS., London. It should also be noted that Clap informed Mortimer that he "had thoughts" to raise a subscription to purchase scientific apparatus. He inquired of Mortimer the prices of the basic items. That the American colonies were deficient of even the most fundamental of scientific equipment is revealed by Clap's action in sending the telescope belonging to the college to England in 1750 for a speculum. Yale Corporation Records, I, 94, Yale Univ.
78. Cheyney, *History of the University of Pennsylvania, 1740-1940* (Philadelphia, 1940), 61-67. Smith was unquestionably the most active, as well as most successful,

By his less professional efforts, Clap managed to procure a considerable quantity of scientific equipment for Yale. In 1757, for
example, a Londoner donated some astronomical instruments. A
few years later, Philip Schuyler, the New York land baron (and
Alexander Hamilton's future father-in-law), contributed an un-
specified "electrical instrument," possibly a Leyden jar.[79] Another
benefactor was that noted citizen of the eighteenth century, Benjamin Franklin, who corresponded frequently with Clap on scientific subjects and advised him of new types of apparatus being
developed in England.[80] The peripatetic Franklin contributed his
valuable volume on electrical experiments and a Leyden jar.[81]
These philanthropic acts may have played some part in Yale's
decision to award Franklin an honorary M.A. degree in 1753,
although the Corporation Records maintain, with undeniable
plausibility, that the degree was granted in recognition of Franklin's "ingenious experiments and theory of electrical fire." [82]

Franklin's greatest contribution to the dissemination of scien-

---

solicitor among colonial academic administrators. The above-mentioned trip brought
to the College of Philadelphia £8,700; Jay collected £7,500 for King's College. The
combined figure represented the largest sum (for a single plea) obtained from Great
Britain by American solicitors to 1776. There were over 800 donors, from the King
to "Master Tommy Ellis," who contributed about a half-crown. Smith's success was
emphasized by a London clergyman who wrote to a Philadelphian: "You ought
to welcome him [Smith] Home with Ringing of Bells, Illuminations and Bonefires.
The Professors of the College . . . ought to meet him at least Half Way to New York,
and from thence usher him into Philadelphia with all the Magnificence and Pomp
in their Power." Quoted in William L. Sachse, *The Colonial American in Britain*
(Madison, Wis., 1956), 112. The general subject of solicitations by the colleges is
fully treated in Beverly McAnear, "The Raising of Funds by the Colonial Colleges,"
Mississippi Valley Historical Review, 38 (1951-52), 591-612.

79. Dexter, ed., *Literary Diary of Stiles*, II, 348-49.

80. In Nov. 1753, for example, Franklin, at the request of Clap, furnished information on a new air pump developed in England. Judging the instrument superior
to the general type of air pump, Franklin urged Clap to secure such a model for
the college. Bigelow, comp. and ed., *Works of Benjamin Franklin*, II, 435-37. Clap's
personal library also benefited from the friendship. The American Antiquarian
Society has a copy of *Cato Major*, presented to Clap by Franklin.

81. In earlier correspondence, Clap had informed Franklin that he planned to
raise money to provide Yale with a "compleat Apparatus for Natural Philosophy."
Franklin promised to contribute the "Electrical Part" if Clap was successful in the
plan. See Franklin to Clap, Nov. 28, 1751, American Philosophical Society, *Proceedings*, 34 (1895), 484.

82. I, 101. The jar, or "friction machine," is now housed in the Franklin room
of the Sterling Memorial Library where the papers of the Philadelphian polymath
are being assembled for publication. Its classroom function was to demonstrate how
static electricity could be generated by means of friction.

tific knowledge at Yale came about indirectly through his establishment of a newspaper at New Haven. When he came to accept his degree from the college, Clap suggested that he found a newspaper at New Haven, since the funds required were beyond the means of any local inhabitants. Clap vigorously pursued the subject in subsequent correspondence, and Franklin was finally convinced that the project was a good investment. He wrote to William Strahan in October 1753: "I am now about to establish a small printing-office in favour of another nephew, at New Haven, in the Colony of Connecticut, in New England; a considerable town, in which there is a university, and a prospect that a bookseller shop, with a printing-house, may do pretty well." [83] The valuable press arrived from England in the fall of 1754, and by Christmas the office was open for business; the first publication, a Latin edition of Clap's "College Laws," symbolized the president's role in the establishment of the office.[84] The press was utilized for publishing the annual commencement sheets and master's *quaestiones,* both of which contained a large number of propositions dealing with science. The local townspeople benefited from Franklin's largesse in the form of the *Connecticut Gazette,* New Haven's first newspaper. Here, Clap published reports of his personal astronomical observations.

The success of Clap's various maneuvers to gain scientific apparatus for Yale is attested by a volume of land records begun in 1747, in which the president listed the "Mathematical Instruments belonging to college." [85] Although some of this equipment had been acquired by Rector Williams, Clap shares credit for attaining what was then a reasonably full component of scientific apparatus:

A Telescope with a Tripod; two Setts of Posts and a Glass to be [lowered?] on to look on the Sun.

83. Bigelow, comp. and ed., *Works of Benjamin Franklin,* X, 267. For unknown reasons, Franklin's nephew could not undertake the management of the business, whereupon the plant was sold to James Parker; Franklin also appointed Parker as postmaster for New Haven in 1754.

84. See Winnifred R. Reid, "Beginnings of Printing in New Haven," *Papers in Honor of Andrew Keogh,* 67-88.

85. Land Book, Yale MS. For a description and discussion of the function of such instruments, consult Cohen, *Early Tools of Science.* Many are pictured in this work.

A Pair of Globes, Celestial and Terrestrial with Quadrants of
   altitudes.
A Pair of old Globes.
A Theodolite with a Tripod, plain Table, and Brass Scale and
   Sights for it needles and Glasses.
Two measuring Wheels.
A Gunters Chain.
A short wooden Scale.
A Pair of Dividers.
A protractor.
A Loadstone set in Brass with Steel Arms.
A Microscope with [?] Apparatus.
A Barometer and Thermometer.
An Orrery.
A concave Glass.
A curve Glass.
A multiplying Glass.
A Pair of small neat Ballances, or Scales with all proper Weights.
A Landscape Box.
Two Prisms, with a Stand.
A brass Syringe.
About Ten glass Tubes.

Even more impressive evidence of Clap's success as a promoter is
a 1779 list compiled by President Ezra Stiles of the apparatus
owned by the college.[86] The great majority of the items had been
gathered together during Clap's tenure, and the collection, while
not as extensive as that of Harvard, was in the judgment of one
modern authority, "clearly well-chosen and of high quality." [87]

One piece of scientific equipment vitally essential for astronomical instruction Clap was unable to acquire. This was an
orrery, an instrument that illustrated the known major bodies of
the solar system in their relative sizes and positions. In 1744, Clap
put his inventive abilities to work and constructed one. Although
crude in comparison with the mechanical wonder built by David
Rittenhouse,[88] it holds the distinction of being the first of its kind

86. Dexter, ed., *Literary Diary of Stiles,* II, 348-49.
87. Cohen, *Early Tools of Science,* 10.
88. Of Rittenhouse and his orrery, Jefferson wrote in his *Notes on Virginia:* "He
has not indeed made a world; but he has by imitation approached nearer its Maker
than any man who has lived from the creation to this day." *Notes on the State of
Virginia,* ed. William Peden (Chapel Hill, 1955), 64.

to be constructed in the American colonies.[89] The machine was seven feet in diameter, and its component parts were held in place by pins and wires. Metal plates represented the earth, sun, moon, and the major and secondary planets. Even the celebrated Comet of 1682 (later renamed Halley's Comet) was represented. Unlike the more expensive and more elaborately constructed European models, the movements of which were controlled by one central lever, Clap's orrery necessitated hand movements of all the various heavenly bodies with corresponding arithmetical calculations for precise positioning. The operation of the orrery, therefore, provided the students with an intensely practical type of mathematical and astronomical training. Though "rough and unpolished," it permitted them to witness, with a sweep of the eye, the complex movements of the earth and planets, and offered a visual explanation for such natural phenomena as eclipses and the reappearance of comets.[90]

Clap was too perceptive an administrator to believe that mathematical and scientific instruction would inevitably improve after the curriculum was properly stocked and philosophical apparatus secured. He was acutely aware of the need of good teachers. A strikingly high percentage of the twenty-eight tutors he appointed were proficient in mathematics and natural philosophy. Several were outstanding: Thomas Darling (1743-45), John Whiting (1743-46), Ezra Stiles (1749-55), Elizur Goodrich (1755-56), Nehemiah Strong (1751-60), Richard Woodhull (1756-61, 1763-65), and Punderson Austin (1765-66).

There is evidence to suggest that Clap started a sort of teacher training program for the purpose of assuring a competent faculty. The Yale teaching staff, it is to be remembered, was academically inbred. Tutors were recent graduates of the college who served short terms, usually two to three years, and then moved on to other

---

89. Howard Rice, Jr., *The Rittenhouse Orrery, Princeton's Eighteenth-Century Planetarium* (Princeton, N.J., 1954), 12-13. Harrold E. Gillingham, in "The First Orreries in America," Franklin Institute, *Journal*, 229 (1940), 81-99, fails to mention Clap's machine and credits Rittenhouse with the honor of constructing the first orrery in America.

90. Chauncey Whittelsey, "A Description of an Orrery or Planetarium in the Library of Yale-College in New-Haven, lately projected and made by the Rev. Rector Clap, to represent the Motions of all the celestial Bodies," *American Magazine and Historical Chronicle*, 1 (Jan. 1743/4), 202-3.

professions—tutoring was conceived of as an interim career. Ezra
Stiles, one of Clap's more brilliant students and himself a competent Newtonian scientist, wrote that Clap "always spoke to the
Person on whom he set his eyes for Tutor and desired him to adapt
his Studies preparatory." [91] Tutorial candidates apparently underwent a special, more intensive course of preparation. There can
be little doubt that they received a concentrated dosage of mathematics and science during their senior year, when they studied
directly with Clap.

In sum, Clap's legacy to science at Yale was of great proportions.
By modernizing and revitalizing the curriculum, by procuring apparatus and introducing more up-to-date texts, and by providing
for a well-trained tutorial staff, he converted Yale into an important center of Newtonian science. He was personally responsible for the first systematic teaching of mathematics and science.
Moreover, the headwaters of Yale's brilliant tradition of experimental science originated in the latter portion of Clap's administration, when students assembled in the library, located in the
chapel, and "a select Number, with proper Instruments in their
Hands" were instructed "in all Delineations and Calculations." [92]
Slight and undramatic as they may be, these exercises mark the
beginning of laboratory science at Yale.

Clap's invigoration of the Yale curriculum affected colonial
society in many ways. He instilled in a generation of Yale youth
the main elements of the new science, along with a knowledge of
surveying, navigation, and other "practical" subjects. And he was
the chief agent in the training of a cadre of teachers who carried
the torch of science to another generation. Ezra Stiles and Nehemiah Strong [93] preached the gospel of Newton at Yale through the
Revolutionary period; Bezaleel Woodward (B.A., 1764), another
Clap-trained educator and scientist, had a long and illustrious
career as professor of mathematics and natural philosophy at Dart-

91. Dexter, ed., *Literary Diary of Stiles*, II, 514.
92. Clap, *Annals of Yale*, 82.
93. Dexter, *Yale Graduates*, II, 383-88. Strong was the first occupant of the chair
of Professor of Mathematics and Natural Philosophy, a position created in 1770.
After a protracted struggle with the Corporation, he resigned his professorship in
1781.

mouth College.[94] Hundreds of ministers and schoolmasters trained at Yale under Clap's direction helped promote the scientific revolution of the Enlightenment in America by implanting the first principles of Newtonian thought in the minds of youth. Clap had a strong hand in shaping the cultural bent of American civilization.

Louis McKeehan has written that, with Clap's departure in 1766, scientific endeavor at Yale sank substantially "to zero." [95] This is a high tribute to Clap, but it mistakenly gives the impression that the whole program rested on his personal abilities. Although it is true that advanced mathematical instruction (conics and fluxions) was temporarily suspended for want of a qualified instructor, mathematics and science continued as central curricular studies, and instruction was carried out in the tradition of the past. Clap's departure did not result in a general scientific slump. The president himself had taken the necessary precautions to prevent such a mishap.

This, then, was the credit side of the ledger of one of colonial America's most accomplished academicians. It was this impressive record that prompted the elder Timothy Dwight to write, "He was the greatest man who ever sat at the head of the institution," [96] and led to Charles Thwing's judgment that Clap was colonial America's "first greatly efficient president." [97] Certainly during the 1750's Yale ranked in importance and in influence with Harvard, William and Mary, and the Jesuit college in Quebec; and it compared favorably with the older Spanish universities in Mexico City, Lima (Peru), and San Carlos (Guatemala). Under Clap's dynamic leadership, Yale College rose to a position of prominence among institutions of higher learning in the New World.

94. Dexter, *Yale Graduates*, III, 89-92.
95. McKeehan, *Yale Science*, 41.
96. Quoted in Woolsey, *Historical Discourse to Yale Graduates*, 114.
97. *Higher Education in America*, 85.

Chapter Five

DISCIPLE OF NEWTON

APART from his duties as a teacher of science, Clap was an active member of an unorganized but surprisingly close-knit circle of academic scientists in colonial America. Like such accomplished academicians as John Winthrop IV and William Small, he concentrated largely on the scientific trinity of mathematics, physics, and astronomy. During the colonial period, it was the academic scientist who conducted the most serious, as well as the most productive, research in these subjects. Scientists who lacked formal academic training could perform creditably in the biological sciences, delineating the characteristics of flora and fauna, but, lacking a sufficient grasp of mathematics, they could not do effective research in physical astronomy.

The scientific aspect of Clap's career stands out as an apparent paradox. Whereas in religious and philosophical thought he exhibited a rigid conservatism, he was a modernist or progressive in his scientific orientation, a foremost expositor of Newtonian theory. Indeed, as he put down the Bible and took up the quadrant, he ceased to represent the medieval point of view and became a herald of the modern order. In this propensity he was by no means singular; New England history is dotted with Puritan intellectuals who displayed a similar dualism. Actually, Clap falls within a long Puritan tradition dating from the inception of that religious movement in England. Rationalism was one foundation of the intellectual structure of Puritanism. But Clap's scientific outlook was not entirely that of a prototypal seventeenth-century Puritan. It is true that his basic scientific orientation was grounded on the proposition that all phenomena were inextricably linked with the doings of Deity; at Harvard he had been fed Newton with a spiritual spoon, trained—in the grandiloquent phrase of Cotton Mather—to combine his scientific studies with "continual Contemplations and agreeable Acknowledgements of the infinite God." [1] Yet his extant scientific writings deviate from conventional Puritan thought in one particular: they betray a greater preoccupation with observed fact than with theological implications. In a word, he was far more rationalistic, far more secular, than his counterparts of an earlier day.[2]

Between Clap and his contemporaries the distinction was one of degree. Unlike other scientific-minded Puritans, he was not zealously intent upon demonstrating the reality of the spiritual world or the majesty of God through his scientific observations. His writings are conspicuously empty of ecstatic statements on the marvels wrought by God. The overwhelming emphasis is on "how" not "why." In his most important scientific treatise, *Conjectures Upon Meteors* (1781), there are but three allusions to God or divine purpose. He relied on naturalistic explanations in accounting for the size of terrestrial meteors, their rate of motion, and the reasons why they remained solid in flight (so he believed). He did not invoke supernatural agency, nor did he discuss scientific matters in a religious idiom, as did Cotton Mather in *The Christian Philosopher* (1721). Utilizing the terminology of the

1. Mather, *Manductio ad Ministerium*, 47.
2. The inevitable exception must be acknowledged. The Yale Library has a manuscript sermon by Clap pertaining to the "Propriety of Using Natural, not Artificial Light." The document suggests an anti-scientific attitude. Clap initially developed the point that the use of artificial light is dangerous to Christian morals. When discussing the advantages of natural light, however, he assumed a more "scientific" attitude. He pointed out, for example, that students studying by artificial light and who had a proclivity to move their eyes from light to darkness would eventually suffer discomfort because of the "instant contractions and dilations." Professor Dexter has dated the sermon as one of Clap's earlier writings. I would be inclined to agree with Dexter.

new age, he set forth hypotheses and sought to confirm them through empirical observation and inductive reasoning.

From the scientific standpoint, Clap was indeed a citizen of the Enlightenment. The Newtonian framework provided the foundation for his conceptual scientific scheme. Newton's theories and rarified principles were as absolute and incontrovertible to him as Puritan religious tenets: "There are many important Truths in natural Philosophy and Mathematics, which, when they come to be fairly proposed, were never doubted of; such as the general Laws of Attraction, the Weight of the Atmosphere, Rules of Fluxions, etc. and yet it is probably that these Things never came into the Mind of any Mortal, till they were suggested by the great Genius of Sir Isaac Newton." [3] He revered Newton's classic, the *Principia,* as a book of scientific revelation. Ezra Stiles once wrote of Clap: "I have known him to elucidate so many of the abstrusest theorems and ratiocinia of Newton, that, I doubt not, the whole *Principia* of the illustrious philosopher was comprehended by him; a comprehension which, it is presumed, very few mathematicians of the present age have attained." [4]

Science in this period, as Whitfield Bell, Jr., writes, "was not yet compartmentalized, each tight little box jealously guarded by guildsmen who talked to themselves and one another in a private jargon." [5] True to prevailing fashion, Clap dabbled in many and diverse types of investigation. All the world of science, from medicine to astronomy, was his domain. He maintained temperature charts,[6] devised agricultural tools, and participated in the project of raising silk in Connecticut; [7] he speculated on the medicinal value of mineral springs; [8] he collected eyewitness accounts of

3. Clap, *An Essay on the Nature and Foundation of Moral Virtue and Obligation; Being a Short Introduction to the Study of Ethics* (New Haven, 1765), 46 (hereafter cited as Clap, *Essay on Moral Virtue*).

4. Stiles to Naphtali Daggett, July 28, 1767, Yale MS.

5. Whitfield J. Bell, Jr., *Early American Science — Needs and Opportunities for Study* (Williamsburg, Va., 1955), 9.

6. Dexter, ed., *Stiles's Itineraries,* 221.

7. See below, p. 98.

8. In 1765, a Connecticut resident afflicted with a severe skin disorder was miraculously cured after bathing in the mineral waters of Stafford Springs, Conn. Overnight Stafford became the "Mecca of New England's hypochondriacs." Clap bathed in the springs in 1766 and came away convinced of their therapeutic value. In a letter to the editor of the *Connecticut Courant* (Hartford), Aug. 18, 1766, he

comets, meteors, sun spots, eclipses, and transits of Mercury and wrote theoretical explanations of these phenomena.[9]

His Baconian breadth of interest was complemented by a passionate desire to be informed on recent scientific developments, especially in astronomy. He kept abreast of events primarily through correspondence with some of the more illustrious scientists of his day, both English and colonial, including Benjamin Franklin, Cadwallader Colden, Samuel Johnson, Cromwell Mortimer, John Pringle, and William Whiston.[10] He had an omnivorous appetite for published scientific tracts; the *Gentleman's Magazine* and the *Philosophical Transactions* of the Royal Society kept him informed of scientific currents in England and elsewhere. Furthermore, his writings reveal that he read extensively in the standard scientific works of the day. His personal library contained a liberal portion of books on science, the greater number of which pertained to astronomy.[11] And, of course, he had access to the rich collections in the college library.

His traits as a scientist also clearly reveal his rapport with the

---

called upon physicians and other learned men from the Stafford area to formulate a program to exploit the springs to the best advantage. In an 8-point plan, he proposed that experiments be conducted to determine the effect of the water upon different types of disorders and that the results be announced to the general public. He also urged that a skilled physician be maintained at the springs to advise the "unskilled Multitudes" flocking there. Clap had become concerned by the improper use of the springs and by the fraudulent practices that had developed. His letter to the *Boston Gazette*, Aug. 4, 1766, reprinted in the *Boston Post Boy*, Sept. 6, 1766, contained this account: a group of invalids in Boston hired a carter to haul water to them from Stafford. Enroute to Boston, the carter began to sell the water, and when the barrels ran dry, he refilled from the nearest brook. His unsuspecting clients in Boston drank the brook water and, in their collective opinion, benefited immeasurably from it. On the mineral springs of Stafford, see Carl Bridenbaugh's delightful article, "Baths and Watering Places of Colonial America," *Wm. and Mary Qtly.*, 3d Ser., 3 (1946), 151-81.

9. See below, pp. 102-11.

10. Clap constantly sought to widen his relationships with British scientists. In a letter to William Whiston, July 1752 (Yale MS.), he requested the names of some "ingenious Astronomical Gentlemen in London" with whom he might correspond. With this letter, incidentally, Clap sent a plan for reducing Halley's astronomical tables into decimals so as to achieve greater accuracy in tracking celestial objects. The plan was to be distributed among English astronomers. In the summer of 1959, I made an intensive search of archival and manuscript repositories in Scotland and England but was able to locate only a few of Clap's letters.

11. Clap's book list is contained in Probate Records of Thomas Clap, Feb. 14, 1768, Conn. State Lib.

Enlightenment. Initially, he was imbued with a robust scientific optimism. Confident that human reason was capable of penetrating the innermost secrets of nature, in at least one instance he allowed optimism to carry him to lofty, and, for a Puritan, somewhat incredible, heights of speculation. He wrote in his *Essay on Moral Virtue*: "It is possible that a Man, by contemplating his own Ideas, the visible Works of Creation, and the Course of Causes and Effects, might by Degrees, find out the Being and Perfections of God." [12] Even the most liberal-minded of earlier Puritans would have regarded this idea as presumptuous if not blasphemous.

Complementing this optimism was a tolerant and liberal attitude noticeably absent in his religious personality. While locked in bitter controversy with Jared Eliot and Benjamin Gale over issues fundamentally religious in character, he freely assisted these two men in simplifying the design of Jethro Tull's "wheat plow." In its current design, the Englishman's plow was too costly for the farmers of Connecticut. At Eliot's request, Clap applied his "mathematical Learning and mechanical Genius" to the problem of reducing its number of intricate parts while preserving its utility. Eliot wrote later that Clap's efforts had resulted in the development of a plow that "can be made with a Fourth Part of what Mr. Tull's will cost." [13] Clap also served amiably with Eliot as a two-man committee representing the Society for the Encouragement of Arts, Manufactures and Commerce of London; their job was to promote silk-raising in Connecticut and confer monetary premiums upon farmers who were successful in this enterprise. [14]

While Clap disagreed with Eliot and Gale over religion, he shared with them a common Congregational Puritan heritage. Yet, his tolerance in scientific matters extended to men whose re-

12. P. 46.
13. Jared Eliot, *Essays Upon Field Husbandry in New England and Other Papers, 1748-1762*, ed. Harry J. Carman and Rexford G. Tugwell (N.Y., 1934), 116-17.
14. *Ibid.*, 128-29; *New London Summary*, Sept. 12, 1760; *Pennsylvania Gazette* (Philadelphia), Aug. 10, 1758; Thomas Clap to Royal Society of Arts, June 2, 1760, Royal Society of Arts Library MS., London. Clap informed the London officials that Connecticut was well suited for the raising of silk. His only concern was that the farmers would be reluctant to take up this form of agriculture since they were receiving high prices for general provisions. However, he had communicated the information to a "great number of gentlemen" and had taken steps to procure mulberry trees.

ligious views differed much more radically. He carried on a warm correspondence with Peter Collinson, a Quaker; with William Whiston, an Arian, whose heresies had resulted in his being sacked at Cambridge University; with Benjamin Franklin, who read Collins and Shaftesbury as a youngster, becoming "a real doubter in many points of religious doctrine" (as he informs us in his *Autobiography*), and as an oldster veered dangerously close to Deism; and finally, with Cadwallader Colden, a downright materialist in philosophical conviction.

The dualism of Clap's mind stands out in the markedly different spirit with which he approached science on the one hand and religion on the other. He implicitly believed in, and practiced, the principles of free scientific investigation, the unrestricted communication of scientific information, and the mutual criticism of theories. Further, he was a relativist in his attitude toward science, not an absolutist. He accepted the fact that scientific truth of the present would be superseded in the future. He was fully aware that his own cherished theory of meteors was but a waypoint on the long road of astronomical science. In his essay on meteors he prefaced his conclusions with a comment to his reader: "Let us, then, conjecture for the present, until we have further light by more accurate observations." [15] But in matters of faith, Clap's mind was closed as tight as the windows of his home in mid-winter. There was no room for conjecture on the doctrines of original sin or the divinity of Christ. These propositions were eternal truths, confirmed for all time.

In his "scientific personality," on the other hand, the president showed no traces of Philistinism. His relationship with Cadwallader Colden best illustrates the point. In 1753, Clap received some of Colden's scientific treatises, one of which was *The Principles of Action in Matter*.[16] In this work Colden sought to extend the Newtonian synthesis by ascertaining the cause of gravitation,

15. Clap, *Conjectures Upon the Nature and Motion of Meteors Which Are Above the Atmosphere* (Norwich, Conn., 1781), 12. Colden, *The Principles of Action in Matter, the Gravitation of Bodies, and the Motion of Planets, Explained from those Principles* (London, 1751).

16. Colden's writings, it is interesting to note, had been forwarded by Samuel Johnson with whom Clap was feuding violently at the time over religious matters.

no small feat for a provincial scientist.[17] Working in the light of
the Newtonian conception of the universe, Colden posited a
theory which pointed to ether as the basic element responsible for
gravitational stress; Newton himself had projected this thesis but
had not bothered to develop it. Colden gave it a full-dress treatment, although his terminology did no honor to clarity.

Clap worked his way through Colden's scientific-metaphysical
maze and later drew up a critique which he sent off to Samuel
Johnson.[18] Clap's criticism of Colden's epochal theory was one of
the most perceptive advanced by a colonial scientist.[19] Indeed,
many prominent natural philosophers, both in the colonies and
Europe, candidly admitted that they could not cut a path through
Colden's ideational jungle. Writing directly to Colden in July
1753, Clap briefly commented on the New Yorker's central theses,
after first informing him that "the many curious Thoughts in them
[his pamphlets], especially relating to Astronomy, have entertained
my Mind with much Pleasure and Satisfaction." With Colden's
philosophical belief "that we have no Knowledge of Substances or
any Being or Thing upon us," he heartily concurred—a surprising
fact in view of the materialistic overtones of the concept. He was
skeptical, however, of the validity of another of Colden's key
propositions, the "Idea of [ascribing] a Power or Principle of self
Motion, or Agency to a *non intelligent.*" This was an area of
thought in which Puritans traditionally feared to tread. But Clap
felt no hesitation in asserting that reason demonstrated that the
universe was governed by an intelligent force, namely God. Clap
did not state it as bluntly as that, but his meaning was perfectly
clear: "We plainly perceive the *Fact* that Bodies gravitate tend or
go towards the Earth, but the efficient *Cause* of this Phenomenon,

17. Brooke Hindle, "Cadwallader Colden's Extension of the Newtonian Principles," *Wm. and Mary Qtly.*, 3d Ser., 13 (1956), 459-75. This article has a penetrating
appraisal of Colden's theory. It has the additional virtue of clarity, an important
factor considering the complexity of Colden's theory as it is outlined in his *Principles of Action in Matter.* (Peter Collinson called the essay "the Work for a Man's
Life.") See also, I. Woodbridge Riley, *American Philosophy: The Early Schools*
(N. Y., 1907), 21 (hereafter cited as Riley, *American Philosophy*).

18. Johnson referred to one of Clap's basic criticisms in a letter to Colden,
Samuel Johnson to Cadwallader Colden, Jan. 12, 1746/7, New-York Historical Society, *Collections*, 52 (1920), 330-32.

19. Hindle, "Colden's Extension of Newtonian Principles," *Wm. and Mary Qtly.*,
3d Ser., 13 (1956), 470.

we do not perceive by our Senses and can only conjecture by our Reason and I can't conceive of any Cause capable of producing any such Effect, but an *INTELLIGENT* one." Nevertheless, he intended to reread and study Colden's "ingenious Theory." He was certain that his own "Conception of those Things, would be much enlarged." [20]

The significance of Clap's statements lies in their temperate and critical assessment of a scientific theory that had staggering and unorthodox religious implications. God was a neutral spectator in the Newtonian scheme, but Colden took no account of God in the universe. Yet Clap read Colden's materialistic writings for the purpose of acquiring understanding, not to confute. When he read John Taylor's attacks on the doctrine of original sin, he instinctively responded in a negative manner, refusing to consider the merits of the argument. But when the scientist Colden theorized that the mainspring of action in the workings of the universe was a physical principle, independent of divine will, Clap allowed the thought to play freely about his mind. Only in science was he receptive to the novel and the strange.

Although Clap manifested an interest in many areas of science, his first love was astronomy, and the bulk of his personal research focused on this subject: "He delighted to survey the Heavens," Naphtali Daggett recalled in his sermon at Clap's funeral, "and travel among the Stars, and calculate their wonderfully regular Motions." [21] At least one portion of the president's research was directed to the determination of the size of the solar system. Like the cause of gravitation, this was a central mystery of astronomical science in the eighteenth century. In the belief of contemporary astronomers, the key to the mystery was to be found in the determination of the solar parallax, that is, the angle formed at the sun by imaginary lines drawn to the sun from the center of the earth and from the edge of the earth. When this angle was known, astronomers could figure the distance to the sun since they could closely estimate the distance to the center of the earth. Once this astronomical unit was computed, the way would be clear to establish the scalar dimensions of the universe through the application

20. Pa. Hist. Soc. MS.
21. *Faithful Serving of God*, 32.

of Kepler's third law. The frame of the world would then be fixed, the cosmological synthesis of Newton completed.[22]

And how was the mean distance to the sun to be determined? In the early years of the eighteenth century, it was thought that the infrequent transits of Mercury and Venus would provide a key to the solution. Considerable difference of opinion existed among British and French astronomers as to whether the transits of Mercury or the transits of Venus would provide a better occasion for determining the solar parallax. By the 1740's, however, astronomers on both sides of the Channel seemed to agree with Edmund Halley, who had concluded that the transits of Mercury were of use only as practice exercises for the main events of 1761 and 1769, when transits of Venus were scheduled to take place.[23]

Clap was very much alive to the currents of astronomical thought running between Europe and the colonies, and as a good Newtonian he was especially aware of the importance of this phase of astronomical research. When a transit of Mercury took place in October 1742, he was at his post. He observed the passage of the planet across the face of the sun through the thirty-inch reflecting telescope belonging to the college. Observation was the full extent of his activity, much to his chagrin. Lacking the necessary instruments for measurement, he was unable to make vital mathematical computations.[24]

Clap was better prepared for the transit of 1753. As a matter of fact, every important astronomer in colonial America was ready for the celestial phenomenon, thanks to the concerted efforts of Benjamin Franklin and James Alexander of New York. Recognizing the value of the transit of Mercury as a rehearsal for the forthcoming transits of Venus, and seeking to stimulate interest in those events, Alexander urged Franklin to lend his prestige to the project. More explicitly, he requested the Philadelphian to notify qualified astronomers in the colonies of the transit of Mercury. In

22. Harry Woolf, *The Transits of Venus—A Study of Eighteenth-Century Science* (Princeton, N.J., 1959), chap. 1.

23. *Ibid.*, 27-29, 71.

24. Clap to Cromwell Mortimer, May 31, 1743, Royal Society MS., London. The president also observed at this time sun spots, an eclipse of the moon, and Saturn's ring. The inopportune appearance of clouds prevented him from making critical observations of the eclipse of the moon.

effect, Franklin was to act as a publicist. In a letter to Franklin, Alexander emphasized the need of the co-operation of the colonial colleges: "It Would be a great honour To our young Colledges in America if they forthwith prepared themselves with a proper apparatus for that Observation and made it." In compliance with Alexander's request, Franklin prepared fifty copies of a brief pamphlet, which emphasized the importance of the transit of Mercury, listed the equipment needed for observation, and detailed the procedure that was to be followed. Franklin distributed the pamphlets among "my ingenious acquaintances in North America." [25] While positive evidence is lacking, from what passed between Alexander and Franklin there can be no question but that Clap received one.

But Clap really did not need Franklin's stimulant; his interest was already fully generated. He made "great Preparations" to view the spectacle, due to take place just before six o'clock on the morning of May 6. This time he was equipped to make calculations. A quadrant and an astronomical clock lay close at hand. The telescope stood poised. Only one element could thwart his efforts— and he confronted it when he arose in the morning! Not only New Haven but the entire Atlantic seaboard was blanketed with heavy clouds. Clap, Winthrop, Franklin—the entire lot of colonial astronomers—cast no shadows that morning. In the British colonies in America, only one astronomer, an observer in Antigua, got a clear view of the transit. In short time, Clap learned of his "very accurate observation" and anxiously, if not excitedly, looked forward to receiving more detailed information.[26]

The leading astronomical event of the century was the transit of Venus in 1761. While it is certain that the president maintained a keen interest in it, there is no evidence that he actively participated in the enormous co-operative scientific enterprise that accompanied it. One would be justified in speculating that Clap was profoundly envious of John Winthrop of Harvard, whose fortune

25. I. Bernard Cohen, "Benjamin Franklin and the Transit of Mercury in 1753," *Amer. Philos. Soc., Proceedings,* 94 (1950), 222-32. A facsimile of the pamphlet is included in this article.

26. See *ibid.* for a discussion of colonial efforts to observe the transit of Mercury. Clap related the sad tale in his letter to Colden (see above, *n.* 20).

it was to receive generous financial support from the Massachusetts government in outfitting a scientific expedition to St. Johns, Newfoundland, for the purpose of observing the transit; it could not be witnessed from New Haven because it occurred before sunrise in that area. This circumstance, and his lack of essential equipment, thwarted Clap's desire to assist in the resolution of the problem of scalar dimension. His sole contribution to the enterprise was that of educating those around him as to the significance of determining the solar parallax. In the cultural wilderness of colonial Connecticut, such a contribution was in itself of profound importance. Education of this sort, however ephemeral it may appear by modern standards, was a necessary prerequisite for the establishment of a tradition of astronomical research.

A second phase of his work in observational astronomy involved the tracking of comets. The sight, or news, of a comet in the New England sky spurred him into feverish activity. To acquire data that would enable him to plot the comet's trajectory and determine its distinctive physical characteristics, he dispatched letters to fellow astronomers in New England, sifted newspaper accounts, and not infrequently journeyed to those areas where the comet had been most conspicuously visible. Two of his accounts were published in the *Connecticut Gazette*.[27]

Clap shared in the general excitement that prevailed among astronomers of the western world in the last months of 1758 over the impending appearance of Halley's Comet.[28] Since the comet came within telescopic sight of the earth but once in a span of 76 to 77 years, it was the sole opportunity of the century to witness one of the most spectacular of all natural phenomena. The precise date of the comet's appearance was not known. Halley had predicted just prior to his death in 1742 that it would return from the unknown and reach its perihelion (at which it could be seen from earth) in late May 1759. French astronomers, after correcting errors in Halley's mathematical computations, predicted that its

27. (New Haven), May 5, 1759; Jan. 12, 1760.
28. After calculating the orbit of the Comet of 1682, Edmund Halley (1656-1742) predicted that this particular comet reappeared after intervals of approximately 76-77 years. When his prediction was borne out in 1759, the comet was named for him.

perihelion would occur at least one month earlier.[29] Whether Clap knew of these revisions cannot be determined. The close ties between the members of the European astronomical circle, coupled with the fact that Clap corresponded with English astronomers, would suggest that he had been informed of developments concerning this most dramatic event. At any rate, it is certain that the president took up his station and spent many anxious moments peering at the heavens from the end of 1758 through the early months of 1759, as did John Winthrop at Cambridge, Ezra Stiles at Newport, Theophilus Grew at Philadelphia, and numerous astronomers throughout western Europe.

Astronomers in continental Europe sighted the comet during Christmas week, 1758, but it was first seen in America by sharp-eyed watchers at Charleston, South Carolina, in late March 1759.[30] Two weeks later the New England observers caught sight of the prodigal. Winthrop tracked it in his telescope on April 3. An account of his observations appeared in the Boston newspapers one month later.[31] In early April, Clap caught sight of the fiery object, whose unique tail of gas molecules, according to modern astronomers, stretches to the phenomenal length of some ninety million miles. A month later, his observations were published in the *Connecticut Gazette,* the report opening dramatically, "The long expected comet now appears." [32] His account was later reprinted in the *Boston Evening Post.*[33] According to Clap's computations, the comet was approximately forty-seven million miles from the earth when it reached perihelion, and came closest to earth on April 26. It is of interest to note that Clap's major generalizations, derived from independent research, approximated those of the renowned Winthrop.

Clap's third area of astronomical specialization, the study of meteors, was closely connected with his work on comets. He had conducted extensive research on meteors since his ministerial days in Windham, but it was not until the 1750's that he announced a theory that certain meteors had the main characteristics of comets,

29. McKeehan, *Yale Science,* 20.
30. *Boston News-Letter,* May 3, 1759.
31. *Ibid.; Boston Evening Post,* May 7, 1759.
32. (New Haven), May 5, 1759.
33. May 14, 1759.

in that they made elliptical orbits and did not fall to earth as meteorites or dissipate into gas. Clap's theory, in brief, embodied these points: the "superior Meteors," or terrestrial meteors, were solid bodies about one-half mile in diameter, which revolved around the earth, their center of focus, in elliptical orbits; the meteors were twenty to thirty miles above the earth at perigee; through friction with the atmosphere they made a constant rumbling noise, similar to earthquakes, and achieved a brilliant luminosity; explosions which usually accompanied these meteors were caused by spark discharges resulting from overcharging; their rate of speed was five hundred miles per minute.[34]

Although Clap may have arrived at this theory of terrestrial meteors on the basis of his own research, its seminal idea had been first set in print by an unknown contributor to the *Gentleman's Magazine* in October 1755.[35] After giving an account of a meteor that had passed over Holland early in that year, the writer made this parenthetical observation: "I have this one further remark to add, that supposing this body had been projected parallel to the horizon with an initial velocity of 4, 95 miles in a second of time, and that its ignition would not have dissipated or consumed it, nor the atmosphere retarded it, it would have assumed the nature of a sattelite or moon, and revolved around the earth perpetually in a circular orbit." An avid reader of the *Gentleman's Magazine* (when he could lay his hands on it), Clap assuredly noticed this account.[36]

The knowledge that at least one European astronomer was conducting research along the same theoretical lines as his own

34. Clap, *Conjectures Upon Meteors*, 11-13.
35. The article was signed "B. J." One authority speculates that it was John Bevis (the initials reversed), a prominent English astronomer and mathematician.
36. The account certainly gave Ezra Stiles a mental jolt when he read it a few years later. Stiles immediately noticed the similarity in theories. He had previously assumed that Clap was the first astronomer to develop the theory of terrestrial meteors. Now he was not so certain but that Clap had borrowed the idea. Puzzled by the coincidence, he wrote his onetime mentor, informing him of his discovery. He tactfully concluded, however, "I still call it your [hypothesis] though I imagine that Mr. B. J. and yourself both hit upon the same hypothesis by separate and distinct efforts of genius." Clap later sent word to Stiles through a courier that his conclusion was correct. If Stiles had other thoughts on the matter, he refrained from publicizing them. See the manuscript note by Stiles on the verso of page 1 of John Noyes to Stiles, July 5, 1756, Yale MS.; and Stiles to Clap, Feb. 19, 1766, Yale MS.

gave a sudden thrust to his desire to gain recognition as the author of the theory. In 1756 he set his thoughts down on paper and circulated the manuscript among astronomical colleagues in the American colonies.[37] The action came none too soon, for three years later there appeared in the *Philosophical Transactions* an article by Sir John Pringle,[38] in which a theory closely paralleling Clap's was presented. Pringle had earlier published a series of accounts of a meteor seen over Europe in June 1758.[39] In his follow-up article, in the process of stating his conclusions, Pringle theorized that some meteors remained solid while in flight and maintained regular elliptical orbits.[40]

The president now intensified his research. On May 10, 1759, a meteor was observed along the coastal area of Massachusetts. Shortly after, Clap, who was en route to Boston on business, traveled through the towns of that locale and interviewed "many people." The information he acquired was sketchy and of a primitive order, offering full testimony to the difficulties of the eighteenth-century astronomer. Residents of Taunton informed him they had heard rumbling noises persisting for two minutes. A man in Roxbury had observed a ball of fire of white transparent brightness about six inches in diameter. A sailor in Boston told him that he had witnessed the phenomenon "about a league SE" from Cape Cod. He estimated the meteor to be about "50 to 60 degrees high" and passing from west to east. When it was about one-half mile from him, it burst into a "thousand pieces"; from the standpoint of Clap's theory, this was a shattering observation.

After collating these superficial and oftentimes contradictory observations, Clap drew up a report and forwarded it to John Winthrop, who had issued an appeal in the Boston newspapers for such data. The report, presented in the form of a letter to Winthrop, was published in the *Boston News-Letter*.[41] Two years later

37. McKeehan, *Yale Science*, 23-24.

38. On Pringle, see Dorothy Singer, "Sir John Pringle and His Circle," *Annals of Science*, 6 (1949-50), 127-80.

39. "Several Accounts of the Fiery Meteor, Which Appeared on Sunday the 26th of November, 1758, Between Eight and Nine at Night; Collected by John Pringle," *Philosophical Transactions*, 51 (1758-59), 218-59.

40. *Ibid.*, 259-74. There were still other points of similarity between their theories (size of the phenomena and rates of motion).

41. May 31, 1759.

Winthrop sent an account of the meteor to the Royal Society. The report, which was substantially identical with Clap's, was read before the Society and later published in the *Philosophical Transactions,* Winthrop receiving the credit for publication.[42] Clap received not a mention (which lends credibility to Louis McKeehan's statement that the colonial scientists were adept at "stealing the thunder" from each other).[43]

In 1763, after re-working certain points in his theory, Clap sent his manuscript to John Pringle in London.[44] Pringle was to offer it to the Royal Society for a reading and, if merited, publication in the *Philosophical Transactions.* Although the paper was read before the Society on July 21, 1764, there was no decision for publication. In June of the following year, Peter Collinson, who served as a sort of clearinghouse, or *via media,* between the colonial scientists and the Royal Society, provided Clap with the comforting news that his essay had been received "with Approbation." He made no mention of publication, however, confining himself to the editor's timeless platitude that the Society was keenly interested in his research and anxiously looked forward to receiving additional accounts.[45]

Even before the receipt of Collinson's communication, Clap had returned to his research. Hearing of a meteor that had passed over Massachusetts, New York, and eastern Pennsylvania on May 10, 1765, he directed a letter of inquiry to Ezra Stiles, then serving as a minister in Newport, Rhode Island. Did he have any informa-

42. Winthrop, "An Account of a Meteor Seen in New England, And of a Whirlwind Felt in That Country: in a Letter to the Rev. Thomas Birch," *Philos. Trans.,* 52 (1760-61), 6-16. In another co-operative venture with Winthrop, Clap fared much better. When a meteor passed over southern New England in Nov. 1742, he drew up a report and relayed it to the Harvard scientist. Some 22 years later, Winthrop inserted Clap's report, with a proper acknowledgement, in a more comprehensive document and sent it off to John Pringle of the Royal Society. Winthrop's paper was read before the Society on June 4, 1764, and published in the *Philosophical Transactions* the same year (54 [1763-64], 185-91). This marked the only time that an astronomical report credited to Clap appeared in the famed journal. Clap did forward to the Society (via Pringle) in 1763 "An Account of Three Fiery Meteors Seen in New England," which was read on June 7, 1764. He reported on meteors seen in 1711, 1743, and 1748. The document is in the Royal Society. For Royal Society's acknowledgment, see Journal Book of Royal Society, XXV, 1763-66, 251-52.
43. McKeehan, *Yale Science,* 34.
44. The manuscript is in the Royal Society, London.
45. Dexter, ed., *Stiles's Itineraries,* 452-53.

tion on this "very Remarkable Meteor...as big and as bright as the sun...? I am in quest of more critical observations." He urged Stiles to keep him informed of any news he might gather.[46] Meanwhile, he made a public appeal, through the *Connecticut Courant,* to "all ministers and all other gentlemen of learning and ingenuity" to correspond with people in the areas in which the meteor had been sighted. If they should travel through those districts, they were to interview people who had witnessed the phenomenon and have them point out with their hands the approximate course of the meteor's movement. The men of education were then to compute the point of compass and the altitude at which the meteor had been first and last seen. In the event their informants did not understand degrees of elevation, they were to describe it "by its being nearly overhead, or half-way between overhead, and on the horizon, or as high as the sun as three or four hours, or the like." This information was then either to be forwarded to Clap personally or published in the newspapers.[47]

When another meteor shot across the sky of southwestern Connecticut on September 18, 1765, Clap gathered together compass and quadrant,[48] hitched horse to chaise, and scurried off on another scientific "journey"; about the same time, many of his non-scientific-minded fellow citizens in Connecticut were perambulating through the countryside, staves under arm, seeking out Jared Ingersoll, distributor of stamps for the Crown. Although many of the reports Clap gathered came from people "not skilled in Angles," he was certain that he had tracked down another "terrestrial" meteor. His final calculations showed it to be one-half mile in diameter and at a height of thirty-two miles. In October his report appeared in the *Connecticut Gazette;* it also contained the standard appeal for co-operation from the public, especially the educated men of the colony.[49]

46. *Ibid.*
47. June 17, 1765. By Oct. Clap had received reports from observers in Coldenham, Salisbury, and Northampton.
48. Clap utilized the scientific equipment belonging to the college in his personal research. He did own a quadrant, however; see Naphtali Daggett to Mary Wooster and Temperance Pitkin, Jan. 14, 1767, Boston Pub. Lib. MS. One of the injunctions in "President Clap's Directions to His Children After His Decease" (1757, Mass. Hist. Soc. photostat) was to return to the college the scientific apparatus he had borrowed.
49. (New Haven), Oct. 4, 1765.

Clap made his final appearance in print on March 3, 1766, just three months before he tendered his resignation to the Yale Corporation. He reported on a meteor that had passed over Hartford the previous month. Once again his observations pointed to a terrestrial meteor. He implored observers who had taken compass readings and made a determination of the meteor's altitude and angle of descent to publish their accounts in the newspapers.[50] In this way the altitude and course of the meteor could be more accurately determined.

The implicit confidence that Clap retained in his theory was not shared by the astronomers of the Royal Society. This probably explains why the Society failed to publish the essay. That Clap's theory was based on some tenuous propositions was apparent. Its weak points have been exposed by a modern authority: "The orbits had to be very nicely adjusted to miss the earth by about twenty miles every time, and yet the orbits had to change rather rapidly to prevent monotonous repetitions of the observed passages at the same latitudes. (The difference in polar and equatorial radii is so slight as to be unimportant.) Worse yet, the earth wobbles so much about the center of the earth-moon system, nearly 3,000 miles from the center of the earth, that a terrestrial comet which ever got as far away as the moon would have to follow a very remarkable orbit indeed to go on missing the earth so narrowly time after time." [51] Moreover, as every schoolboy of the rocket age knows, the earth's gravitational pull at an altitude of twenty to thirty miles is much too powerful to allow an object, whatever its size, to maintain a perpetual orbit. The famous Russian sputnik launched in October 1957, while admittedly a marble compared to Clap's theoretical meteors (the sputnik was only 23 inches in diameter and weighed but 184 pounds), was 150 miles from the earth at the lowest point in its orbit (perigee). Yet it disintegrated shortly after two months of earth-circling, a victim of atmospheric friction. Modern astronomical science has also demonstrated that meteorites, even those of substantial size, passing between the earth and sun would be shattered by the tidal forces of the sun's gravitational field. In the scheme of the universe, meteors are

50. *Connecticut Courant* (Hartford), Mar. 3, 1766.
51. McKeehan, *Yale Science,* 30.

flimsy things, easily disturbed and easily destroyed by the greater forces of nature.

Although displaying a notable ingeniousness in formulating his theory, Clap was conspicuously lacking in what McKeehan aptly calls "physical intuition." The president's essay was published posthumously in 1781 through the efforts of Ezra Stiles.[52] It stands today as a quaint museum piece of early American astronomy. Nevertheless, it represents one of the earliest efforts by a colonial American to comprehend in a scientific manner a most mysterious aspect of astronomy. Even today, with hypersensitive telescopes (both reflecting and refracting), chronographs, spectroscopes, spectrographs, radio equipment, and photometers at the disposal of astronomers, there is a cloud of uncertainty surrounding movements of larger meteors. One fact is certain, however. Through such primitive and naive speculation, through such conspicuous errors of judgment, astronomical knowledge was advanced. That failure is an important component of progress is a fact often overlooked. Clap's efforts to provide a rational explanation of meteors represent one link in the chain of knowledge leading to the greater understanding of the mysteries of outer space.

Not to be disregarded or minimized are Clap's efforts as a popularizer of astronomical science. His published reports of comets and meteors reached a wide audience. However elementary in content, they contributed to the education of the general public in observational astronomy. This type of promotional effort played a part in making astronomical research the most widely practiced scientific activity in New England during the post-Revolutionary period.

To the colonial scientists of his day, Clap stood out as a formidable figure. Friend and foe alike acknowledged his competence as a "natural philosopher," particularly in the areas of physics, mathematics, and astronomy. The reliable Stiles wrote these words of high praise: "In mathematics and natural philosophy, I have not reason to think that he was equalled by any man in America, except the most learned Professor Winthrop. Many others excelled

---

52. Stiles presented a copy of the work to the Royal Society in 1784. Dexter, ed., *Literary Diary of Stiles*, III, 119.

him in the mechanic application of the lower branches of the
mathematics, but he rose to sublime heights, and became conversant in the application of this noble science to those extensive
laws of nature, which regulate the most extensive phenomena,
and obtain through the stellary universe." [53] At another time, Stiles
affirmed that Clap surpassed Elisha Williams "(as well as all the
Presidents in Harv[ard] Coll., and in all American Colleges) in
Mathematics, Philosophy and *Astronomy*." [54] Chauncey Whittelsey, a tutor under Clap and one who held him in something less
than esteem, echoed Stiles's judgment when he wrote that in
"Mathematical and Philosophical Learning [Clap] was neither
surpassed nor equalled by any man on this Continent, except
Professor Winthrop." [55]

Some reputable later authorities have also heaped encomia upon
Clap for his scientific skills. Franklin Dexter has written that his
"attainments in mathematics, astronomy, and physics, placed him
beyond doubt in the first rank of Americans in his generation." [56]
Less glowing, but suggestively flattering, is Theodore Hornberger's
statement that "Clap, had he been properly encouraged, suitably
paid, and freed of administrative responsibilities, might perhaps
have been another Winthrop." [57]

"Might have been" perhaps best sums up Clap's scientific life.
Whatever his abilities, and they were considerable in certain
fields—mathematics, for example—the president cannot be ac-

53. Stiles to Daggett, July 28, 1767, Yale MS. Stiles frequently solicited Clap's
aid in his astronomical research. See, for example, Clap to Stiles, Sept. 1, 1757,
Yale MS. Clap assisted in determining the orbit of a comet.

54. Dexter, ed., *Literary Diary of Stiles*, II, 336. This statement takes on added
significance when it is noted that Stiles was "personally acquainted" with 16
college presidents. He lists them in *ibid.*, II, 335.

55. Dexter, ed., *Stiles's Itineraries*, 461. Another contemporary, the historian
Samuel Miller, who was usually too ostentatious in his praise, as well as uncertain
in his facts, judged Clap to be "one of the most profound and accurate scholars ever
bred in Connecticut." The judgment is open to question on a number of counts; in
the first place, Clap was "bred in Massachusetts." Miller was closer to the truth
when he wrote that Clap succeeded in producing at Yale a greater interest in the
abstruse sciences, particularly mathematics and astronomy, than had been done
before. *A Brief Retrospect of the Eighteenth Century*, in *Wm. and Mary Qtly.*, 3d
Ser., 10 (1953), 600, 615.

56. Dexter, "Clap and Writings," New Haven Colony Hist. Soc., *Papers*, 5 (1894),
268.

57. McKeehan, *Yale Science*, preface.

corded the status of an Olympian. He was actually a cut below America's best. The available evidence would indicate that he was not of the class of Winthrop and Franklin. He lacked the qualities that made for their greatness—the analytical ability of Winthrop, the pragmatic temperament of Franklin. Lacking the architectonic mind, he neither constructed an imposing or monumental scientific synthesis nor produced any remarkable scientific discoveries. In the larger issue of synthesis he was not vitally interested. While he boldly grappled with the advanced problems posed by Cartesian and Newtonian scientific thought, he did so for the express purpose of amplifying rather than creating. He was essentially an improver or enlarger, not a creator. His mission was merely to advance science along rational lines through the doctrines of the "perpetual Dictator," as Cotton Mather reverently alluded to Newton,[58] not to establish a school of scientific thought. Viewed in the perspective of colonial American science, he sailed well beyond the known frontiers of astronomical science, but there were definite limits to his range of investigation and speculation. He was not an intellectual adventurer. Try as he might, he could not in conscience consistently follow Pope's exhortation and "mount where Science guides." [59]

58. *Manductio ad Ministerium,* 50.
59. The couplet reads:
      Go wond'rous creature! mount where Science guides
      Go, measure earth, weigh air, and state the tides;
Alexander Pope, *An Essay on Man,* ed. Maynard Mack (London and New Haven, 1950 and 1951), 56.

Chapter Six

NEW RELIGION AND
AN OLD LIGHT

IN mid-September of 1740, while Rector Clap was busily
planning the reorganization of Yale, George Whitefield, twenty-
five years of age and already the most famous revivalist of his day,
arrived by sloop in Newport, Rhode Island. Whitefield had recently completed a successful sweep of the southern and middle
colonies, and now, at the request of the Reverend Benjamin Colman of Boston, was undertaking a tour of New England.[1] His
arrival marked a new era in that area's religious history.

For the next six weeks this young and pompous preacher held
New England spellbound. With his flaming oratory and gesticulating delivery, Whitefield overpowered his audiences.[2] To a people
long accustomed to prepared, prosaic sermons, the extemporaneous offerings of the itinerant came to represent the words of an

1. Whitefield's New England tour is traced in detail in this portion of his
Journal: *A Continuation of the Reverend Mr. Whitefield's Journal, From a Few
Days After His Arrival at Savannah, June the Fourth, to His Leaving Stanford
[Stamford], the Last Town in New England, October 29, 1740* (Philadelphia, 1741),
48-126 (hereafter cited as Whitefield, *Continuation of Journal, Savannah to Stamford*).

2. The irascible Dr. Johnson commented on Whitefield's monumental success as a
preacher as follows: "His popularity, Sir, is chiefly owing to the peculiarity of his
manner. He would be followed by crowds were he to wear a nightcap in the pulpit,
or were he to preach from a tree." James Boswell, *The Life of Samuel Johnson*,
Oxford ed. (London, 1946), I, 386-87.

inspired prophet. Even the staid ministers of Boston were impressed. Thomas Prince, a chief Brahmin among the Boston clergy, expressed the sentiments of many of his colleagues when he wrote: "Surely God is with this Man of a Truth." [3] An equally enamored Colman designated the Sunday on which Whitefield graced his pulpit as the "happiest day he ever saw in his life." [4]

Upon the general populace the revivalist made an even more profound impact. Moved by an urge for religious experience and braving all forms of personal inconvenience and hardship, thousands flocked to his sermons, overflowing the tiny churches and meeting halls, listening from the streets. "He lookt almost Angelical," wrote Nathan Cole, a semi-literate farmer-carpenter of Kensington Parish, Connecticut, who had dropped his farm implement and raced from the field at the news of Whitefield's impending arrival in Middletown, and driven his horse at breakneck speed so as to be on time for the "Sarmon." The evangelist, Cole further noted, was a "young, Slim, slender youth before some thousands of people with a bold undaunted Countenance, and my hearing how God was with him every where as he came along it Solemnized my mind; and put me into a trembling fear before he began to preach; for he looked as if he was Cloathed with Authority from the Great God; and a sweet sollome solemnity sat upon his brow And my hearing him preach, gave me a heart wound; By Gods blessing: my old Foundation was broken up, and I saw that my righteousness would not save me." [5]

Wherever the "Pied Piper" (as Whitefield was dubbed by some critics) paused, the mobs assembled and gaped. Whole towns fell under his sway. All eyes and ears hung on his lips; audiences greedily devoured his every word. Frequently the hugeness of the crowds necessitated a transfer of meetings from churches to town commons or open fields. On one occasion in Boston the transfer

3. Thomas Prince, Jr., ed., *The Christian History, Containing Accounts of the Revival and Propagation of Religion in Great-Britain and America for the Year 1744* (Boston, 1745), II, 360 (Vol. I concentrates on the events of 1743).

4. Quoted in E. Edwards Beardsley, *The History of the Episcopal Church in Connecticut* (Boston, 1883), I, 123.

5. From Cole's "Spiritual Travels." See Leonard W. Labaree, "George Whitefield Comes to Middletown," *Wm. and Mary Qtly.*, 3d Ser., 7 (1950), 588-91. Cole provides an extremely vivid account of the frenetic activities preceding the actual meeting.

was delayed and tragic consequences resulted. Five obviously distraught devotees of the sermonizer plunged to their deaths from an overloaded gallery. The incident had no adverse effect either on Whitefield's popularity or on attendance at subsequent meetings. As Charles Chauncy, one of the few Bostonians not at all charmed by Whitefield's eloquence, surlily informed a European correspondent: "The grand Subject of Conversation was Mr. *Whitefield,* and the whole Business of the Town to run, from Place to Place, to hear him preach." [6]

In this auspicious manner the Great Awakening came to New England. From the Rhode Island rum center, Whitefield moved northward to Boston and, later, to what is now southern Maine. He retraced his steps to Boston and, after preaching a farewell sermon to an audience estimated at between twenty to thirty thousand, swung westward to Northampton, the precinct of Jonathan Edwards, one of the principal "river gods," who had promoted a "little" Awakening five years earlier. Whitefield preached—and Edwards wept.

Accompanied by Edwards, who was en route to his parents' home in South Windsor (Connecticut), Whitefield started down the Connecticut River valley on Monday, October 20. It was a triumphal tour. There was standing room only wherever he preached and, as Whitefield wrote, "I did not spare them." He performed in Westfield and Springfield on Monday; Suffield and Windsor on Tuesday; Hartford and "Withersfield" on Wednesday; Middletown and Wallingford on Thursday. The tour almost opened on a tragic note. Outside of Springfield, the revivalist's horse fell while crossing a bridge and Whitefield was thrown to the ground, falling "directly upon my Nose: The Fall stunned me for awhile. My Mouth was full of Dust. I bled a little." Shaken but unhurt, he remounted and set out again, whereupon "God so filled me with a Sense of his sovereign, distinguishing Love, and my own Unworthiness, that my Eyes gushed out with Tears; but they were all Tears of Love. Oh how did I want to sink before the high and

6. "A Letter From a Gentleman in Boston [Charles Chauncy] to Mr. George Wishart, One of the Ministers of Edinburgh Concerning the State of Religion in New England 1742," Clarendon Historical Society, *Reprints,* 1st Ser. (1882), 74.

lofty One that inhabited Eternity. I felt myself less than nothing, and yet knew that my Jesus was my ALL in ALL." [7]

Arriving in New Haven on Friday morning, Whitefield "declined preaching . . . because it was wet, the People had no Notice of my Coming, and I had much private Business upon my Hands." He preached an afternoon sermon, two sermons on Saturday ("There were sweet Meltings discernable both Times."), and two on Sunday. During the evenings he held court at his lodgings where he "expounded" to small groups and collected £40 for his orphanage in Georgia. He captivated all in New Haven, including the members of the colonial government, then sitting in session, and the venerable Governor Joseph Talcott. After the Sunday sermon, the governor, "an aged, grave old Gentleman," held an audience with the itinerant. Stirred to his spiritual depths, the Governor was barely able to speak. "The Tears trickled down his aged Cheeks like Drops of Rain," Whitefield wrote later with satisfaction. "He was thankful to God, he said, for such Refreshings in the Way to our Rest. Food does us good, added he, when we eat it with an Appetite. And indeed I believe, he had fed upon the Word." From all accounts, there were many in New Haven who shared Governor Talcott's appetite for Whitefield's theological morsels and who "had fed upon the Word." About eight o'clock on Sunday evening, with the moon shining brightly, Whitefield left New Haven.[8] Three days later he arrived in New York City. The tour was at an end. New England was in spiritual shambles, never to be the same.[9]

The most immediate and discernible effect of Whitefield's preaching was a renewed interest in religion. Thousands were shaken out of their indifference. Church attendance swelled wherever he had appeared.[10] Religious meetings were held on all days

---

7. *Continuation of Journal, Savannah to Stamford,* 108-14. Whitefield's march through central Connecticut is also recounted in the *Boston Weekly News-Letter,* Oct. 30–Nov. 6, 1740.

8. On Whitefield's activities in New Haven, see *Continuation of Journal, Savannah to Stamford,* 114-19.

9. The most complete secondary account of the early years of the revival in New England is Edwin Gaustad, *The Great Awakening in New England* (N. Y., 1957).

10. Benjamin Trumbull estimated that 30 or 40,000 people in New England "were born into the family of heaven" as a result of the revival; *History of Connecticut,* II, 218.

and at all hours and in all places. In many cases, a single meeting would consume the entire day and continue well into the night by flickering candlelight. Ordinary table talk focused on religious questions; for the moment, salvation, predestination, and the like supplanted the price of codfish and the European political situation as the main topic of social conversation. In the vernacular of the clergy, "a waxing of the dry bones" had taken place. The spirit of God was apparently hovering over New Zion.

A second noticeable effect of Whitefield's evangelical campaign was a growing emotionalism in religious practice. Many of his meetings had been characterized by a moderate degree of disorder, with people fainting and exhibiting other types of frenzy. The frequency of these scenes prompted some of the more conservative New Englanders, mostly ministers and magistrates, to regard Whitefield with disfavor and his doings as a travesty of religion. They were aghast at this new religious development. Whitefield stubbornly insisted that people were witnessing the outpouring of the spirit of God. The conservatives were more inclined to credit these scenes of emotional orgy to overwrought imagination, or, as it was generally designated, "Enthusiasm," which was once defined by Charles Chauncy as a "disease—a Sort of Madness." [11] In their view, New England had gone raving mad. They preferred, in the words of Edwin Gaustad, to dismiss the revival as "satanic seduction." [12]

"Separatism," or the fragmentation of the Congregational church system in Massachusetts and Connecticut, was still another religious consequence stemming directly from Whitefield's tour. In the course of his wanderings, in addition to preaching the need of true conversion, Whitefield hammered on the theme that the generality of New England ministers were "unconverted," that they were therefore incapable of preaching a truly spiritual religion. If the members of the church judged their minister to be of this unsanctified order, it logically followed that they should desist from attending his services and institute private meetings. With a rapidity that alarmed the conservative elements, a score of separate churches sprang up in Massachusetts and Connecticut.

11. Chauncy, *Enthusiasm Described and Cautioned Against* (Boston, 1742), 2-3.
12. *Great Awakening in New England*, 80.

Separation was fast becoming the order of the day. The conservatives were inclined to believe that all too many were taking literally Paul's dictum: "Come out from among them, and be ye separate, . . . and touch not the unclean Thing." Events in New England seemed to be bearing out Jacques-Bénigne Bossuet's prophecy of the eventual destruction of Protestantism through schism and internal disorder.

The vacuum created by Whitefield's departure was very quickly filled by a horde of itinerant preachers. As described by a New Haven missionary of the Society for the Propagation of the Gospel in Foreign Parts, they were "furious preachers that Whitefield has set a madding." [13] Of this group, some were untrained exhorters, while others were established ministers who had descended to the wandering habit. Whereas Whitefield had had the tact to generalize his charge that the majority of practicing ministers were unconverted, the itinerants did not scruple to particularize. With monotonous regularity they castigated the established clergy as hypocrites, Pharisees, and carnal, unregenerate wretches. This type of abuse became their stock in trade. If there were a few learned and distinguished clerical figures among these "strollers," there were a great many more who were unlearned and unkempt. That they were unimpeachably sincere in their efforts to make the spiritual pulse of New England beat faster is beyond question; but that they were lacking in tact and charity is equally evident. Like the Ranters of an earlier age, the greater number of them concentrated on denouncing and censuring the established ministers and terrorizing the populace into seeking spiritual rebirth. Their zeal outran discretion. With the appearance of the itinerants, experiential religion, a stranger to New England religious life, came into prominence. Passion replaced cool conviction. Ramus gave way to Pascal.

While Whitefield's meetings often presented scenes of mild disorder, those of the itinerants almost always produced mass madness. At a typical meeting "some would be *praying*, some *ex-*

13. Theophilus Morris to S.P.G., May 4, 1742, MS. Letters to the Society for the Propagation of the Gospel in Foreign Parts, Case B10, No. 47. Unless otherwise specified, all references to S.P.G. MSS., including the S.P.G. Journal and Journal of Minutes, relate to materials in the S.P.G. Library, London.

horting, some *singing,* some *clapping their Hands,* some *laughing,* some *crying,* some *shrieking and roaring out."* [14] The itinerants themselves, often overwrought with emotion, joined in the spiritual writhings. On occasion, James Davenport became so aroused while preaching that he would remove his clothes from the waist up and, while gesticulating wildly with his arms, shout and scream in the highest decibel he could attain.[15] Gilbert Tennent was especially renowned for the bodily gyrations that accompanied his preaching.[16] The disorderly character of itinerant meetings drew this biased, but nonetheless perceptive, observation from arch-critic Charles Chauncy: "Religion of late has been more a commotion in the Passions than a change in the Temper of the Mind." [17]

By 1741, New England was in a state of religious turmoil; the "civil war of the Lords" was in full swing. The population was roughly divided into two religious "parties," designated as Old Lights and New Lights. The Old Lights, largely composed of representatives of the Standing Order, were for the most part convinced that what was transpiring was utterly destructive of true religion and not even remotely connected with the doings of God. A more moderate group among the Old Lights, while admitting that the Awakening had been originally the handiwork of God, asserted that human weakness had permitted the devil to infiltrate the movement. In their view, this fact accounted for the tumultuous meetings and the prevailing religious disorder. All of the Old Lights seemed to agree that "Enthusiasm" and separatism were the two major evils of the Great Awakening that outweighed any good it might achieve.

In Connecticut, the conflict between supporters and detractors of the revival was sharpened by a division of thought over the Saybrook Platform. Embodied in this document was the Half-Way

14. "[Chauncy] to Wishart," Clarendon Hist. Soc., *Reprints,* 1st Ser. (1882), 77. See also, Schneider, eds., *Writings of Johnson,* I, 28-29.

15. Chauncy, *Enthusiasm Described and Cautioned Against,* 98-99. Other examples are provided in Chauncy's *Seasonable Thoughts On the State of Religion in New England* (Boston, 1743).

16. For an uncomplimentary account of Tennent's "beastly brayings," see Luke Tyerman, *The Life of the Reverend George Whitefield* (London, 1890), II, 124-25. The account is by Timothy Cutler.

17. *Seasonable Thoughts,* 109.

Covenant, the religious compromise granting provisional church membership to persons who had not experienced conversion. They were given all the usual privileges except the right to participate in the Lord's Supper. According to the New Lights, however, membership in the true church could be granted only to "visible saints," only to those who had experienced the soul labors of spiritual rebirth. To them, the Half-Way Covenant was, as Eleazar Wheelock sarcastically phrased it, "half-way nonsense." [18] Having thus reaffirmed the doctrinal position of the Puritan founding fathers, the New Lights repudiated the Saybrook Platform—and "Mr. [Solomon] Stoddard's Way"—and declared the established churches of Connecticut false and corrupt. It was on this basis that the New Lights justified separation and the establishment of separate churches. Of equal importance, the New Lights were also dead set against the Presbyterian form of polity (association and consociation framework) set forth in the Saybrook Platform. They insisted on retaining the decentralized, independent-type polity of the Cambridge Platform.[19]

In no portion of Connecticut did the controversy over the Awakening and the Saybrook Platform rage as heatedly as it did in the New Haven area. The "eye" of the religious hurricane sweeping through the colony was centered in New Haven. This commercial and cultural capital of Connecticut became a mecca for wandering itinerants, a key stop on the circuit. As already noted, Whitefield paused here for the unusually lengthy period of three days and preached five times to large, "remarkably attentive" crowds. The itinerants moved in on Whitefield's heels. Tennent, Davenport, Bellamy, Mills, Parsons, Graham, and a host of others came to spread the gospel.

Their meetings produced the characteristic excesses. One observer from Hartford, who was attending the Yale commencement in September 1741, sat in on two revival meetings conducted by itinerants and wrote in his diary: "Much confusion this day at New Haven, and at night; the most strange management and a

18. "Yale College One Hundred Years Ago," *Hours at Home*, 10 (Feb. 1870), 329.
19. On the revival in Connecticut, see Oscar Zeichner, *Connecticut's Years of Controversy* (Chapel Hill, 1949), 21-24.

pretence of religion that ever I saw." [20] Samuel Hopkins, then a student at Yale, was more explicit, noting during a meeting conducted by Gilbert Tennent that "many cried out with distress and horror of mind, under a conviction of God's anger, and their constant exposedness to fall into endless destruction." [21] One effect of itinerant activity was a division of the First Church, heretofore the only Congregational church in the town. As a consequence of the repeated charge by the itinerants that the Reverend Joseph Noyes was unconverted, a group of parishioners severed ties with the First Church and began holding separate meetings.[22] This development further intensified the rift between the local Old Light and New Light elements.

It was only natural that the college should feel the full impact of the revival, for the college was an integral part of the town and most of its members received a good portion of their spiritual sustenance at the First Church. From the outset, the students became a favorite target of the itinerants; indeed, the college was a primary reason for the heavy concentration of itinerants in the New Haven area. Whitefield himself had addressed the students, speaking "very closely on the dreadful ill consequences of an unconverted Ministry," and on the moral dangers of "mixed dancing and frolicing of males and females together." [23]

Such sentiments had a powerful impact upon the impressionable students of Yale. The boys were quickly swept up by the winds of revivalism [24]—in the medical metaphor of one anti-revivalist, they were "much affected with the Disease of the Day." The general mood was expressed by John Maltby, a student, who wrote to his parents that his soul was "Dried up in this wilderness of Sin and Corruption .... O that the Lord would Shine into my Soul and

20. Walker, ed., *Daniel Wadsworth's Diary*, 72.

21. Hopkins, *Sketches of the Life of the Late, Rev. Samuel Hopkins D.D., Pastor of the First Congregational Church in Newport, Written by Himself* (Hartford, 1805), 31-34 (hereafter cited as *Life of Hopkins*).

22. Discussed in Leonard Bacon, *Thirteen Historical Discourses on the Completion of Two Hundred Years, From the Beginning of the First Church in New Haven With an Appendix* (New Haven, 1839), 211-42.

23. Hopkins, *Life of Hopkins*, 30; Whitefield, *Continuation of Journal, Savannah to Stamford*, 117.

24. See Chauncey Goodrich, "Narrative of Revivals of Religion in Yale," *American Quarterly Register*, 10 (1838), 290-93.

Set it on fier with his Love."[25] Maltby was soon ablaze. Others were likewise consumed with religious conviction. Emotion ran riot in the hall. Overstimulated by the preaching of the itinerants, the boys conducted private meetings; prayed individually and in small groups in their chambers; joined in the singing of hymns; discoursed on religion in the evenings, the discussions oftentimes outlasting the candles; and regularly attended local revival meetings.[26] The more deeply affected students, David Brainerd, for example, went about the college hall questioning classmates at length on their spiritual condition. So intense was the religious fervor that traditional student "customs" were ignored. For the moment, the freshmen were released from bondage, mingling freely and on a level of equality with their academic overlords.

A few of the more zealous students abandoned dull academic routine and themselves set out as itinerants. One such religious knight-errant carried the word to Boston where he was heard by Judge Samuel Sewall and Benjamin Cooper. Cooper was not impressed by the boy's performance. He informed Benjamin Colman that the youth "needed more to be at his studies." Colman reached the same conclusion; he found him "to be greatly Spirited to serve Souls but wanting Furniture." Colman later wrote Whitefield that at Harvard the students had been advised "not to rush forth so ill-prepared, but to be waiting upon God for Gifts, Grace and holy Zeal." [27]

Gilbert Tennent, who had been urged by Whitefield to tour New England so as to "blow up the divine fire lately kindled there," was especially popular with the students during his week's stay in New Haven. As one Bostonian correctly reported, he produced a "great shock" at Yale.[28] Of the seventeen sermons Tennent preached in New Haven, at least three were delivered in the college hall. After listening to two of these thundering sermons,

25. Nov. 18, 1742, Dartmouth College MS.

26. For a contemporary account of the religious activities of the Yale youth, see the John Cleaveland Diary, Yale photostat. The diary runs for a four-month period beginning in Jan. 1741/2.

27. Colman to Whitefield, June 3, 1742, Mass. Hist. Soc., *Proceedings*, 53 (1919-20), 214-15. The boy was apparently Samuel Buell. See Buell to Eleazar Wheelock, Apr. 20, 1742, and Silas Brett to Wheelock, Mar. 29, 1742, Dartmouth College MSS.

28. "Extract of a Letter From Benjamin Colman to George Whitefield," *Glasgow-Weekly-History* (1743), Mass. Hist. Soc., *Proceedings*, 53 (1920), 198-99.

which were delivered in one day, thirty students walked ten miles to hear Tennent speak again.[29] Samuel Hopkins became so intoxicated by the religious offerings of the dynamic New Jersey revivalist that he decided then and there to study divinity under him when he graduated. "When I heard Mr. Tennent," Hopkins later wrote, "I thought he was the greatest and best man, and the best preacher that I had ever seen or heard. His words were to me 'like apples of gold in pictures of silver'. And I then thought that when I should leave the college . . . I would go and live with him, wherever I should find him." [30] As it turned out, the impressionable young theologian-to-be later heard Jonathan Edwards sermonize and came to the conclusion that the Northampton minister was the greatest and best man and the best preacher he had ever seen or heard. Subsequently, he placed himself under Edwards's tutelage.

While Tennent was whipping up religious enthusiasm among the student body, he was simultaneously agitating the latent suspicions of Rector Clap. In the incipient stage of the revival, Clap had been its staunch supporter, favoring and furthering it at every turn. He had welcomed Whitefield to New Haven, invited him to address the students, and had even broken bread with him in his home.[31] He also had granted the use of the college hall to the itinerants.[32] With the appearance of Tennent in New Haven (April 1741), however, Clap underwent a noticeable change in his attitude toward the revival in general and the itinerants in particular.[33] A more powerful and searching preacher than Whitefield, but boorish in appearance and manner, Tennent wreaked emotional havoc on his audiences with his "fire and brimstone" ser-

29. Gilbert Tennent to William Tennent, Jan. 24, 1740/1, *ibid.*, 195.

30. *Life of Hopkins*, 37.

31. Whitefield, *Continuation of Journal, Savannah to Stamford*, 115-17; George Fisher, *A Discourse Commemorative of the History of the Church of Christ in Yale College During the First Century of Its Existence* (New Haven, 1858), 68 (hereafter cited as Fisher, *Discourse on Church of Christ*).

32. For example, Ebenezer Pemberton, *The Knowledge of Christ Recommended, in a Sermon Preached in the Public Hall at Yale-College in New Haven April 19th, 1741* (New London, 1741).

33. In a letter to Solomon Williams on July 16, 1742, Clap wrote that Tennent, while in New Haven, ran into all "extravagancies" with the exception of "Singing in the Streets." He credited Tennent with being the "Leading Cause of all our Difficulties and Confusions." Pa. Hist. Soc. MS.

monizing. In keeping with the main convention of the itinerants, he delivered hard words with respect to established ministers. In one intemperate outburst during a sermon in Pennsylvania, Tennent had characterized them as "hirelings, caterpillars, letter-learned Pharisees, Hypocrites, Varlets, Seed of the Serpent, foolish Builders whom the Devil drives into the ministry, dead dogs that cannot bark, blind men, dead men, men possessed of the devil, rebels and enemies of God." [34] Similar words of extravagant abuse passed from his lips in New Haven. More often than not, Tennent's meetings degenerated into scenes of bedlam and mass hysteria. Clap now became uncertain as to whether he was witnessing the outpouring of the spirit of God in man, or the welling up of the Old Adam.[35]

If the activities of Tennent instilled doubts in Clap's mind and aroused his suspicions as to the merits of the Awakening, the subsequent lunatic caperings of James Davenport served to crystallize these doubts and confirm these suspicions. A brilliant scholar at Yale in his undergraduate career [36] and a descendant of one of the most distinguished clerical families of New England, Davenport had seemingly been destined to a dull career as minister of the small, rural parish of Southold, on Long Island. Then the Great Awakening opened to him new vistas of religious service. Filled with the spirit of revivalism, drunk with the assurance of righteousness, he decided to quit his post as an established minister and strike out as an itinerant. Before embarking on his new career, however, he thought it appropriate and necessary to convert his own parishioners. He gathered them together and addressed them in the meetinghouse. The meeting came to an end twenty-four hours later. It was the opinion of some critics that Davenport made the short passage from genius to mental derangement on this

---

34. Quoted in Maria Greene, *The Development of Religious Liberty in Connecticut* (Boston, 1905), 237-38; taken from Chauncy's *Seasonable Thoughts.*

35. With things in such a topsy-turvy state at Yale, Samuel Johnson's enterprising son, William, then a sophomore, deemed the time propitious to carry out some proselytizing on behalf of the Church of England. He asked his father to forward Daniel Whitby's *Discourse Concerning . . . Election and Reprobation* (London, 1710), an anti-Calvinist tract. Johnson wished to convert the tutors as well as fellow students. See George Groce, *William Samuel Johnson; A Maker of the Constitution* (N. Y., 1937), 5-6.

36. For Davenport's biographical sketch, see Dexter, *Yale Graduates,* I, 447-50.

particular day, but his more implacable enemies attributed his subsequent behavioral peculiarities, especially his corporeal frenzies, to a "hereditary sense of enthusiasm." [37] Davenport first traveled to the middle colonies where he joined Whitefield's entourage.[38] From this "training school" he graduated *cum laude*, and the ensuing summer he moved out on his own. In July 1741, his peregrinations carried him to New Haven.

Davenport was outstanding even among the itinerants. Chauncy, who had become somewhat of an authority on the new class of clerics, honored him with the title, "the *wildest Enthusiast* I ever saw." [39] Samuel Johnson, who was ordinarily more restrained than Chauncy in his criticism of itinerants, listened to him preach, or "rave," as Johnson phrased it, for five minutes and then cast this judgment: "this I humbly conceive could not be called going to meeting any more than a visit to Bedlam." [40] On the subject of Davenport, the Congregationalist and the Anglican were of one mind. As noted earlier, one of Davenport's customary techniques was to tear off his clothes to the waist; by so doing he gave dramatic expression to the point that man should renounce all worldly pretensions. His style of preaching contributed even more to his singularity. According to Benjamin Trumbull, "he gave an unrestrained liberty to noise and outcry, both of distress and joy, in time of divine service. He promoted both with all his might, raising his voice to the highest pitch, together with the most violent agitations of body. With his unnatural and violent agitations of the body, he united a strange singing tone which mightily tended to raise the feelings of weak and undiscerning people, and consequently to heighten the confusion among the passionate of his hearers." [41] Critics emphasized the point that Davenport's greatest successes were achieved during the candlelight services.

In New Haven, in addition to performing his usual feats of

37. "A Dissertation on the State of Religion in North America," *American Magazine* (Sept. 1743), 3.

38. Eleazar Wheelock, in letters to Stephen Williams, May 22, 1740, and June 6, 1740, Dartmouth College MSS., reported that Davenport had become very ill while preaching in the middle colonies, which may have accounted for his strange behavior.

39. "[Chauncy] to Wishart," Clarendon Hist. Soc., *Reprints*, 1st Ser. (1882), 82.

40. Schneider, eds., *Writings of Johnson*, I, 106.

41. *History of Connecticut*, II, 126. See also the *Boston Evening Post*, July 5, 1742.

frenzy and damning the local citizenry as carnal wretches who were on the verge of plunging into the "Bottom of Hell," Davenport unleashed an unprovoked torrent of invective upon the Reverend Joseph Noyes. His chief stricture was that Noyes's spiritual state was that of a Pharisee. He urged the First Church parishioners to desert their unsanctified minister and set up separate worship. Davenport went too far. Attacking Noyes was in itself ill-advised, but consigning him to perdition from the pulpit of the First Church was a classic bit of stupidity. The Reverend Mr. Noyes did not take kindly to the remarks of his guest, nor did Rector Clap.

The fanatic Davenport was the catalyst that precipitated Clap's anti-revival tendencies and made him an inveterate foe of the Awakening. "Enthusiasm," separatism, the appearance of ranting, boorish and arrogant lay exhorters who made fierce and reckless assaults upon learning and an educated ministry and who usurped the prestige and the privileges of the established ministerial caste, a growing tendency to place individual judgment above moral and religious sanction—all of these developments terrified Clap. They ran counter to his Puritan grain, irritated his hypersensitive feelings on social order and religious unity, and drove him inexorably toward the Old Lights. Clearly, to his mind, these developments were foreign to the New England way; they vulgarized the church and violated the Puritan tradition of a rational approach to religion. To his practiced eye this emotional approach to religion was without depth or ground of intellectual apprehension. Clap now made it known that he was opposed to those who persisted in revival practices. It was at this stage of the Awakening, in July 1741, that he not only announced his opposition to the revival but, characteristically, assumed the leadership of the Old Light movement in the New Haven area.[42]

As the leader of the New Haven Old Lights, Clap's first order of business was to sweep the madman Davenport out of New Haven's religious life. The president took the initiative in having him ar-

42. Joseph Noyes and Isaac Stiles, minister of the North Haven Church, were also key figures in the Old Light reaction. The latter delivered the election sermon of 1742 in which, after the conventional pious exhortations, he called upon the civil authority to take action against the separatists who were "subversive of Peace, Discipline and Government" and who had broken the "Laws of God." *A Prospect of the City of Jerusalem* (New London, 1742), see 46-58 in particular.

raigned before a committee of the First Church, of which he was
chairman. The committee intended to demand an explanation of
Davenport's public accusations against Noyes. On the appointed
day, the rump court assembled in the home of Noyes and undertook its inquiry. In the course of the questioning, while Clap and
his colleagues discoursed among themselves, Davenport suddenly
began to sing and pray in his inimitable style, "but there being
so much Noise in the Room he was hardly heard at first, many
kept on talking, others cryed out stop him, the Rev. Mr. Noyes
spoke once or twice and said, Mr. Davenport, I forbid you Praying
in my House without my leave; but he persisted and went on in
the midst of the greatest Noise, Confusion and Consternation, and
declared Mr. Noyes an unconverted Man and his People to be as
Sheep without a Shepherd." The meeting soon came to an end in
"a great Consternation." [43]

The Clap-led group then took positive action to rid themselves
of the pestiferous itinerant. He was denied the use of the First
Church and harried by the Clap group from every side. Persuaded
at last that he had done all in his power to restore New Haven to
God's kingdom, Davenport drifted off to eastern Connecticut,
where he continued his disruptive activities. The New Haven Old
Lights, in conjunction with others from Davenport-ravaged townships, then applied pressure upon the colonial Assembly to declare
him insane and have him removed from the colony. Not much
prodding was required. As early as September 1741, a disillusioned
Governor Talcott suggested that "perhaps the least difficult and
Most safe Method of dealing with so boysterous a person [Daven-
port] . . . might . . . be, to send him by boat or otherwise out of this
Government, that he may go to his own people." [44] In May 1742,
the Assembly judged Davenport to be *non compos mentis* ("disturbed in the rational Faculties of his Mind"). In June he was
forcibly placed aboard a ship and "deported" to his former parish
at Southold, Long Island.[45]

43. *Boston Post Boy*, Oct. 5, 1741; Chauncy, *Seasonable Thoughts*, 157-61.
44. "Talcott Papers," 1724-41, 2 vols., Conn. Hist. Soc., *Collections*, 4 (1892), II, 373.
45. *Boston Evening Post*, June 14, 1742; Jared Ingersoll, An Historical Account of Some Affairs Relating to the Church, Especially in Connecticut, Together With Some Other Things of a Different Nature, 11-12, Lib. Cong. MS. (hereafter cited as

Clap's next bit of anti-revival activity was to have a more far-reaching effect. In collaboration with other Old Lights of the New Haven area, he formed a plan to stop the more offensive revival practices and, correspondingly, to strengthen the established church system. The first step was to convoke representatives from the established churches of Connecticut. As chairman of a five-man committee, the president drafted and directed a petition to the legislature requesting that body to issue a call for a meeting of the General Consociation in Guilford on November 24, 1741. The purpose of the meeting, as Clap informed the Assembly, was to discuss matters of "serious Religious Concern" in view of the "Division and Confusion" precipitated by the revival.[46] Heavily Old Light in its membership, the Assembly approved the petition and directed the established churches to appoint delegates.[47] Clap himself distributed copies of this document to the proper ministerial authorities in the colony.[48]

From the November meeting came the "Guilford Resolves," [49] a document that is singularly significant for its delineation of the Old Light attitude toward the revival. After opening with words

---

Ingersoll, An Historical Account, Lib. Cong. MS.). Davenport refused to stay put on Long Island. Before the end of June he returned to the mainland and set out for Boston. It was an unwise course of action. The Boston Old Light ministers censured him, and the civil authorities clapped him in prison. After being declared insane by the legislature, he was returned to Long Island (*Boston Weekly News-Letter*, June 24–July 1, 1742). He made one more ill-fated return to the Connecticut area, this time to New London, in July 1741. He went singing through the streets with an "armour bearer" by his side. With the help of his equally distracted followers, the irrepressible itinerant started bonfires in the streets; his chief fuel was "heretical" books (including Cotton Mather's works) and articles of wearing apparel. Quickly thereafter, revival leaders of the area appealed to Eleazar Wheelock and Benjamin Pomeroy, mainsprings of the New Light faction in Connecticut, to come to New London and deal with Davenport (Solomon Williams to Wheelock, July 17, 1741, Dartmouth College MS.). Davenport himself settled the issue by suffering a mental breakdown, virtually everyone regarding it as providential intrusion. In 1744, he returned to his senses and made a public declaration of his errors in the *Boston Gazette* (August). See also *Two Letters From the Reverend Mr. Williams and Wheelock of Lebanon, to the Rev. Mr. James Davenport, Which Were the Principal Means of his Late Conviction and Retraction* (Boston, 1744).

46. Connecticut Archives: Ecclesiastical Affairs, VII, 243, Conn. State Lib.

47. *Ibid.*, VII, 244; Trumbull and Hoadly, eds., *Conn. Recs.*, VIII, 438-39.

48. Solomon Williams to Eleazar Wheelock, Oct. 30, 1741, Dartmouth College MS.

49. There is a manuscript copy of the Resolves in the Case Memorial Library, Hartford. The Resolves are printed in the "Law Papers," Conn. Hist. Soc., *Collections*, 11 (1907), I, 5-10.

of praise to God for initiating the Awakening, the paper enumerated the "imperfections and imprudences" that had accompanied the event. To curb further irregularity, it was resolved that the followers of the faith should secure ministers of "piety, learning and wisdom"; that they should attend only the meetings approved by the county consociations; that only those ministers who have "prudence wisdom and learning and have a true piety and Experimental acquaintance with Christ" should be granted a license; that the only lawful ministers in Connecticut were those licensed by the proper authorities; that it was illegal for people to censure their established minister, remove him from office, or reform the church; that separations were to be handled by the county consociations in accordance with the procedure outlined in the Saybrook Platform; and that it was unlawful for a minister to enter into another minister's parish without first acquiring the latter's consent.

Separatism was treated in a special section. To eliminate this practice, which was creating "hard thoughts and Evil murmurings among Professing Christians," it was proposed that those parishes which were infected with separatist tendencies should hold a day of fasting and prayer "to Seek wisdom and Light from God." Also, the ministers of churches threatened by separation were to render advice to those "under mistakes and prejudices" and dissuade them from leaving the established church.

Having outlined the steps by which religious order could be restored in Connecticut, the Guilford representatives submitted the "Resolves" to the legislature and called for the passage of implemental legislation. The legislature responded in 1742-43 with a series of acts designed to crush the New Light movement. They were patterned on the "Guilford Resolves." Hereafter, established ministers who preached from other ministers' pulpits without permission were denied the benefit of any law made for their support; unlicensed preachers were to be fined initially, and jailed if they persisted in preaching; itinerants from other colonies were to be considered as *persona non grata* and were to be deported.[50] That the Connecticut officials were deadly serious in their

50. Trumbull and Hoadly, eds., *Conn. Recs.*, VIII, 454-57, 501-2; *Boston Weekly News-Letter*, Nov. 12, 1742.

intention to enforce these measures (and others) was shown by their arrest of the respected Samuel Finley, later to become president of Princeton, while on his way to preach to a separatist congregation. The charge was vagrancy. Judged guilty, Finley was expelled from Connecticut.[51] In the "land of steady habits" all the animus of sectarian passion was unleashed against the supporters of the revival.

It would not be proper to designate Clap as the author of the repressive "correctional legislation" of 1742-43, of which the above is but a portion. Yet it is certain that he was a prime force in the Old Light reaction. Trumbull has written that the measures passed by the General Assembly in May 1742, although embodied in the "Guilford Resolves," actually originated in the New Haven County Consociation,[52] of which Clap was the dominant figure. There can be little doubt that Clap heartily endorsed the government's policy of repression against the New Lights, a policy which included the fining and incarceration of itinerants without due process of law; depriving New Lights of rights of citizenship; ousting them from governmental offices, even from those positions won through the elective process; and declaring illegal the marriages and baptisms performed by New Light clergymen.[53]

Clap also joined Charles Chauncy and other anti-revival clergymen of Boston in keeping their English clerical brethren informed of the negative effects of the revival. It was perhaps the only issue on which Clap and Chauncy saw eye-to-eye. To Isaac Watts, the great English divine, Clap forwarded "some papers and some pamphlets all relating to the irregularitys and the abuses" that had crept into the religious life of New England. Watts later informed Benjamin Colman that he was fully aware that such errors were in evidence but that, as he had told Rector Clap, defenses had been everywhere raised against them, "and these guards are ready and are practised by him and you at New Haven and Boston." [54] With regard to Clap, in particular, Watts never wrote a truer word.

51. Trumbull, *History of Connecticut*, II, 141.
52. *Ibid.*, II, 130n.
53. For reaction to the revival in Connecticut, see Ingersoll, An Historical Account, Lib. Cong. MS.; Larned, *History of Windham*, I, 477-85; Trumbull, *History of Connecticut*, II, chap. 8.
54. "Letters of Isaac Watts," Mass. Hist. Soc., *Proceedings*, 2d Ser., 9 (1895), 396-97.

Clap's personal authority and influence were circumscribed on the colony level, but his imperium within the college was supreme. Having thrown in his lot with the Old Lights, he immediately took steps to stamp out New Light influence and tendencies at Yale. At his insistence, the trustees, predominantly Old Light in sentiment, passed a measure making it punishable for any student to state directly or indirectly that the rector, trustees, or the tutors were "Hypocrites, carnall or unconverted men." [55] With the reopening of school in September 1741, Clap barred itinerants from the college and ordered the students to desist from attending their meetings.[56] To provide the students with the "proper" type of religious instruction, he journeyed into the neighboring countryside, sought out approved ministers, and, like a theatrical agent, booked them for future appearances. Frequently, he himself mounted the rostrum and imparted words of Old Light wisdom, warning students against the intemperance engendered by the revival and cautioning them that "it is our great and indispensable duty to make our calling and election sure." [57]

If some of the students were prone to regard the New Lights as subversives intent upon overthrowing Christianity and the Connecticut "way of life," such thoughts may well have stemmed from Clap's incessant pounding on these themes. From the rostrum he heaped coals of fire upon those who threatened to destroy the established religious system. "He seemed to talk as if these people were quakers, who go under the name of New Lights," a student noted in his diary upon returning from one of Clap's lectures. "I think he said that they had taken oath against the religion of the country, and also he said it would not do for the Colony to bring up scholars to swear against the religion of the Colony. He said that our religion is the true religion of Jesus Christ, and we should find it so, if we would compare it with the word of God." [58]

Perhaps the propensity of youth to defy constituted authority was responsible, but Clap's measures of repression failed to arrest

55. Yale Corporation Records, I, 69, Yale Univ.
56. William Allen, "Memoir of Rev. Eleazar Wheelock, D.D." *Amer. Qtly. Reg.*, 10 (1838), 17; Wheelock to Mrs. Wheelock, June 28, 1742, Dartmouth College MS.; John Cleaveland Diary, Yale photostat.
57. John Cleaveland Diary, Yale photostat.
58. *Ibid.*

the progress of the Great Awakening on the Yale campus. His "words of wisdom" were flouted by the majority of students. In open defiance of the college head and newly enacted legislation, they continued to frequent itinerant meetings in the New Haven area. Some refused to attend services sponsored by the college. With the situation rapidly getting out of hand, Clap began imposing severe disciplinary measures. He levied heavy fines upon those who failed to attend religious meetings conducted within the college. One New Light was fined five shillings, as a sympathizer explained, for "speaking the truth . . . and the truth was, that he staid at home, because of the coldness of the air and the preacher." [59] In another instance, the president denied degrees to two seniors for their "disorderly and restless endeavors" to propagate New Light principles in the college.[60] David Brainerd, the leading junior scholar and destined to become one of the saints of New England Protestantism, was banished outright from the college. Brainerd previously had aroused Clap's ire by attending itinerant meetings and influencing other students to participate in these extramural activities. He effectively terminated his collegiate career by remarking of Tutor Chauncey Whittelsey, whose prayer meeting he had attended: "He has no more grace than this chair." A freshman overheard the comment and passed it on to a woman in town, who tattled to Clap. Upon being questioned by the president, the freshman promptly implicated Brainerd. Brainerd was then called before Clap and ordered to prepare and submit a public confession. Objecting to the irregular method of investigation and to the inquisitorial tactics of Clap, Brainerd refused to comply with the directive, whereupon he was peremptorily expelled.[61] Not even the impassioned solicitations of the Reverend Aaron Burr, the New Jersey religious leader, who traveled to New Haven for the specific purpose of pleading Brainerd's cause, could induce Clap to alter his decision.

The breaking point between Clap and the students came in the

59. *Ibid.*
60. Schneider, eds., *Writings of Johnson*, I, 102-3.
61. On Brainerd, see Ingersoll, An Historical Account, 5, 15, Lib. Cong. MS.; Bacon, *Thirteen Historical Discourses*, 249; Woolsey, *Historical Discourse to Yale Graduates*, 105; Brainerd's spiritual character is sympathetically delineated by Jonathan Edwards in *Works of Edwards*, I, 656-72.

spring of 1742. Realizing that he no longer could maintain rigid discipline, the president suspended classes and ordered the boys to their homes.[62] The General Assembly, alarmed by the sudden dissolution, promptly dispatched a commission of inquiry to New Haven. Old Light in sentiment, the commission exonerated Clap of any improper action. Its report stated that Clap's course of action was entirely justified in that the students had fallen into "Several Errors in principal [*sic*] and disorders in practice, which may be very hurtfull to Religion." It further noted that the students were "rash Judgeing" those in authority at Yale; that they were calling their instructors "unconverted, unexperienced and unskillfull guids"; that they refused to attend religious exercises; and that some were roaming the streets of New Haven and other towns, preaching against the college and urging other students to separate.[63] As indicated by the tenor of this report, social unity, deference for personal authority, and compliance with the edicts of established authority were canons of paramount importance to the Old Lights, Clap included. Governor Law further revealed the social conservatism of the Old Lights when, in an address to the legislature regarding the dispersal of the students, he instructed Clap to make and duly execute "good and wholsom laws," "for youth there to be traind up in Disobedience to them will lay a foundation for Sedition and Disregard to all humane laws." [64]

Although most of his attention was directed to the college during the trying days of 1741-42, Clap also became implicated in the dispute raging in the dissension-wracked First Church, in which a separatist movement had developed. His active concern in the affair was largely prompted by the fact that Noyes's church functioned as the college parish. From the outset, Clap vehemently had opposed the separatist movement, but by 1742 he saw the futility of trying to force dissenters to remain in the church under the same conditions as had prevailed before the revival. The division be-

62. Dexter, ed., *Documentary History of Yale*, 355-56; *Boston Evening Post*, Apr. 26, 1742. On the problems Clap faced, see Clap to Jonathan Dickenson, May 3, 1742, Haverford College MS., Haverford, Pa.

63. Connecticut Archives: Colleges and Schools, 1st Ser., Pt. ii, I, 269a, Conn. State Lib.; Dexter, ed., *Documentary History of Yale*, 356-58.

64. "Oliver Wolcott Papers," Conn. Hist. Soc., *Collections*, 16 (1916), 458. The committee of inquiry had instructed Clap to keep the students "from all such Error as they may be in danger of Imbibing from Strangers and foraigners."

tween the two groups was irreconcilable. The dissenters were resolute in the conviction that the Reverend Mr. Noyes, as the itinerants had charged, could not lay claim to a saving religious experience. To placate the anti-Noyes element, Clap, in company with the officers of the First Church, made plans to appoint a second minister to assist Noyes. While Noyes was chafed by the proposal,[65] he was obliged to yield, whereupon Clap and his colleagues offered the position to the Reverend Aaron Burr, a New Light but a man of learning, dignity, and respectability.[66] For reasons unknown, Burr refused the job, but even while the negotiations were going on, the anticipated separation took place. In May 1742, the dissenters broke from the First Church and formed a separate society, the act being solemnized by four ministers from nearby Fairfield County.[67]

Clap was unable to prevent the organization of the separate church, but he did his utmost, along with other New Haven Old Lights, to hinder the separates in their efforts to ordain a minister, acquire land on which to build a meetinghouse, seek a division of First Church property, and gain relief from providing for the financial support of the First Church. It was not until 1748 that the separates received legislative permission to build a meetinghouse, and not until 1751 that they were able to ordain a minister.[68]

In 1745, Clap exacted a measure of personal vengeance against the separates by ousting from the Corporation the Reverend Samuel Cooke. Cooke, an avid New Light, had been a leading promoter of the separate movement [69] and had served on the council of solemnization. For his activity in this affair, he was directed to appear before the Corporation and make answer to a set of charges drawn up by Clap and his Old Light colleagues. Ostensibly because of illness in his family, Cooke failed to appear on the appointed day. Later, he was informed that a measure call-

65. Mr. A. [unknown] to Eleazar Wheelock, Mar. 28, 1743, Dartmouth College MS.
66. Clap to Solomon Williams, June 8, July 16, 1742, Pa. Hist. Soc. MS.; Clap to Jonathan Dickenson, May 3, 1742, Haverford College MS.
67. Bacon, *Thirteen Historical Discourses,* 220-21.
68. New Haven First Church Records, I, 50, 73-74, Conn. State Lib.
69. Cooke was also active in organizing the New Lights on a colony-wide basis. See Jonathan Edwards to Eleazar Wheelock, July 13, 1744, Pa. Hist. Soc. MS.

ing for his expulsion had been passed *in absentia* but had not yet been publicly announced. Cooke chose "not to stand the brunt" and in April 1746 submitted his resignation.[70] The New Lights railed bitterly against Clap and his technique of drumhead justice, but to no avail.

By 1745 there were a good many people, of both high and low social standing, who bristled at the bare mention of Clap's name. One of these was Gilbert Tennent. In July 1742, Tennent experienced a change of heart over the revival. In a letter to the Reverend Jonathan Dickenson of New Jersey, he recanted his own excesses and condemned such revival practices as enthusiasm and separatism. Dickenson gave the letter to Clap, who immediately realized its value as an influence upon public opinion and thereupon sent it off for publication to the *Boston Evening Post*.[71] Tennent was outraged by Clap's action. He had not wished to bare his private feelings to public scrutiny, and although not disposed to cross quills with Clap over the issue, he did communicate his displeasure and harbored a lasting grudge against Clap over the incident. A second New Light leader, Eleazar Wheelock, was irate because he was refused permission to preach within the college. Wheelock did not sever relations with Clap, but he did reprove the Yale head for his principles and practices which, as he put it, were contrary to the "Natural Rights and Liberties of all man-kind." Yale, he charged, did not breathe a "Catholick air." [72]

Jonathan Edwards was still another New Light who regarded Clap with feelings other than friendly. Their personal relations had steadily deteriorated since September of 1741. At that time, in the high tide of the revival and just after Clap had begun his campaign to eliminate New Lightism, Edwards had been invited to deliver the commencement address at Yale. Appropriately, he discoursed on the revival, choosing for his theme "The Distinguishing Marks of a Work of the Spirit of God, Applied to that uncommon Operation that has lately appeared on the Minds of many of the People in New England." As was to be expected, the

70. William Bliss, *The Charter of Yale College: the Import and Reach of its Several Changes* (New Haven, 1882), 26.

71. Clap to Solomon Williams, July 16, 1742, Pa. Hist. Soc. MS.; *Boston Evening Post*, July 26, 1742.

72. Wheelock to Clap, Sept. 1743, Dartmouth College MS.

tenor of his sermon was defensive. He made a careful analysis of emotion, noting the differences between the genuine and the spurious. He candidly acknowledged the irregularities that had accompanied the revival, but passed them off as negligible in importance. Whatever the excesses that had developed, the overriding consideration was "that the extraordinary influence that has lately appeared causing an uncommon concern and engagedness of mind about the things of religion, is undoubtedly, in the general, from the Spirit of God." [73] Later, in carefully measured words that were obviously tailored for a predominantly Old Light audience, Edwards cautioned: "Let us all be hence warned, by no means to oppose, or do any thing in the least to clog or hinder, the work; but, on the contrary, do our utmost to promote it." [74] As far as Clap was concerned, Edwards's admonition was wasted breath; he already had been doing his utmost to "clog and hinder" the revival. Relations between the two clerical leaders soon cooled.

In May of 1743 the two men met by chance at the switching station of Brookfield, Massachusetts, from whence they shared a coach en route to a ministerial convention in Boston. While they held no affection for each other, they were not averse to passing the time of day in conversation, the bulk of which naturally dealt with religious issues. As Edwards later wrote, Clap "fell upon me . . . about some passages in my Book [*Thoughts on the Revival*] concerning the Revival of Religion, greatly blaming me, earnestly disputing, I suppose, for Hours together"; after which, inasmuch as they still had some distance to go, they had "another Dispute" about Connecticut laws.[75]

Nothing more developed from the incident until the following year [1744]. Clap then tossed a bomb into the Harvard commencement proceedings by announcing that on the ride to Boston the previous year Edwards divulged that Whitefield had informed him of a "Design" to turn out the generality of New England ministers and replace them with clergy from England, Scotland, and Ire-

73. Edwards, *Works of Edwards*, I, 546.
74. *Ibid.*, I, 552.
75. Edwards, *Copies of the Two Letters by the Rev. Mr. Clap, Rector of the College at New Haven, in His Late Printed Letter to a Friend in Boston, Concerning What He Has Reported, as From Mr. Edwards of Northampton, Concerning the Rev. Mr. Whitefield . . .* (Boston, 1745), 14-15.

land.[76] The announcement was as absurd as it was spectacular. Edwards was outraged by the statement. He cried out that he had been misquoted. While clerical leaders in New England, particularly in the Boston area, buzzed excitedly, he lashed Clap in personal letters; subsequently, both vilified each other in a pamphlet battle.[77] Edwards unequivocally denied having made the statement Clap attributed to him. He accused the rector of misrepresentation, if not premeditated lying. He affirmed that Clap had "confounded Things" in his mind; that he had exaggerated, discolored, and misconstrued the facts; that "some strange and wonderful Mis-apprehension and Confusion" had obviously arisen in his mind. Even more cutting was Edwards's statement that he certainly would not provide Clap with information that he had not revealed even to his closest friend. The implication was all too obvious. He demanded that Clap publish a retraction of his statement, that he acknowledge it to be a canard.

Clap struck off replies to Edwards's letters, but they were not retractions. On the contrary, the rector insisted that what he had stated in Boston was not wild imaginings but the unvarnished truth just as it had passed from Edwards's lips. As for Edwards's letters of denial, Clap brusquely tossed them aside with the quip: "I hope for the future your Time will be better employ'd."

And so the matter stood. Clap never again invited Edwards to deliver a commencement address. In fact, the commencement of 1741 marked the last time that Edwards, the most illustrious "son of Yale" of his generation, attended such an exercise at his alma mater; thereafter, he became a "son" of Princeton. Since both men were of obstinate temperament, they remained bitterly at odds until the last breath passed from their bodies.

Clap's relentless war against the New Lights reached a climax in 1745 with the expulsion of the Cleaveland brothers from the college. The incident represented Clap's first serious breach with the students since their dispersion in the spring of 1742. In the

76. *Ibid.*, 2.

77. In addition to the work cited in *n*. 75, these pamphlets also appeared: Edwards, *An Expostulatory Letter From the Rev. Mr. Edwards of Northampton, to the Rev. Mr. Clap* ... (Boston, 1745); Clap, *A Letter From the Reverend Mr. Thomas Clap* ... *To a Friend in Boston* ... (Boston, 1745); Clap, *A Letter From the Reverend Mr. Clap* ... *To the Rev. Mr. Edwards* ... (Boston, 1745).

interim, he had maintained a rigid control over the youth and had not experienced any severe disciplinary problems. His task was aided considerably in the fall of 1742 when many of the extreme New Light students dropped out of Yale and enrolled in Timothy Green's so-called "Shepherd's Tent" in New London—which the General Assembly promptly legislated out of existence. There was an occasional minor incident. In 1743, for example, Clap suspended a sophomore who was popularizing the notion that the Reverend Mr. Noyes's preaching had a direct tendency to lead souls to Hell.[78] But the general tranquillity remained undisturbed.

The Cleaveland affair began in the late summer of 1744. During the post-commencement vacation, John Cleaveland, a junior, went to his home in Canterbury, Connecticut. He and his brother, Ebenezer, about to enter Yale as a freshman, accompanied their parents to a separate meeting; the separatist minister, Solomon Paine, was the boys' uncle. When the brothers began the school term in November, they were promptly haled before Clap and the tutors, who had been informed of their activities, and upbraided for violating the "laws of the colony and the college." Surprised innocence was their initial reaction. They claimed that they were unaware they had done wrong or broken any law. The elder Cleaveland testified that he had inquired of a trustee whether there was a college law explicitly forbidding a student's attendance at separate meetings, and had been told that such a law had been prepared but not passed; which answer elicited Clap's icy response, "The laws of God and the College are one."

As the interrogation continued, the Cleavelands became more obdurate in their conviction that Clap's accusations were unreasonable. Growing a trifle belligerent, they took to "flagging the bull." When asked if they had attended a separate church, John Cleaveland replied that they had attended a "meeting" at which a "major part" of the Canterbury citizens were in attendance. This sophistical response brought forth from Clap a classic aphorism: "A few more than half makes no difference." Clap abruptly terminated the meeting and announced on the following day that both boys were suspended until they had drawn up a confession admitting

78. Ingersoll, An Historical Account, 17, Lib. Cong. MS.

their violation of the "laws of God, of the Colony and of the College," and had read it before the student body. A few days later,
the elder Cleaveland submitted a pathetically humble petition
asking for reinstatement, but because the petition failed to acknowledge that transgressions had been committed, Clap rejected
it. Many sharp debates followed, the boys resolutely maintaining
their innocence.[79] Clap then drew up a formal admonition to them
which was read to the student body; its substance was—confess or
be expelled. Still insisting upon their innocence and refusing to
comply with Clap's demands, the boys were finally brought before
the student body and ceremoniously expelled. Their names were
"blotted" from the school records. Following custom, Clap warned
the students not to receive them in their rooms or converse with
them, lest they be "infected" thereby.[80]

The summary expulsion of the Cleavelands precipitated a storm
of reaction throughout the colony. Clap was again peppered with
criticism. The New Lights roundly denounced him for his "late
Stretch of Collede [sic] Power." In a letter published in the *New-
York Weekly Post-Boy,* one Connecticut New Light likened the
expulsion to an act of "Popery." [81] The students also took up the
Cleavelands' cause. The elder Cleaveland's senior classmates pooled
their finances and published Locke's *Essay on Toleration,* which
was then distributed among the student body.

The Cleavelands themselves reacted sharply to their dismissal.
Following the advice of prominent New Light leaders,[82] they
petitioned the General Assembly for redress and readmission.
Clap was ordered to appear before the Assembly. Still heavily
Old Light in composition, the Assembly, as expected, refused to

79. The Cleavelands' side of the story is related in John Cleaveland's Narrative
of the Proceedings of the Government of Yale College in the Expulsion of John
and Ebenezer Cleaveland, Essex Institute MS.

80. Years later (1763), Chauncey Whittelsey, a tutor at Yale when the Cleaveland
incident occurred, recalled that he and his fellow tutors had expostulated with Clap
over his decision for expulsion, but they were unsuccessful in having it changed.
Connecticut Archives: Colleges and Schools, 1st Ser., II, 69, Conn. State Lib. The
following year, during his "visitation defense" (see below, chap. 9), Clap affirmed that
a prime consideration in his decision for expulsion was the Cleavelands' proclivity
for casting censorious reflections upon established ministers, especially those in
Windham County.

81. Mar. 18, 1745.

82. Eleazar Wheelock to John Cleaveland, Mar. 9, 1745, Essex Institute MS.

act on the petition.[83] Meanwhile, Clap had presented his side of the story in a pamphlet and in a communication to a New York newspaper.[84] He inveighed against revival practices in general and charged specifically that the Cleavelands had imbibed "erroneous Doctrines" to such an extent that they "were filled with such a strong and lively Impression of divine Things as made them come home Singing along the Streets." The Cleavelands eventually took degrees at Yale without the formality of attendance: John received his degree in 1763,[85] Ebenezer in 1775, eight years after Clap's death.[86] In matters involving religion, Clap's memory was long.

Clap's final public act against the Awakening, the censuring of George Whitefield, was a symbolic act. It was only fitting that he should vent his spleen, through a public declaration, upon the man who had been the principal originator of the movement in New England. It was chiefly Whitefield who had blasted the institutions of Puritanism to pieces. But there were other reasons which prompted Clap to censure the English revivalist. In his widely circulated *Journal,* which was published after he left New England, Whitefield had made some disparaging statements on the state of religion both at Harvard and Yale. In Cambridge he had noted that the "Tutors neglect to pray with and examine the Hearts of their Pupils. Discipline is at too low an ebb. Bad Books are become fashionable amongst them." After three days in New Haven, he became convinced that Yale was in an equally irreligious state. In his view, both schools had sunk into seminaries of paganism. "As for the Universities," he had recorded, "I believe, it may be said, their Light is now become Darkness, Darkness that may be felt, and is complain'd of by the most godly Ministers." [87] The most immediate reason, however, for Clap's concern about Whitefield and the public indictment of him issued in the *Yale Declaration* was the return of the itinerant to New England for another revival

83. Connecticut Archives: Colleges and Schools, 1st Ser., Pt. ii, I, 280, 280c, 280d, Conn. State Lib.

84. *The Judgement of the Rector and Tutors of Yale College, Concerning Two of the Students Who Were Expelled: Together With the Reasons of It* (New London, 1745); *New-York Weekly Post-Boy,* Apr. 29, 1745.

85. Clap to John Cleaveland, Dec. 26, 1763, Yale MS.; Dexter, *Yale Graduates,* II, 29-33.

86. Dexter, *Yale Graduates,* II, 149-52.

87. Whitefield, *Continuation of Journal, Savannah to Stamford,* 71, 125.

tour. The conservatives, Clap included, blanched at the thought of a second season of religious turmoil.

Harvard was the first to issue a formal pronouncement against Whitefield.[88] The Yale pamphlet, which in all likelihood was drafted by Clap, followed shortly after. The *Declaration* [89] ran Whitefield through the gauntlet of the standard Old Light charges. He was particularly castigated for creating confusions and disorders unparalleled in church history, advocating and sanctioning separation, censuring ministers, and casting slanderous remarks on the colleges. He was branded as a disturber of the peace.

While these accusations were in themselves of a serious order, they were subordinate in importance to the general charge that Whitefield was subverting the institutions of New England. The accusations referred to a "Scheme" and "divisive plots and Design." At numerous points, the *Declaration* reasserted the major contention that Clap had set forth in his dispute with Edwards: Whitefield's principal aim was to cast out the established ministers and bring in ministers from England, Ireland, and Scotland—in effect, to overthrow the religious system of New England. The *Declaration* also consciously exploited the technique of implying guilt through association: it was pointed out that Whitefield was a known "Friend and Patron" of the Moravians, "Papists in disguise," who had made efforts to ally the Indians with the French in the war against England and the colonies.

When the famous English revivalist reached New Haven in June of 1745, he confronted the unyielding hostility of Clap and other Old Lights.[90] Acting on the request of the General Association of Connecticut, Clap's clerical contingent refused to grant him the use of the First Church. Denied a pulpit, the itinerant became a "preacher in the fields," booming out his sermon from a platform hastily constructed on the green. It was just as well, for

88. *The Testimony of the President, Professors, Tutors, and Hebrew Instructor of Harvard College in Cambridge, Against the Reverend Mr. George Whitefield, and His Conduct* (Boston, 1744).

89. The complete title is *The Declaration of the Rector and Tutors of Yale College in New Haven, Against the Reverend Mr. George Whitefield, His Principles and Designs* (Boston, 1745).

90. *The Declaration of the Association of the County of New Haven in Connecticut, Conven'd at New Haven, February 19, 1744/5, Concerning the Reverend Mr. George Whitefield, His Conduct, and the State of Religion at this Day* (Boston, 1745).

the crowd was too large for the local meetinghouse.[91] On this visit, Whitefield did not dine at Clap's home.[92]

By 1745, however, the major tremors of the great religious earthquake were at an end, although minor convulsions continued to be felt in scattered portions of New England. Sanity had returned with somewhat of a rush. As the European political situation began to darken, and the specter of war with France appeared, religious issues lost their appeal as prime foci of public attention. Political affairs suddenly became the all-absorbing interest. Everyday conversation of the "common sort" shifted from salvation to the hated "Papist" French who lurked menacingly to the north. The New England air was soon to ring with one persistent cry: "On to Louisbourg!"

Although Clap was himself disturbed by the French threat,[93] he perceived more deadly foes at home. Rationalism was slowly but steadily infiltrating New Zion and eroding the inner substance of the Puritan theological system. Secondly, the Church of England was rapidly expanding in numbers and extending its influence into every corner of New England, especially in Connecticut. Clap felt that Puritanism could withstand French military force, but he was apprehensive that a clear field existed for the penetration of rationalism and Anglicanism. While New England made feverish preparations for the impending clash with France, President Clap laid plans to do battle against the "new scheme of religion" and against the Church of England, the historical enemy of Puritanism.

91. Bacon, *Thirteen Historical Discourses*, 222-23; Fisher, *Discourse on Church of Christ*, 29-31.

92. In later years, Clap laid aside his grudge and became a warm friend to Whitefield. In 1754, he permitted Whitefield to preach to the students and treated him "much like a Gentleman." *Boston Gazette*, Dec. 31, 1754.

93. See, for example, "Law Papers," Conn. Hist. Soc., *Collections*, 13 (1911), II, 128-29. Clap informed Governor Law of a French "Spy come from Canada."

Chapter Seven

RATIONALISM AND ANGLICANISM

WHILE rationalism has a history reaching to the very taproots of western civilization, it is most generally identified with the Enlightenment, that great intellectual flowering of the seventeenth and eighteenth centuries. It was, as Carl Becker has written, an age when God was placed on trial; an age when miracle stood before the bar of Reason. Riding on the wave of optimism that had risen with the revolutionary findings of seventeenth-century science, "the century of genius," as it has been called by Alfred North Whitehead, the rationalists began to propagate a set of ideas antithetical to the standard Christian body of belief. Seeking to emancipate man from the shackling grip of medieval superstition and theological dogma, they posited that it was within the power of man to erect the "heavenly city" on earth. The central tenet of rationalism was, in sum, the belief that man was capable of achieving the "good life" in his natural, rather than beatific, state.

For the rationalists, reason was the magic key that would unlock the mysteries of the universe. They regarded it as the source of all valid knowledge, the final arbiter in determining truth. Their "angle of vision" has been reduced to concrete terms by Professor Crane Brinton: "Reason applied to human relations will show us that kings are not fathers of their people, that if meat is good to eat on Thursdays it is good to eat on Fridays, that if pork is nourishing to a Gentile it is nourishing to a Jew. Reason will enable us to find human institutions, human relations that are 'natural'; once we find such institutions, we shall conform to them and be happy. Reason will clear up the mess that superstition, revelation, faith (the devil of the Rationalists) have piled up here on earth." [1] The rationalists affirmed that there were eternal, immutable truths (Newton's laws of celestial mechanics were often cited as an example) readily discoverable through the application of reason alone. In this scheme of thought there was no room for Christian revelation or any other supernatural experience.

As the standard of reason was applied to society, government, the experimental sciences, literature, and art, so too was it applied to religion. The result was the development of a "natural religion," or "religion of reason," which came to be known as Deism. There were various degrees of Deism but, in general, the creed was based on these pivotal beliefs: the universe was created by God but once set in motion functioned on a system of natural law; God does not interfere in the workings of the universe, nor does He reveal himself directly to man; Jesus was a paragon of moral virtue but was not of divine substance; man could lead a moral life and achieve salvation merely by adhering to the code devised by Jesus. As indicated by this creed, the Deists demystified Christianity, discarding such supernatural elements as revelation, the divinity of Christ, Biblical miracles, and the plenary inspiration of the Scriptures. All beliefs that would not conform to, or stand the test of, "noble reason" were looked upon as untrue, as a tissue of lies and fables.

In addition to propagating Deism, rationalism was instrumental in recalling into prominence a number of other religious "isms," all of which were Christian in substance but opposed to specific doctrines of orthodox Christianity. Rationalism was intimately linked with the recrudescence of Arminianism, Socinianism, Arianism, and Pelegianism—liberal movements dating from the middle ages; and rationalism had a direct hand in the outgrowth

1. Brinton, *Ideas and Men—The Story of Western Thought* (N. Y., 1950), 371. Chap. 11 contains an excellent account of intellectual currents of the Enlightenment.

of the new liberal offshoots of Universalism and Unitarianism late in the eighteenth century.

The rise and spreading influence of Deism, and the propagation of the "heterodox" principles of the appurtenant religious "isms," produced a doctrinal crisis of major proportions in both old and New England in the post-Awakening period. In New England, the crisis had been mounting steadily since the adoption of the Half-Way Covenant in 1662. Already experiencing grave difficulties in their attempt to preserve the high idealism of the ancient faith, the defenders of orthodoxy were now confronted with the problem of warding off attacks upon the very fundamentals of Puritanism.

Slowly but perceptibly the great bastion of Puritanism was crumbling. Interestingly, the process was given a spur by some within the fortress. Under the sway of the anthropocentric, rationalistic spirit of the Enlightenment, a few prominent Puritan clerical figures, most notably Charles Chauncy and Jonathan Mayhew, reacted against the harshness of certain key doctrines of the traditional creed. This group particularly began to disclaim the Augustinian-Calvinistic concepts of Deity and man. In place of Calvin's wrathful, glory-seeking God, they substituted a benevolent Deity, one of infinite goodness, justice, and mercy. At the same time, they stressed the natural goodness of man, minimized, and in many cases refused to acknowledge, his depravity. If they were not as yet prepared to sanction Hamlet's image of man as "noble in reason," they were, conversely, no longer willing to accede to the French theologian's gloomy view that he was but a cut above the Yahoos.

While some rationalists were chipping away at the doctrines of an impersonal, self-centered Deity and original sin, others, opprobriously called Arminians by the adherents of orthodoxy, were laying the ax to the tenets of predestination and necessity of divine grace for salvation. To delineate with precision the nature of the Arminian movement in the eighteenth century is most difficult. Arminianism was a broad designation conveying multitudinous nuances of meaning. The word itself has a checkered etymology. In its original sense, the core of Arminianism was the belief that man had free will and was an independent agent in the determination of his terrestrial fate. The movement took its name from Jacob Arminius, the seventeenth-century Dutch Remonstrant. By the eighteenth century, however, the term had become an all-inclusive catchall denoting any deviation from orthodox Christian belief. More frequently than not, it came to be used as a smear word connoting heresy. Generally, in its theological structure, Arminianism stressed man rather than God. It magnified the capacities and potentialities of man, minified the sovereignty and majesty of God; the creature was inflated, the Creator deflated. With such a focus, the happiness of man became the great desideratum of religion. The Arminians repudiated the doctrine of original sin, affirming that man was a free moral agent capable of achieving salvation solely through leading a life of moral excellence.

Socinianism, Arianism, and Pelegianism were also exercising a corrosive influence upon Puritanism, but to a lesser extent. Again, there is a problem in precise definition. Socinianism was opposed to the doctrine of the trinity, its adherents holding to the belief that Christ was of mortal substance. But through indiscriminate usage Socinianism also came to denote that man was neither endowed with prenatal sin nor predestined to eternal damnation. The doctrinal significance of Socinianism was that, in rejecting the belief that Christ was of the Godhead, it replaced the vital emphasis upon faith with an emphasis upon works; it substituted worthy behavior or "means" in place of divine grace in the process of salvation. The Arians, unlike the Socinians, acknowledged the divinity of Christ, but they made a profoundly significant semantic distinction: they described Christ as being of "like" substance, but not of the "same" substance as God, thereby relegating Christ to a subordinate position in the Godhead. By so doing, the Arians cut out the very heart of Christian (and Puritan) belief. The doctrine of Christ's atonement was now reduced to virtual insignificance. The Pelegians were significant mainly for the position they took on original sin; their central idea was that man was not irremediably tainted with Adam's guilt.

By 1750 these liberal movements posed a threat to religious and philosophical Puritanism, but defenders of the faith were quick to react. On June 22, 1750, the Reverend Jonathan Edwards, who had been ousted from his pulpit, took leave of his parishioners with a warning against the rising tide of religious liberalism. At one point in his farewell sermon the thin-lipped Edwards, speaking in his customary quiet voice, admonished his people:

You were, many of you, as I well remember, much alarmed with the apprehension of the danger of the prevailing of these corrupt principles, near sixteen years ago. But the danger then was small in comparison of what appears now. These doctrines at this day are much more prevalent than they were then: the progress they have made in the land, within this seven years, seems to have been vastly greater than at any time in the like space before: and they are still prevailing and creeping into almost all parts of the land, threatening the utter ruin of the credit of those doctrines which are the peculiar glory of the gospel, and the interests of vital piety.[2]

Shortly after, Edwards made a lonely retreat to the frontier outpost of Stockbridge, Massachusetts, where he became a philosophical recluse. Here in the primeval wilderness of the Berkshires the metaphysically-minded Edwards gave himself to thought and formulated a new and more forceful Calvinism; a Calvinism based on a synthesis of the historic "five points" with the "new philosophy"; a Calvinism that reasserted in a systematic, "scientific" form the allness of God and the nothingness (or, at most, the limited power) of man.

While the peerless Massachusetts logician was in the process of refashioning Calvinism, and Chauncy and Mayhew were seeking to blunt the sharp edges of the old faith, President Clap raised his influential voice on behalf of "orthodoxy." The religious system that Clap defended was actually a *via media* between the "New Divinity" of Edwards and the rationalistic, humanistic theology of Chauncy and Mayhew.

It should be noted at the outset that Clap was no Olympian among the theological scholars of New England. To compare him with Edwards, for example, would be inappropriate. Unlike Edwards, he was not a relentless searcher into mysteries of the soul, or

2. Edwards, *Works of Edwards*, I, 79. On the rise of religious liberalism in New England, see Conrad Wright, *The Beginnings of Unitarianism in America* (Boston, 1955); Herbert Morais, *Deism in Eighteenth Century America* (N. Y., 1960).

an expounder of the fine points of theology. He made no attempt to climb the ladder of abstraction and explore the character of religious affections, define the nature of true religious experience, or analyze the essence of virtue and the will. Nor did he indulge in the practice of extracting novel or arresting theses out of Biblical texts. It may well be that he was not intellectually equipped to journey into the trackless depths of inner thought. Indeed, according to some informed contemporaries, he had his difficulties comprehending conventional theology. Ezra Stiles, who probably knew Clap's intellectual capabilities better than any contemporary, affirmed that he was weak in polemical divinity "and it is doubted, whether he had the happiest talent of conceiving and presenting the sentiments, principles and views of Arminians, Arians and deists." [3] Chauncey Whittelsey, another close associate, delivered a similar appraisal: "for a Man of his strong Judgment and clear perception, he failed in polemical Divinity, and had no talent of entering into the views and systems of Heretics, Deists, Romanists (his Arminians, Arians, Socinians etc. were very foreign and reverse from Realities)—witness his new System of Divinity." [4] Both assessments appear to be just. Certainly, no theological *Summa* flowed from his pen.

In extenuation of Clap, however, notice should be taken of the disadvantages under which he was placed by reason of his professional position. His was an active, not a speculative, life. Unlike Edwards, who spent on the average thirteen hours a day in his study poring over theological tracts and writing out his ideas on controversial points of divinity, Clap was constantly wound up in a coil of activity. He once candidly confessed to a fellow minister that "much writing is always tedious to me and a great Consumer of precious time." [5] In the last years of his life, he ruefully lamented that he had not even had sufficient leisure to search his own heart for evidences of grace.[6] It was admittedly a common lament of the times, but it does underscore his uncommon absorption in nonspeculative affairs. In apologizing for the brevity of his

3. Stiles to Daggett, July 28, 1767, Yale MS.
4. Dexter, ed., *Stiles's Itineraries*, 461.
5. Clap to the Rev. Solomon Williams, July 16, 1742, Pa. Hist. Soc. MS.
6. Clap, Memoirs, July 7, 1763, Yale MS.

Essay on Moral Virtue, his only treatise of a philosophical nature, Clap wrote in the preface that he would publish a more comprehensive work as soon as he could gain "some Relaxation from my present Multiplicity of Business." [7] The period of leisure never materialized while he remained in office. And while he was deeply interested, and surprisingly well read, in the many doctrinal disputes of the period, both in England and in the colonies, he contributed but one pamphlet to the enormous literature of religious controversy.[8]

Yet, there is no denying Clap's importance as a religious leader, an importance derived entirely from his position. As president of Yale, he stood as the ceremonial head, as the high priest, of Connecticut Congregationalism. He was interpreter of the faith and moral spokesman all in one. He was a powerful force in setting the religious standards of Connecticut. His religious prominence was out of all proportion to his talents as a theological scholar.

Taken as a whole, Clap's extant religious writings for the period 1745-66 are noteworthy only for their belligerent anti-rationalist tone. They are scarcely profound in doctrinal analysis. Judged by these writings, his theology represents a hodgepodge of the traditional precepts of Christianity and the refined Calvinism of New England Puritanism. In no single writing is his theological system completely elucidated. Overwhelmingly commonplace in form, his religious ideas were almost always placed in the form of massive generalizations. Examination of these generalities suggests both vagueness and ambivalence in his thought. It is not at all unusual, for example, to find the president asserting with one breath that the doctrines of St. Augustine are conformable to the word of God and should be accepted as the standard tenets of Christianity,[9] and in another endorsing the Westminster and Savoy Confessions of Faith, which were the standard formulations of Puritan doctrine.[10] The two systems are difficult to square on

7. Stiles (see above, *n.* 3) wrote that the labors of Clap's office "left a most contemplative mind but a few hours for reading."

8. Clap, *A Brief History and Vindication of the Doctrines Received and Established in the Churches of New England* (New Haven, 1755). The theological controversies of the day in England are ably recounted by Roland N. Stromberg, *Religious Liberalism in Eighteenth-Century England* (London, 1954).

9. Clap, *Brief History and Vindication,* 32.

10. *Ibid.,* 26.

many points. To cite another example, Clap's concept of Deity approximates at times the stern, inscrutable, glory-seeking God of Genevan Calvinism, while on other occasions it strangely mirrors the benign, benevolent Deity of the rationalists.[11] To search for the systematic exegesis is to search in vain.

The clue to Clap's religious orientation during the post-Awakening period is to be found in these few words: "Arminianism, Arianism and other Errors approaching toward Deism, have greatly prevailed in our Nation and Land and are likely more and more to prevail unless a proper stand be made against them." [12] This statement struck the keynote of his religious life. From 1745 on, President Clap made a "proper stand" against those who "have risen up openly to oppose and deny" Christian principles and sought to introduce a "new Scheme of Religion and an easy Way of Salvation, unknown to the Gospel of Christ." [13] The prime object of his life was to save Puritan doctrine from the pollutions of religious rationalism and to prevent it from being reduced to a mere code of morality. With every fiber of his being, he worked to this end.

In defending orthodoxy from the attacks of the rationalists, Clap set up the postulate of original sin as his main line of defense. The fundamental principle of human existence, the first great fact in the science of man, was the depravity of the human animal. The concept of man's innate goodness he condemned as pure fantasy and a fundamental heresy. He unequivocally repudiated the contention that man entered the world "like a clean white Piece of Paper." [14] While he drew much of value from Locke, he would have no dealings with the Englishman's epistemology.

11. Compare in Clap's Sermon Outline Book (Yale MS.) his outline of "Original Sin" with that of "O Love the Lord All his Saints." Clap's notes on his Thanksgiving sermon of Nov. 13, 1754, "That the infinite goodness and mercy of God lays us under the urgent obligation to be thankful to him and to bless and hail him in the most perfect manner," definitely betray a tinge of "benevolence." Unfortunately, Clap's extant religious writings offer no clue as to his position on the covenant theory and other technical areas of Puritanism. Nor have I been able to uncover a shred of evidence to indicate that Clap was predestinarian in outlook. The negative evidence is even more convincing.
12. Clap, Thots on the Present State of Religion Occasionally Minuted Down, Yale MS.
13. Clap, *Brief History and Vindication*, 18.
14. *Ibid.*, 37.

Locke's theory of cognition (*tabula rasa*) was from Clap's point of view not in accord with spiritual truth. That man had been placed under the curse of original sin as a consequence of Adam's transgression was an incontrovertible proposition. Since that fateful day in the Garden of Eden, man was born under the "wrath and curse" of God, and was subject to misery and tribulation in his mortal existence. He was deprived of his former divine qualities, blinded from truth and goodness, doomed to suffer in this life "inward and bodily afflictions" and "spiritual trouble." Since the fall, man's "Understanding is darkened, his Judgement is perverted, his Taste and Relish of Things corrupted, and his Mind and Conscience is defiled." [15] Man had broken divine law and stood condemned. In this manner, with the grim overtones of Calvin, the doctrine of original sin was instilled into the impressionable minds of Yale youth. Although not a genuine Genevan Calvinist, Clap worked in the light of the great theologian's pervasive critique of the human condition. Man was born sinful and corrupt, and he could not escape the moral obliquity at the core of his personality.

Clap's reaction to the "new Scheme" of salvation was equally sharp. He scornfully derided the optimistic affirmation that man can be saved simply by leading a life of moral excellence or by living up to the "Light of Nature." This method of salvation was, in his judgment, "the most pleasing to corrupt Nature of any that ever was invented." [16] "Except a man be born again he cannot enter the kingdom of God" was a sermon doubtless well known to Clap's students. "The Doctrine of the new Birth," Clap wrote of the conversion experience, "is of the utmost Consequence in Christianity[;] it is the very Foundation of all practical Religion and of all our hopes of eternal life." [17]

As Clap saw it, there was but one true *modus operandi* for salvation. It began with conversion, with God cleansing the human soul of original sin and imparting his divine grace. With sin expiated, man's understanding was illumined; he could again see the "excellency and glory of God." And man was in dire need

15. "Original Sin," Sermon Outline Book, Yale MS.
16. Clap, *Brief History and Vindication*, 27, 41.
17. Yale MS.

of divine revelation to instruct him in the nature and perfections of God, to teach him his duty, and to obtain a restoration of divine favor. Once having received God's redeeming grace, man was obliged to place unfeigned faith in Jesus Christ.[18] But conversion was fundamental to the process. It was the sign of the miracle of a human being's redemption, which must be wrought, not by his own efforts, but by God.

Clap's "proper stand" also included a stubborn defense of the doctrine of Christ's divinity. To those of Arian tendency, he pointed out that to worship Christ without acknowledging His full divinity was sheer idolatry, somewhat the same as worshiping the Virgin Mary or a "Piece of Wood." [19]

Thus did Clap restate in conventional terms the standard Christian dogma in the vital areas of original sin, necessity of divine grace in salvation, and the divinity and satisfaction of Christ. "In these doctrines," Stiles wrote, "he conceived the essence of religion to consist." [20] For Clap, they constituted the underpinning of Christianity, and because they formed the core of Christian belief, they must be accepted as a unity; to deny but one was to render impotent the entire system.[21]

The prominent question of reason versus revelation was a knotty one for the president since he was a scientist of progressive bent. Yet, when faced squarely with the issue in his capacity as a religious leader, he was obliged to promulgate the standard "party line" of his forefathers. In laying out his brief for revelation, he devalued reason. While admitting that reason was a "great and noble" endowment, he insisted that it was subject to many limitations and imperfections in "this fallen state" and to many "Delusions and pernicious Errors." Reason, therefore, was not an "infallible Guide," not the final revealer of truth. It had been originally transmitted to man in a pure form, but since the Fall it had shared in the general contagion of sin and was of a "carnal"

18. See Clap, *Essay on Moral Virtue*, 41-42.
19. Clap, *Brief History and Vindication*, 34-35. Lashing out further, he wrote: "They [Arians] will give Christ the Title of God, the Son of God, a divine Person, a glorious Being, a mighty Saviour, etc.... Whereas they ascribe no attribute of Perfection to him, but what may belong to a Creature...."
20. Stiles to Daggett, July 28, 1767.
21. Clap, *Brief History and Vindication*, 38-40.

nature. It therefore followed that natural reason was subordinate
to divine grace as a source of truth. As long as this faculty remained
unregenerate, man was not capable of distinguishing true excellence. In his *Essay on Moral Virtue,* Clap admitted that man could
use the "light of nature"—or reason—to learn something of moral
law. But he was quick to add that the knowledge derived through
the application of reason was insufficient for discovering a method
that would enable man to gain reconciliation with an "offended"
God.[22] "A man by his own natural Reason," reads one of the president's manuscript sermons, "may see that he is a sinful and corrupt creature yet he cant by any means root out the sinful Inclination from his Heart." There was still a mystical realm which
reason could not penetrate. It would always be so.

Some of Clap's heaviest barrages were unleashed against the
rising anthropocentrism represented by the belief that "the happiness of the creature is the sole end of Creation," a belief which was,
in substance, an extension of the Epicurean moral tradition. To a
Puritan it was a perversion of the true faith, the rankest form of
heresy. Clap bluntly declared: "For a Man to make the sole,
supreme, or ultimate End of all Being and Action to be for himself alone or his own Happiness, as the Summum Bonum; and to
regard God and all other Beings, only so far as they may serve himself or be subservient to his own Happiness, or gratify his Principle
of Self-Love is the most absolute Inversion of the Order, Dignity
and Perfection of Beings: and one of the worst Principles that can
be in human Nature, that a small Part is bigger than the Whole." [23]
God, not man, is the central actor on the stage of history. God, not
man, is the measure of all things. And salvation, not the pursuit
of happiness, is the object of life.

It was President Clap's deep-seated conviction that the rationalists were actively seeking to undermine the ideological foundations of Puritanism; that they were conspiring to overthrow the
Congregational "way of life." To prevent this became one of the
dominant passions of his life. In 1755, he published his *A Brief
History and Vindication of the Doctrines Received and Established*

22. See Clap's discussion on pp. 25-30, 53.
23. Clap, *Essay on Moral Virtue,* 16-17.

in the Churches of New England, With a Specimen of the New Scheme of Religion Beginning to Prevail. The pamphlet was well-received in New England. Within two years the initial supply was exhausted and a second edition run off. Historical in form, the work animadverted against religious liberalism in general. The president stoutly denounced those who were propagating the new beliefs. Near the conclusion of his work, he invoked the time-honored theme of subversion. To clinch his point, he inserted a quotation from a standard anti-rationalist polemic [24] describing the conspiratorial methods of the rationalists:

But men of this Character [rationalists] are not always open and frank in declaring their Sentiments, but choose to lie concealed, until they have been able to ingratiate themselves with those whom they intend to bring over to their Sentiments; and watch for some favourable Opportunity of Advantage, which they will never fail to improve. The Doctrines which it may be they have no Relish for, some in their congregations firmly believe; and therefore they dare not at once, in a plain Manner, deny them, and now and then covertly advancing Principles not consistent with them, they insensibly instil them into the minds of their Hearer; and draw them off from that regard they once had to those other Principles. It is very sad, what Influence such conduct has had, and still has in many places, I had almost said, to the total subversion of Christianity.[25]

If Clap rarely agreed with Jared Eliot on religious matters, he certainly was in accord with Eliot's belief that "the Deists are a Set of men not to be trusted." [26]

Within Connecticut itself Clap took other defensive measures. He rang the warning bell against rationalism at ministerial meetings and sought to mobilize the clergy. To educate the ministers and learned lay public in the insidiously secretive character of the threat, he saw to it that each tutor, each fellow of the Corporation, each of the nine ministerial associations in Connecticut, and every "large" public library in the colony received a set of John Leland's *A View of the Deistical Writers* (2 volumes); while not stated, the

24. John Brine, *A Treatise on Various Subjects* (London, 1750). Brine (1703-65) was one of the chief English critics of Arminianism.
25. P. 42.
26. Eliot to Ezra Stiles, Nov. 4, 1758, Yale MS.

cost was apparently assumed by the college.[27] Leland's work contained convenient capsule summaries of the major writings of the chief English Deists and the author's refutations of the principal deistical tenets. It was a well-integrated discussion, but loaded heavily in favor of orthodoxy. Finally, Clap labored tirelessly, but without success, to establish a "Supreme Ecclesiastical Court" whose function it would be to pass judgment on all religious disputes and debates in Connecticut. Such an organization, had it been established, would have exercised a dominant influence over religious life in the colony.[28] It perhaps would have insured doctrinal orthodoxy within the colony. Clap's plan, however, was a century behind the times.

The president's efforts to prevent the infiltration of rationalist ideology at the college were conducted with greater success but not without occasional difficulties. The most infectious source of rationalism was the collection of latitudinarian tracts in the library, particularly Samuel Clarke's deistic-tinged *Sermons*. Clap knew from past experience there were inherent dangers in allowing not only the students but the officers as well the run of the library. The record already contained one shattering experience, the Cutler defection of 1722. Therefore, he simply pulled Clarke's work from the library shelves and placed it beyond the reach of the students.[29]

The action came back to haunt him in 1759 when the celebrated Collins incident took place. Henry Collins, a Baptist merchant of Newport, Rhode Island, seriously considered presenting a collection of books to Yale, most of which were Baptist tracts. Having learned of the removal of Clarke's *Sermons*, he decided against making the bequest since it appeared that Clap would not permit "free use" of his donation. At this point, Ezra Stiles, then serving as a minister in Newport, intervened. He assured Collins that Clap would not put the Baptist writings under lock and key. Stiles even agreed to arrange for the transfer of the books to New Haven.

27. Yale Corporation Records, I, 142, Yale Univ.
28. Thomas Darling, *Some Remarks on Mr. President Clap's 'History and Vindication of the Doctrines etc. of the New England Churches'* (New Haven, 1757), 107 (hereafter cited as Darling, *Remarks on Clap's History of Doctrines in New England*).
29. According to Darling, Clap "locks up a Number of Books from the Scholars to prevent their reading of them." *Ibid.*, 127.

Writing to Clap, he explained Collins's offer and the condition upon which the books had been presented. Going beyond his original purpose in writing, Stiles then took his former teacher to task, with measured restraint, of course, for his former action of removing Clarke's book from the shelves. In the spirit of Milton's *Areopagitica,* he urged that there be fair, free, and candid inquiry of religious beliefs, and that the issue of orthodoxy versus rationalism be haggled out in the market place of ideas. *"Truth* and this alone being *our* Aim in fact, open, frank and generous, we shall avoid the very Appearance of Evil," wrote the universal scholar. He summed up his position as follows: "Deism has got such Head in this Age of Licentious Liberty, that it would be in vain to try and stop it by hiding the Deistical Writings: and the only Way left to conquer and demolish it, is to come forth into the open Field and Dispute this matter on even Footing." [30] Stiles's letter, which forcefully argues that it is not proper to impose a quarantine upon ideas, unquestionably ranks as one of the noblest expressions of intellectual liberty during the colonial period.

But this passionate plea for a more "catholic spirit" fell on deaf ears. Clap refused to accept Collins's benefaction. Stiles, of course, was deeply disappointed by the decision. The people in the Newport area, he informed Jared Eliot, now regarded Yale as a seat of prejudice; Clap's action had fixed its reputation for "contracted Bigotry." [31] Stiles was heartsick at the turn of events, for he looked upon Yale as an "excellent and generous Institution both for Science and Religion," as an institution where scholars were permitted to examine and compare the religious principles of all sects. But Clap regarded such sentiments as romantic nonsense and was not of mind or mood to accede to such a point of view. On such matters, teacher and ex-student were a century apart.

The affair ultimately concluded on the sour note of personal diatribe between Clap and Collins, with poor Stiles placed between. Collins set the stage for the clash by freely expressing his unflattering opinion of the president and the fellows. These as-

30. Stiles to Clap, Aug. 6, 1759, Yale MS. Large portions of the letter have been printed in Riley, *American Philosophy,* 217; Abiel Holmes, *The Life of Ezra Stiles ... President of Yale College* (Boston, 1789), 79; Riley, "The Rise of Deism in Yale College," *American Journal of Theology,* 9 (1905), 481-82.
31. Stiles to Jared Eliot, Sept. 24, 1759, Yale MS.

persions became known to Clap, who then informed Stiles that he did not take kindly to such insolence. Stiles showed the letter to Collins and the latter took umbrage. That gentleman, as Stiles in turn informed Clap, meant not to cast "dishonorable Implications or Reflexions" on Clap and the fellows, but his patience was now at an end. "He therefore directs me to signify to you," concluded Stiles, "that you may please to return the books to me when opportunity presents." [32]

Clap's grave concern over the reading habits of the Yale youth is understandable in the context of Yale's relationship to the religious life of the community it served. Whether Connecticut would continue to embrace orthodoxy or turn in the direction of religious liberalism would depend in large measure upon the religious attitudes of the colony's clergy and lay leaders. Most of these men made—or reinforced—their religious commitments during their collegiate experience; therefore the character of the religious training offered by the college heavily influenced the type of theology disseminated throughout the colony. If there was any single key to victory in orthodoxy's battle against rationalism, that key was Yale. For this reason, Clap was determined that it must remain a bastion of old truth. If the preservation of orthodoxy was contingent upon censorship, the president would resort to censorship. No measure was too extreme.

Clap's realization that the future of religion in Connecticut was linked with the religious program of the college is demonstrated by his act of creating the new category (for Yale, at least) of *Theologicae* on the commencement sheets. The addition was made in 1757. Prior to that year the sheets had featured the six traditional categories of: *Technologicae; Logicae; Grammaticae; Rhetoricae; Mathematicae; Physicae.* The newly added category was defined as "Scientia, quae Deum et ejus Perfectiones contemplatur" (the science which contemplates God and his perfections). Discourse on this subject was one means of communicating orthodox principles to the ministers and lay "First Gentlemen" of the colony who swarmed into New Haven for the commencement exercises. At the Commencement of 1765, for example, the

32. Stiles to Clap, Apr. 16, 1760, Yale MS.

men who molded religious and ethical opinion in Connecticut listened to debates on these three propositions:

Agentis moralis Perfectio, in Dei Imitatione consistit.
(The perfection of the moral agent consists in the imitation of God.)

Obligatio moralis, e Dei Perfectione absoluta praecipuè oritur.
(The moral obligation arises especially from absolute perfection of God.)

Peccatoris Justificatio absque Fide, Legem destruit moralem.
(The justification of a sinner without faith destroys the moral law.)

Listed on the sheet under *Theologicae* were other propositions which focused on the key principles of the orthodox creed, as, for example:

Justitia Christi, Spei Peccatoris est Fundamen.
(The justice of Christ is the foundation of the sinner's hope.)

In Regeneratione, Gratia Dei irresistibilis Voluntatem nullo modo constringit.
(In rebirth, the irresistible grace of God restrains the will in no way.)

Doctrina Peccati originalis negata, Necessitas Mortis Christi negatur.
(The doctrine of original sin having been denied, the necessity of the death of Christ is denied.)

Naturalis Relatio Agentis moralis ad Deitatem, ut Creatorem, Obligationis ipsius una est Origo.
(The natural relation of the moral agent to the Deity, as a Creator, is the sole source of the obligation itself.)

Clap thus strove to make certain that the members of the Standing
Order took leave of New Haven with something more than full
stomachs. For the remainder of his administration, *Theologicae*
remained a fixture on the sheets.

As Clap saw it, there was a pressing need for such a program of
indoctrination. Observation of the religious life of Connecticut and
his own community, plus a reading of the theological tracts that
filtered into the colony from England, provided sufficient evidence
of a startling change in religious orientation; of a change from the
contemplation of the perfection of God to the contemplation of
the perfection of man. This fact was particularly brought home to
him with telling impact when he scanned the ethical formulations of such liberal and popular savants as Francis Hutcheson,
Anthony Ashley Cooper (third Earl of Shaftesbury), James Foster,
Thomas Chubb, and John Taylor, among others. In their writings,
these men sloughed off supernatural sanctions with a vengeance
and stressed humanistic and utilitarian ethical concepts.

The switch in emphasis had indeed been sharp. The revolt from
Christian dogma was all too quickly followed by a breaking away
from traditional Christian ethics. The transcendental ideal was
yielding to rational standards. The new current in ethics was
emphasizing that moral conceptions originate in man himself
and in nature. One school of thought posited the thesis that man
was wholly competent to evolve standards of right and wrong
through the application of rational judgments; reason was regarded as a valid standard for ethical conduct. Others found a
universal basis for conduct in the conscience. It was affirmed that
God had created man with a "moral sense" that existed instinctively, antecedent to, and independent of, all religious beliefs. The
origin of moral conceptions was to be found in an inborn social
instinct; one need only look within to discover truth. Closely akin
to the moral instinctivists, or intuitionalists, were those who
stressed the principle of benevolence, that is, the common good of
all is the supreme end and standard of moral virtue. Therefore,
all action that contributes to the good of society is moral. Some
had become converts to Hobbes's materialistic ethical system,
which centered on the proposition that man's sensations, imagina-
tions, thoughts, and emotions were all appearances of motion in

the interior parts of the body. From this mechanistic basis, any activity that helped stimulate or promote "vital action" (or give pleasure) was morally right, and those activities which hindered "vital action" (or give pain) were wrong. Hobbes's theory of self-interest naturally gave an ethical sanction to all forms of egoistic hedonism, since it was thought that impulses arising out of bodily wants were prompted by an organism's urge to preserve itself. Other ethical theories of similar pragmatic, materialistic, humanistic bent were being espoused in the mid-century period, but reason, moral taste, benevolence, and self-interest had achieved the greatest popular acceptance.

None were acceptable to President Clap. He condemned all natural-scientific interpretations of morality as fallacious. In his teaching of moral philosophy to Yale seniors, he placed total stress on the transcendental ideal. Ethical instruction thus became fixed upon the "right Foundation." An entire generation of Yale youth heard Clap beat the constant refrain that God constituted the one plausible standard of moral virtue and obligation. In the president's own words: "Moral virtue is a conformity to the Moral Perfections of God; or it is an imitation of God in the Moral Perfections of his Nature, so far as they are imitable by his Creatures." [33] Clap's dialectic of ethics began with the proposition that all perfection was originally invested in God. He is all-perfect without any antecedent or concomitant standard to measure Himself by, the highest and best of forms, the supreme actuality. In the process of creation, God communicated a limited degree of His perfection to all the elements in proportion to their rank and order—it is to be remembered that Clap firmly adhered to the classical "Chain of Being" theory, to the concept of the fixity of species.[34] Because of his rational faculty, man holds a unique position in the scheme of creation. He has been endowed with a far higher degree of perfection than any other known form. But he is still a part of a whole. Try as he might, he cannot possibly hope to approximate God's degree of perfection.

Yet he is obliged to attempt to achieve the ideal, that is, he must consciously strive to conform to the moral perfections of God. Such

33. Clap, *Essay on Moral Virtue*, 3.
34. See, for example, *ibid.*, 4, 6.

obligation arises first from the divine nature of God, which makes
of Him an all-perfect standard, and from His declared will, emphasized by His sovereign power and authority. Clap stated it in
this manner: "Indeed all the works of God, as they come from him,
are perfect; and every Part of them congruous and consistent with
each other; so that whenever he makes a moral Agent, he endues
[sic] him with a perfect Disposition and full Powers to do his Duty,
and be perfect, as such a Creature: But if he afterwards, by any
Means, contracts a contrary Disposition, or loses his Power, that
no ways alters the Nature of his Perfection, or the Nature of his
Obligation." [35] Man's obligation to complete conformity with divine perfection is therefore constant. He is never released from
this obligation. When man falls short of a perfect conformity, he
commits a moral transgression, he commits sin.

The third central point of Clap's ethical system held that divine
revelation was the only means by which man could know God's
perfection, or the extent to which man's own disposition and conduct conformed to it. Ethics thereby became, as Clap himself put
it, "nearly connected with true Religion," and proficiency in moral
virtue was contingent upon sanctification.[36] Clap thus furnished
a theological foundation for ethics, and after teaching these ideas
for a quarter of a century, he decided to write them out. In 1765
he published his *Essay On Moral Virtue,* which was utilized as a
text by the seniors in their moral philosophy instruction.

As some discerning critics have noted, Clap's moral philosophy
was nothing more than Puritan dogma covered with a thin veneer
of Platonic idealism. It was ethical instruction in the manner of
William Ames. For Clap's concept of metaphysics was directly
linked with the concept of a Deity who regulated and controlled
the destiny of all elements in the universe. The doctrine of im-
manence was at the apex of his philosophical speculations. In sum,
it was philosophy in a religious idiom. As Professor Franklin Dexter has written, Clap's *Essay On Moral Virtue* was a "meagre and
juiceless compend of familiar commonplaces of theological doctrine." [37]

35. *Ibid.,* 10.
36. *Ibid.,* 1, 53.
37. Dexter, "Clap and Writings," New Haven Colony Hist. Soc., *Papers,* 5 (1894),
264-65.

It would not be proper to conclude a discussion of the ethical instruction provided at Yale without taking notice of William Wollaston's mildly deistic work, *The Religion of Nature Delineated*. Clap's rarefied metaphysics actually comprised but a small portion of the course in moral philosophy, which dealt heavily with the practical application of moral principles. As Leon Howard points out, the major part of the course "was directed toward regulating the sinners rather than gratifying the saints." [38] Wollaston's text, which remained in use throughout Clap's ad ministration, provided the students with a practical, and comprehensible, type of ethical instruction. Clap placed Wollaston's fundamental standard of moral virtue—conformity to the truth of things "as they are"—on his "Index" of fallacious standards,[39] but he found little to criticize in Wollaston's rules of external conduct.

Wollaston's social ideas chimed in perfectly with the distinctively conservative social philosophy of the "land of steady habits." Consider, for example, this passage from Wollaston's discussion of "Truths respecting particular Societies of Men or Governments":

When a man is become a member of a society, if he would behave himself according to truth, he ought to do these things: viz. to consider property as founded not only in nature, but also in law; and men's titles to what they have, as strengthened by that, and even by his own concession and covenants; and therefore by so much the more inviolable and sacred; instead of taking such measures to do himself right, when he is molested, or injured, as his own prudence might suggest in a state of nature, to confine himself to such ways as are with his own consent markt out for him: and, in a word, to behave himself according to his subordination or place in the community, and to observe the laws in it. For it is contained in the idea of a law, that it is intended to be observed; and therefore, he who is a party to any laws, or professes himself member of a society formed upon laws, cannot willingly transgress those laws without denying laws to be what they are, or himself to be what he is supposed or professes himself to be.[40]

38. Howard, *The Connecticut Wits* (Chicago, 1943), 10.
39. Clap, *Essay on Moral Virtue*, 33-35.
40. Wollaston, *The Religion of Nature Delineated*, 6th ed. (London, 1738), 152.

The sanctity and inviolability of property, social stratification, adherence to prescription, deference to civil authority—these were cornerstone principles of Connecticut's social system. In virtually every other area of external conduct, Wollaston's theories harmonized with existing practice. As a social conservative and ranking member of the Standing Order, Clap was rooted to the conviction that the Yale youth should be trained to respect property rights, know their "station" in life, abide by prescription, revere authority, and uphold the social *status quo*. While Wollaston was personally a Deist and many of his thoughts reflected the typically deistic optimism, his social philosophy per se was orthodox.[41] To Clap, these portions of Wollaston's text represented the consummation of all proper ideas. For this reason, he rated the text as the best of the "many Treatises which contain good Rules of external Conduct."

While exercising an unrelenting vigil over the students, Clap maintained surveillance of the tutors, the transmitters of knowledge and potential vehicles of heresy, notwithstanding the fact that they had been carefully screened before appointment to make certain they were aseptic in religious belief. There are recorded instances of tutors being arraigned before, and interrogated by, Clap for alleged deviation from the theological creed. The deviations did not have to occur in a classroom to warrant Clap's intrusion; a tutor was expected to conform to orthodoxy in his personal, as well as professional, life. During the Great Awakening, Eleazar Wheelock, a rabid revivalist but a great friend to learning, wrote Clap that Tutor Chauncey Whittelsey was reported to have broached Arminian principles in the course of a heated conversation with the Reverend Stephen White, the minister who had succeeded Clap at Windham. Whittelsey's words had "created a great stir" in the Windham area. Clap first consulted with two men who had been present at the "dispute." Then he questioned Whittelsey. He found the tutor's beliefs to be orthodox and, in a letter to Wheelock, wrote that "I believe the best way to suppress Arminianism is to be slow in charging, but sure proving of it

41. On social thought in Connecticut, see Charles M. Andrews, "Early Aspects of Connecticut History," *New Eng. Qtly.*, 17 (1944), 3-24.

against any particular person." [42] In 1765, however, Clap gave evidence that his principle "to be slow in charging" was susceptible to change without notice, for he summarily cashiered two tutors who, losing sight of the fact that they were paid purveyors of tradition, had strayed off into the heretical path of Sandemanism.[43]

Bent upon purging Yale of every taint of heresy and guarding against corruption of doctrine in the future, Clap drew up a so-called "orthodoxy act" in 1753.[44] This ten-point document, scornfully designated by many as a "Test Act," granted to Clap and the Corporation members a legal sanction to judge and impose punishment upon college officials who should deviate from the orthodox creed. Should a fellow or the president as much as suspect a college official of having fallen from his profession of faith or gone into a "contrary Scheme of Principles," he was empowered to order the official to appear before the Corporation for an examination. The accused had no recourse; he must submit to the examination.

The act contained other significant provisions which were also aimed at assuring the close religious conformity of Yale officials. Especially significant was the fifth article stating that future officers of Yale must first make a public statement of assent to the doctrines contained in the accepted catechism and confession of faith before they could enter upon the execution of their offices; secondly, they must submit to an examination by the Corporation which would verify the sincerity of their public statement. Should an officer undergo a change in his religious sentiments, that is, entertain a set of principles contrary to, or different from, those he approved at his installation, he was bound by duty to resign his position. Appended to the act was a "loyalty oath," [45] to be taken by those elected to the Corporation. Once having taken the oath, a fellow was placed under the moral obligation of accepting, supporting, and propagating the doctrines contained in the catechism and confession of faith of the Saybrook Platform. He must

42. Clap to Wheelock, Nov. 17, 1743, Boston Pub. Lib. MS.
43. Dexter, *Yale Graduates*, III, 93. For a discussion of the creed of Sandemanism, see Williston Walker, "The Sandemanians of New England," American Historical Association, *Annual Report for the Year 1901* (Washington, 1902), I, 131-62.
44. The document is printed in Clap, *Annals of Yale*, 61-65. See also, Yale Corporation Records, I, 106-7, Yale Univ.
45. Clap, *Annals of Yale*, 65-66.

regard any other creeds as "wrong and erroneous," and abide by
the ecclesiastical discipline of the established churches of Connecticut.

The document was, in effect, a more comprehensive reaffirmation of the act of 1722, which had followed on the heels of the
sensational Cutler apostasy. It was another attempt to enforce
doctrinal uniformity. Clap's act thus intensified the tradition of
candid watchfulness begun at Yale in 1722. It also called attention to the filial relationship of Yale College to the Congregational
Church. For the act was not entirely directed at the threat of
religious liberalism; it was also designed to meet an alternate
threat posed by the rapid upsurge of the Church of England in
Connecticut.

If Clap regarded rationalism as a primary menace to orthodoxy,
he was also deeply disturbed, as were most of the Connecticut
"Saints," by the rapid growth of "Rome's sister," the Church of
England.[46] A scattered handful in the opening years of settlement,
the Anglicans at first increased in numbers only gradually. But
neither restrictive governmental legislation, nor the obdurate and
sometimes violent hostility of the populace could arrest this
growth.[47] The spread of Anglicanism was rapidly accelerated during and after the Great Awakening. In this period of violent religious upheaval, many of "Independent" persuasion—bewildered,
dismayed, disillusioned, or disgusted by the bitter wrangling of
the Old Light—New Light controversies—broke from established

46. Despite its animus against the Congregationalists and, conversely, obsequious
praise for the Anglicans, Beardsley's *Episcopal Church in Connecticut* is still the
best secondary account of Anglicanism in Connecticut; vol. I carries the story to
1796. Also of value are Charles Tiffany, *A History of the Protestant Episcopal Church
in the United States of America*, 2d ed. (N. Y., 1900), chap. 5; Origen Storrs Seymour,
"The Beginnings of the Episcopal Church in Connecticut," Tercentenary Commission of Connecticut, *Publications*, No. 30 (1934). Samuel Johnson's published correspondence contains many of his letters to S.P.G. officials in London, a rich source
for tracing the growth of the Church of England in Connecticut. Undoubtedly the
best window for observing this growth is the well-organized collection of documents
in the S.P.G. Library in London.

47. It should be noted that the Anglicans fared somewhat better than other
minority sects. In 1727, for example, Anglicans who had organized into church
societies were released from financial obligations with the established churches.
Other special exemptions were granted with the passage of time.

churches and took refuge in the Church of England.[48] Anglicanism flourished in the rich soil of Congregational contention. Within twenty-six years after the establishment of the first formal Anglican church in Connecticut (Stratford, 1724), the number of churches had swelled to twenty-four. In the decade of the 1750's an additional ten congregations were founded.[49] By mid-century Anglicans had become the largest minority sect in the "Sturdy and Steady" colony. Connecticut's formerly homogeneous religious structure had been rent. Significantly, the heaviest concentration of Anglican strength was in Fairfield County in southwestern Connecticut, the eastern boundary of which was but a stone's throw from New Haven—and Yale College.

Somewhat paradoxically, Yale had figured prominently in the rapid Anglican upsurge. The cataclysmic Cutler defection, in particular, had aided the Anglican cause immeasurably. The repudiation of Congregationalism by Yale's rector had dealt Connecticut's Congregational System a blow from which it never fully recovered. Conversely, the event proved to be a windfall for Anglicanism. In addition to providing the Anglican cause with two dynamic and first-rate religious and intellectual leaders (Cutler and Samuel Johnson), the explosive incident gave a thrust to the movement as a whole. Within a few years of Cutler's apostasy, Anglicans in increasing numbers were to be found at Yale preparing for ministerial careers. It is important to note that there was not a single Anglican graduate of Yale before 1724,[50] but in the first decade after Cutler's defection one of every ten graduates made the hazardous voyage to London to take Holy Orders in the Church of England.[51]

The Anglican leaders of Connecticut were quick to recognize

---

48. See, for example, Edmund B. O'Callaghan, ed., *Documents Relative to the Colonial History of the State of New-York* (Albany, 1856), VII, 372 (hereafter cited as O'Callaghan, ed., N.-Y. Col. Docs.).

49. For statistical information on Anglican increase, see Dexter, ed., *Stiles's Itineraries*, 110, 112-14; Hawks and Perry, eds., *Documentary History of Episcopal Church*, I, 311.

50. Dexter, *Yale Graduates*, I, 296-98. There is no earlier reference to an Anglican graduate.

51. The 1-to-10 ratio remained constant to the end of Clap's administration. To 1765, Yale had graduated 400 "worthy Ministers," wrote Clap, of whom 40 became Anglican clergymen. *Annals of Yale*, 84.

the paramount importance of the college in their plans for further expansion. They were also anxious to gain a foothold in New Haven, the principal commercial town and co-capital of the colony. As one S.P.G. missionary informed his London superiors in later years, "that mission [church in New Haven] is of greater Consequence than any in the Colony." [52] For the moment, however, the college was of greater import, for it played a vital role in Anglican plans to enlarge their force in Connecticut. Like the Congregationalists, the Anglicans placed a high value on a learned ministry, and the high cost of sending a boy to a college controlled by the Church of England, William and Mary, for example, made it necessary for Anglicans in Connecticut to utilize Yale for training their youth. To increase the number of Anglican students at Yale and thereby expand their influence in the intellectual bastion of Connecticut Congregationalism became a primary objective of the Anglicans after 1722. With single-minded dedication they worked to this end. The guiding spirit of the movement was the ubiquitous Samuel Johnson, then preaching at nearby Stratford. Because of his proselytizing activities, Johnson has rightfully acquired the sobriquet, "father of the Episcopal Church in Connecticut." [53]

The Anglicans soon began to disturb Yale's internal homogeneity. After one of his periodic visits to New Haven in the spring of 1745, Johnson informed the London Secretary of the S.P.G. "that the harvest is large." There were at Yale "ten children of the Church and several sons of dissenting parents, that are much inclined to conform." [54] Heartened by the surprisingly high Anglican representation among candidates for degrees in 1745 and by the liberal character of the questions defended in the disputations, the Reverend James Wetmore of Rye, New York, optimistically predicted that "we may see a great change in that Colony for the better in a very few years." With mixed emotions of pleasure and surprise, Wetmore heard defended, "by those whose

52. Jeremiah Leaming to S.P.G., Sept. 29, 1767, MS. Letter to S.P.G., Case B23, No. 248. A similar sentiment is expressed in Solomon Palmer to S.P.G., July 26, 1763, and June 25, 1765, MS. Letters to S.P.G., Case B23, Nos. 307 and 311.
53. Seymour, "Beginnings of Episcopal Church in Connecticut," Conn. Tercentenary Com., *Publications*, No. 30 (1934), 5.
54. Hawks and Perry, eds., *Documentary History of Episcopal Church*, I, 213-14.

fathers have held, and acted upon their reverse, in their separation from the Church of England," the following propositions:

> Potestas Legislativa est unicuique Societati
> essentialis: affirmat Respondens.
> (The legislative power is essential for every
> single society.)
>
> Res in se indifferentes, sunt proprium
> humanae Potestatis Objectum: Respondens
> affirmat.
> (Things neither good nor bad in them-
> selves are a proper object of human power.)
>
> An conscientiae dictamina conferant jus
> agendi vel cogitandi contra veritatem?
> Negat Respondens.
> (Whether the dictates of conscience con-
> fer a right of thinking or doing against
> truth?) [55]

A year later Johnson was pleased to observe that a "love to the Church is still gaining in the College." Four more students had declared themselves candidates for orders, "and there seems a very growing disposition toward the Church, in the town of New-Haven, as well as in the College, so that I hope there will, 'ere long, be a flourishing Church there." [56] On commencement day, 1748, nine Anglican clergymen were in New Haven, and held a colloquy there, while ten Anglicans took degrees. Among the B.A. candidates were Johnson's own son, William, and Samuel Seabury, son of a prominent S.P.G. missionary. Of young Seabury, the future first Anglican bishop in America, the elder Johnson correctly prophesied, he "may in due time do good service." [57]

Quite naturally, the college officials became deeply alarmed as more and more Anglicans began poaching on their ecclesiastical preserves. They persistently exerted their influence in an attempt to contain the encroachment within and without the college. On

55. Extract of a letter from Wetmore to Secretary of S.P.G., Oct. 3, 1745, in Dexter, *Yale Graduates*, II, 18.
56. Hawks and Perry, eds., *Documentary History of Episcopal Church*, I, 222-23.
57. *Ibid.*, 1, 245.

one occasion they countenanced the use of force and mob violence to prevent the Anglicans from constructing a church in the town. The incident took place in 1735. In that year William Grigson,[58] a London churchman and great-grandson of one of New Haven's original settlers, presented to the Reverend Jonathan Arnold (Yale, 1723), an S.P.G. missionary of West Haven, the deed to a strip of land bordering upon the New Haven Green at the very portals of the college. The land was granted for the purpose of building a church and parsonage. When in the fall of 1738 Arnold announced his intention to execute the design, a legal controversy developed as a local Congregationalist claimed title to the Grigson property. The partisan town fathers sustained the claim of their religious kinsman, declaring Arnold's deed void.

The Reverend Mr. Arnold, however, was an uncommonly stubborn man. Firm in the conviction that he had legal title to the property, he traveled to New Haven and, aided by a servant, set about clearing the undeveloped plot. When the task was near completion, a mob came trooping down the dusty street with the Yale student body acting as vanguard. Arnold and his servant were physically abused and threatened with death if they persisted in their enterprise. His stubbornness deflated, Arnold withdrew and abandoned the project.[59] Years later a satiric Anglican pamphleteer recalled the "noble action" of the students who "quitting soft dalliance with the *muses,* they roughened into sons of *Mars,* and issuing forth in deep and firm array, with courage bold and undaunted, they not only attacked, but bravely routed a YOKE OF OXEN and a poor *Plowman.*"[60] The Anglicans strongly, and rightfully, suspected that Rector Elisha Williams and "other chief

58. Sometimes cited as Gregson.

59. The episode is discussed in Beardsley, *Episcopal Church in Connecticut,* I, 168-71; Frederick Croswell, "History of Trinity Church, New Haven," New Haven Colony Hist. Soc., *Papers,* 1 (1865), 50-55; Dexter, *Yale Graduates,* I, 275-76. Arnold's difficulties over the Grigson property did not terminate with his forced removal. Theophilus Morris, who replaced Arnold as S.P.G. missionary shortly after the abortive attempt to establish a church in New Haven, complained to his London superiors that Arnold had not only carried away the Bible and Common Prayer Book belonging to the mission in Derby, but also a sum of money donated by Bostonians for the construction of churches in New Haven and Derby. Morris affirmed that Arnold had refused to provide him with an accounting of the funds. Morris to S.P.G., May 4, 1742, MS. Letter to S.P.G., Case B10, No. 47.

60. Quoted in Beardsley, *Episcopal Church in Connecticut,* I, 114n.

men in town" were directly implicated in this act of violence. While failing in their attempt to bring the Church of England to Yale's doorstep, the Anglicans were successful in setting up in West Haven two years later a "pretty neat little church," as Samuel Johnson described it.[61] They were now within four miles of the main target.

The West Haven Church was established at the time Clap was installed as rector; his entrance upon the Yale scene coincided with a sudden spurt in Anglican enrollment and a subsequent quickening of Anglican efforts in New Haven. Clap was automatically cast in the role of a chief policymaker for the local Congregationalists.

He immediately found himself locked in the jaws of a predicament. He clearly understood that Yale was making a rich contribution to the Anglican cause, and he deplored the fact. Yet if he took direct action to prevent Anglicans from entering Yale, or if he subjected them to discriminatory indignities while in attendance, there was every likelihood of an appeal to the Crown for redress. And royal interference, as every Connecticut politician knew only too well, could result not only in the destruction of Connecticut's near-autonomous status under its charter, but also in the dissolution of the college. Clap went through an experience which called his attention to this "darned uncomfortable reality" —in the terminology of Artemus Ward. During the Great Awakening, he denied a degree to a senior, a New Light, who had been prominent in promoting a plan to publish Locke's *Essay on Toleration*. The student hired a lawyer and threatened to pursue the case until it reached the King in Council. Clap relented and granted him his degree. The Anglican issue augured the same serious consequences. It was a classic "powder-keg" situation, fraught with the greatest dangers for a Congregationalist policymaker.

With Anglican parents and clergy clamoring for an administrative policy that would permit the sons of Churchmen to attend Sabbath and communion services in the new Anglican church in West Haven, Clap was forced to declare a definite policy. Probably

61. S.P.G. Journal (1747/8-1750/1), 137-38. The Anglicans had established a parish in West Haven as early as 1723, but owing to a lack of finances they did not begin construction of a church until 1740.

after considerable soul-searching and consultation with other
Congregational leaders, including the trustees, he instituted a
"custom" conferring upon the Anglican youth the right to attend
communion services in West Haven when such attendance did
not interfere with regular academic routine.[62] The precise date of
this broad concession is not known, but it assuredly came very
early in his administration.[63]

Clap's liberality to the Anglicans extended beyond permission
to attend Sabbath services in West Haven. When touring Anglican
clergy preached in New Haven or close by, as they frequently did,
Clap allowed the sons of Churchmen to attend, even though he declared these meetings off limits to Congregational youth.[64] He
also permitted William Johnson to serve as a lay reader and
catechist for neighboring Anglican parishes.[65] These concessions
doubtless account for the absence of strife—and it is a notable
absence—between the college officials and Anglicans in the period
1740-53; they also would appear to account for the equally striking
fact that the S.P.G. missionaries of Connecticut offered no criticism
of the college authorities in their letters and reports to superiors in
London.[66] It is important to note that the missionaries made a
fetish of chronicling every discriminatory condition, as well as
the more flagrant offenses committed by the Congregationalists.
Had Anglican students been denied freedom of worship or been
subjected to discriminatory actions, it seems reasonable to assume
that the S.P.G. missionaries would have reported these facts to
the home office in a most detailed manner. Clap's liberality apparently mollified even the most dissident missionary. On the

62. This significant bit of information is to be found in a letter from Samuel
Johnson to Clap, 1754. See Schneider, eds., *Writings of Johnson*, I, 181. In this
period, services in West Haven were very irregular because the S.P.G. missionary
assigned to that mission was obliged to divide his time and energies among a
number of parishes.

63. See the incident related in Hawks and Perry, eds., *Documentary History of
Episcopal Church*, I, 204-5.

64. *Ibid.*, I, 208; the Rev. James Lyon, an S.P.G. missionary, in reporting to the
home office of a tour he had made, wrote as follows: "At Milford and New-Haven
there are a few members of our Church, but care is taken, at the last of those places
especially, that they should not increase, the rector [Clap] and tutors of the College
there having, of late, suffered none of the students (except the children of professed
Churchmen) to attend my lectures."

65. *Ibid.*, I, 252; Journal of Minutes of S.P.G., XII, 295.

66. A close search of materials in the S.P.G. Library reveals this important fact.

surface at least, there was a distinct harmony in the relations between the two antagonistic religious groups.

The harmony abruptly dissolved in October 1753, when Clap made the most fateful administrative decision of his presidential career. Without advance warning he withdrew the Congregational students from the New Haven First Church and announced that in the future all students, including Anglicans, would receive religious instruction and would worship within the college and under the supervision of approved ministers.[67] With one bold stroke, he sealed off the college from the briskly blowing winds of rationalism and Anglicanism.

What prompted this extreme action? A fear of religious liberalism was assuredly one factor. Of greater importance, perhaps, was the startling development that an Anglican church had arisen in the very shadows of Yale. At long last, the Anglicans had fulfilled one of their most cherished ambitions.

The project had not been achieved with ease; indeed, it was the consummation of twenty-odd years of sustained effort. After the Arnold debacle, the New Haven Congregationalists, with rare agreement, closed ranks and presented a united front against the common foe. They persistently refused to sell land in town to church-building Anglicans. The steady thrusts of the churchmen, however, eventually bared a weak spot in this defense, and in July 1752, they managed to purchase a strip of land close to the college. The following year "beautiful little" Trinity Church, sixty feet long and forty broad, looked out upon Yale.[68] Just prior to the building's completion, the sacrament of the Lord's Supper was performed in the liturgy of the Church of England, the first such service in the history of New Haven.[69] The local Congregationalists could not have imagined a more frightening development, unless it had been the appointment of Archbishop Laud himself as the spiritual head of the church.

Clearly, the denouement had been reached. The presence of an Anglican church near Yale threatened to destroy the traditional

67. Clap, *Annals of Yale*, 60-61.
68. S.P.G. Journal of Minutes, XIII, 26-27; Croswell, "History of Trinity Church," New Haven Colony Hist. Soc., *Papers*, 1 (1865), 55.
69. S.P.G. Journal of Minutes, XII, 227-29.

relationship of the college to the established religious system. As Clap analyzed the situation, it appeared that only one course of action remained open to him if the *status quo* was to be preserved. He must separate the students from the First Church and provide compulsory religious instruction within the college for all of the youth. He knew that such a policy would provoke criticism. He was prepared to meet it.

Chapter Eight

THE YALE CONTROVERSY

WITH the announcement of Clap's new policy, a storm broke over New Haven. Militant in mood, the Churchmen were not inclined to remain passive and submit meekly to Clap's order. Bristling with indignation, they raised a hue and a cry against him, smiting him hip and thigh for abridging their right of freedom of worship, for denying them liberty of conscience—and the echo of their slashing criticism still rings in American historiography! Clap soon found himself the target of a withering hail of obloquy. Leading the assault was the Reverend Ebenezer Punderson, S.P.G. missionary and newly appointed spiritual head of Trinity Church.[1] Punderson's anger was intensified by a personal affront. A member of the Class of 1726, he currently had two sons attending Yale. After hearing of Clap's decision to institute separate worship, he requested that the boys (as well as other Anglicans) be excused from Congregational services on the Sabbath so as to attend his church.[2]

The question was now squarely before Clap. Did he intend to carry out his policy to the letter, or was it to be but a paper policy?

1. S.P.G. Journal of Minutes, XII, 229. Punderson was assigned to the New Haven-Guilford-Branford area. So anxiously did he covet the post that he willingly took a slash in salary. See Punderson to S.P.G., Apr. 12, 1761, Case B23, No. 292.
2. Nov. 3, 1753, Yale MS.

Taking account of "darned uncomfortable reality," Clap vacil-
lated. He opened his reply with a denial of Punderson's request,
arguing that every student must conform to the "religion, rule
and order" of the college while in residence. There could be no
exceptions. To permit the Anglicans to attend special religious
services would be inconsistent with the laws and constitution of
the college. Furthermore, should the college officials adopt a
policy of complete toleration, they would run the risk of not providing sufficient spiritual training for the students. And, on a more
mundane level, how could it be determined whether absent students were attending the Anglican church or playing hooky?
Finally, arguing from a political point of view, Clap averred that
the principle of majority rule must be observed in such matters.
Disregarding the aphorism he had once quipped to the Cleaveland
brothers when they had thrown the majority rule argument in his
face—"A few more than half makes no difference"—he affirmed
that it was a known rule in all societies that the "minor Part should
give Way to the Major."

Up to this point intractable in his position, Clap suddenly
changed his tone, offering a sop. While historians have been quick
to seize upon that portion of his letter which affirmed that all
students must comply with the new religious policy, no one has
directed attention to his effort to conciliate the opposition:

And on the other side, he [Clap, writing in the third person], at
discretion does sometime upon special occasion, give liberty to
boys to be absent from prayers, recitations, and Sunday worship;
and the governors of Yale would continue to be, as they always
have been, as complaisant to the Gentlemen of the Church of
England as may be, we shall be willing to give Liberty to those
Students, who have been educated in the Worship of the Church
of England, and are of that Comunion [*sic*], to be absent at those
Times when the Sacrament is administered in that Church, and
at Christmas, and such other Times as shall not be an Infraction
upon the general Order and standing Rules of College, and as
shall be found, by Experience, not to be attended with any considerable Inconvenience to the Society.[3]

3. Nov. 5, 1753, Yale MS.

Half a loaf was not acceptable to the Anglicans. They wanted a clear-cut policy of religious toleration. And they gave voice to their wishes. Their outcry against Clap increased in rancor and intensity; their criticism widened in scope. They assailed him for adhering to a narrow interpretation of the character and purpose of Yale. They charged him with hypocrisy in accepting benefactions from Churchmen while abridging their freedom of worship. They repudiated his contention that Yale was an agency of the Congregational Church, for, they argued, all faiths contributed to its support through the annual legislative grant. His policy was beyond the pale of reason, indefensible by any standard of thought. On this basis, Punderson directed his sons to attend Anglican services and pay no heed to Clap's policy.[4]

Clap had a ready answer to all charges.[5] On the main question of denying liberty of conscience, he countered that there were defined limits to such a freedom. Liberty of conscience, he reasoned, applied only to the admission of students. If Yale denied entrance to Anglicans, then it would be guilty of a breach of the principle. But since it granted entrance to all Protestants it observed liberty of conscience in the "fullest sense." Once a student took up residence in the college, he was morally obliged to abide by the established regulations of that institution. He must therefore attend "our way of Worship." Clap elucidated his position in a letter to Samuel Johnson: "That liberty of conscience consists in this that every man shall act according to his own judgment in all those things wherein he is immediately to act provided he breaks no superior law." A parent who sent his son to Yale and then ordered him to violate the laws of that society—and the reference was directed to Punderson—was guilty of a moral indiscretion, since he was willfully destroying the liberty of conscience of the rightful governors. Thus "liberty of conscience is set in one to destroy liberty of conscience in another where he has a proper right to act." [6]

4. S.P.G. Journal of Minutes, XIII, 57-58.
5. In reconstructing Clap's defense, I have relied on his pamphlet *Religious Constitution of Colleges*, and on his exchange of views with Samuel Johnson. His exegesis was consistent at all times.
6. Clap to Johnson, Jan. 30, 1754, N.-Y. Hist. Soc. MS., New York City; the letter is printed in Schneider, eds., *Writings of Johnson*, I, 174-76.

Clap entrenched himself behind the walls of historical and legal tradition in defense against the charge of hypocrisy. What if the Anglicans did give financial support to Yale through their taxes? The founders of Yale had decreed that the school was to train youth for service in the Congregational Church. It was his responsibility to direct the college in accordance with this decree. To do otherwise would defeat the original purpose of the founders. Clap reminded his critics of the fact that English common law explicitly set forth the principle that a donor did not have a legal right to order the type of worship for an institution. Donations were to be used in accordance with the design of the founders of that institution. The argument now moved smoothly into a well-worn groove. To grant a donor the right to dictate Yale's method of worship would defeat the intentions of the founders and destroy the religious order of the college. It was Clap's conviction that this order "ought, sacredly to be observed." Then, too, had not Yale educated a number of Anglican ministers? Did this not constitute "sufficient compensation" for the relatively small amount of taxes Churchmen contributed to the college? Clap was certain that it did. The Anglicans were inclined to think not.

While the bulk of Clap's opposition was centered in New Haven and its environs, the sharpest Anglican critic was the influential Samuel Johnson, then president of King's College. Johnson had followed the developments in New Haven with keen interest. Consumed with anger at Clap's newly announced policy, he fired off a letter of protest. "It is strange to me," wrote Johnson, "that merely opening a church at New Haven should be considered by any of you, gentlemen, as a justifiable provocation to interrupt the harmony that had subsisted between us." [7] The two academicians and rival religious leaders were soon engaged in a sharp epistolary duel, parrying and thrusting over questions relating to the character of Yale, its function as an educational institution, and its policy of compulsory worship.[8]

7. Schneider, eds., *Writings of Johnson*, I, 180.
8. Two of Johnson's letters are printed in *ibid.*, I, 174-82. Only one of Clap's letters has survived (see above, n. 6), but the main outline of the contents of other letters can be ascertained from Johnson's replies. Johnson's letters are framed as refutations of Clap's arguments.

Johnson's position on these issues was explicit and symptomatic of the new spirit of liberalism that was beginning to permeate American educational theory. His closely reasoned arguments paralleled those expressed by the New Haven Anglicans.

The only point in question, as I humbly conceive [he affirmed], is, whether there ought of right to be any such law in your College as, either in words or by necessary consequence, forbids the liberty we contend for! What we must beg leave to insist on is, that there ought not; and that it is highly injurious to forbid it; unless you can make it appear that you ever had a right to exclude the people of the Church belonging to this colony, from having the benefit of public education in your College, without their submitting to the hard condition of not being allowed to do what they believe in their conscience it is their indispensable duty to do, i.e., to require their children to go to church whenever they have opportunity, and at the same time a right to accept and hold such vast benefactions from gentlemen of the Church in England, wherewith to support you in maintaining such a law in exclusion of such a liberty.[9]

Clap responded with the same old arguments he had been using against the New Haven Anglicans.

After three months of paper warfare, Johnson tired of the argument and threatened to take positive action to change Yale's policy. He made it known that he would first lay his complaint before the Connecticut General Assembly. Should this fail, he would then be forced to employ the ultimate weapon in the Anglican arsenal: appeal to the Crown. As he wrote Clap, he would be bound by duty "in obedience to a rule of the Society [S.P.G.] to join with my brethren in complaining of it [compulsory attendance] to our superiors at home, if it be insisted upon—which is what I abhor and dread to be brought to." If this statement had a disquieting effect upon Clap, what followed was far more frightening in its implications. "It may also deserve to be considered," Johnson wrote, "that the Government at home would probably be so far from going into the formality of repealing this law that they would declare it a nullity in itself; and not only so, but even the corpora-

9. *Ibid.*, I, 176-77. Johnson also made this significant statement: "And I am prodigiously mistaken if you did not tell me it was an allowed and settled rule with you heretofore [to allow the children of dissenting parents to go to their meetings]."

tion that hath enacted it; inasmuch as it seems a principle in law that a corporation cannot make a corporation without his Majesty's Act." [10] It was a chilling observation, designed to arouse Clap's apprehensions. Johnson was reminding him of the uncomfortable fact that Yale rested on a tenuous legal base: its charters (1701 and 1745) had been granted by the Connecticut General Assembly and not, as in customary fashion, by the Crown.

Was Johnson bluffing, or was he seriously intent upon dropping the Damoclean political sword that the Anglicans frequently dangled over the heads of their Congregationalist protagonists? In any case, Clap could not afford to let Johnson make the next move. Perhaps he had learned that Johnson had already informed S.P.G. officials of his intention to carry the case to the King in Council should the Connecticut General Assembly fail to take the necessary remedial action.[11] The stakes were altogether too high for Clap. If he vehemently despised the Church of England, just as vehemently did he love the college he served. Daggett described his deep loyalty to Yale: "his whole heart was bound up in the welfare of this important society. He begrudged no pains or labour to promote its prosperity.... He seemed to care for it naturally, with as much solicitude as if it had been his own private interest, and all the Students his own Children." [12] Clap had sufficient common sense to know that he would be courting disaster for Yale by rigid adherence to his declared policy. Better to concede a point than risk the possible fate of dissolution by royal decree. For Clap, interference by the Crown was a terrifying specter.

Just five days from the date of Johnson's letter, Clap was at his desk drafting a reply. In a condescending manner, he urged Johnson to put a damper on his passions and to consider the gravity of his intended actions.[13] These words had no effect; Johnson was intent upon conquering, not compromising. At last, Clap was forced to capitulate. Without further public announcement, he liberalized the execution of policy. In June 1754, William Johnson, who was close to the college scene, informed his father that

10. *Ibid.*, I, 178.
11. Journal of Minutes of S.P.G., XII, 376-77.
12. *Faithful Serving of God,* 33.
13. The tone and content of Clap's letter are clearly indicated by Johnson's reply of Feb. 19, 1754; Schneider, eds., *Writings of Johnson,* I, 180-82.

Clap "seems to have yielded the point as to the Church scholars, that as many as ask leave to attend, have it, but the scholars are negligent and but few of them trouble their heads about it." [14] Understandably nettled by the news of Anglican apathy, Samuel Johnson directed the Reverend Mr. Punderson, through the medium of his son, William, "to take some pains with those wicked scholars that are so indifferent, and put something into their hands to read that may animate and indoctrinate them better." The "prison doors" had been flung open, Johnson proudly announced. The Anglican youth should pass through them. With regard to Clap, Johnson was pleased as punch to learn that he was so "mortified and humbled." [15]

Thus Yale's policy of repression came to an end after being in effect for only five or six months. Thereafter, Churchmen were once more given the right to worship in their own way, provided such worship did not conflict with scheduled academic exercises. For the remainder of the pre-Revolutionary period (and thereafter), the "prison doors" remained open. The Yale authorities limited their anti-Anglican activities to an occasional act of harassment,[16] and to veiled threats such as those implicit in this significant statement of policy by Clap in 1765:

The Sons of those, who profess themselves to be Episcopalians, have Liberty to go out on the Lord's-Day, and at other Times, to attend on the Mode of Worship in which they were educated, as often as will not be an Infraction on the general Rules of Order in the College. Persons of all Denominations of Protestants are allowed the Advantage of an Education here, and no Inquiry has been made, at their Admission or afterwards, about their particular Sentiments in Religion. Yet, if it should manifestly appear, that any should take Pains to infect the Minds of their Fellow-Students with such pernicious Errors, as are contrary to the Fundamentals of Christianity, and the special Design of founding this College, so that Parents should justly be afraid of venturing their

14. *Ibid.*, I, 190.
15. *Ibid.*, I, 191.
16. In 1759, for example, Clap refused to permit John Beardslee, a freshman, to serve as a lay reader in Trinity Church; Yale Corporation Records, I, 139, Yale Univ. Beardslee transferred as a junior to the more congenial surroundings of King's College; Samuel Johnson to S.P.G., Apr. 30, 1761, Letter Books of S.P.G., Lambeth Palace Library, London.

Children here, it is probable that some Notice would be taken of it.[17]

With the termination of Clap's short-lived repressive policy, Anglican criticism of Yale suddenly ended. The letters and reports of S.P.G. missionaries in New Haven and environs once more lapsed into silence on the matter of religious discrimination at Yale. The battle had been won in this critical area. Freedom of worship had been achieved. Under the pressure of a "dissenting" sect, the orthodox establishment had been forced to accommodate itself to existence in a religiously pluralistic society and to extend a reluctant toleration to a minority group.[18]

On the issue of Yale, Clap, and the Church of England, there remains but one point requiring clarification. Common report has long made out that the administrators of pre-Revolutionary Yale, and particularly Clap, forced Anglican students, under the threat of fines and expulsion, to attend Congregationalist Sabbath services and kept them tied in bonds of discrimination. It would seem that American historians have made the mistake of assuming that the Punderson incident represented a general condition during Clap's tenure. Professor Morison has written, for example: "When Christ Church, the first Episcopal Church in Cambridge, was built in 1760, the Harvard Faculty allowed students to attend service there, instead of at the Congregational meeting, if their parents permitted; but Yale forbade her students to attend Episcopal service in New Haven, well into the next century." [19]

That Yale was out of step with her sister colleges cannot be

17. Clap, *Annals of Yale*, 83-84. These words represented much more than "lip service" to the principle of toleration; see Richard Hofstadter and Walter P. Metzger, *The Development of Academic Freedom in the United States* (N. Y., 1955), 152*n*.

18. So rapidly did passions subside that by 1768 the S.P.G. missionary in New Haven could write in all candor that his people "live at Peace with the Dissenters." The Rev. Bela Hubbard to S.P.G., May 4, 1768, S.P.G. Journal of Minutes, XVII, 520-21.

19. *Three Centuries of Harvard*, 88. See also, Catherine Drinker Bowen, *John Adams and the American Revolution* (N. Y., 1949, 1950), 611; Roland Bainton, *Yale and the Ministry* (N. Y., 1957), 13; Daniel J. Boorstin, *The Americans; the Colonial Experience* (N. Y., 1958), 180. Clifford Shipton, in writing briefly of Clap's struggles with the Churchmen, conveys the traditional impression of protracted discrimination at Yale, although notice is made of Clap's temporizing statement of 1765; see *Harvard Graduates*, VII, 44-45.

denied. The record clearly shows that she tenaciously resisted latitudinarian tendencies and steadfastly sought to maintain the religious ways of the past, especially during Clap's regime. Yet, with regard to the Anglicans, the most careful reading of the evidence would suggest that Yale's policies were far more liberal than is commonly held. Certainly, Clap extended many concessions to the Churchmen. Such liberality, it must be acknowledged, was a tribute rendered to political expediency and was not inspired by deeply rooted convictions on the intellectual and moral propriety of toleration. As Ezra Stiles once pointed out, Clap "was very strenuous for Orthodoxy: and had he been a Cardinal or a Pontiff he would have supported it with the Inquisition and Arms." [20]

If the growing power of the Church of England and the specter of rationalism sweeping triumphantly through New England were the primary determinants of Clap's action in taking Yale's students from the First Church and establishing separate worship at the college, the Reverend Joseph Noyes was another contributing cause. Noyes, who was as much a part of the New Haven scene as the college itself, had become the object of widespread criticism. The criticism did not stem solely from his parishioners. It reached as high as the General Assembly, in which Noyes was the subject of sharp debate. Some people accused him of equivocation and vagueness in doctrine; others, of outright deviation from orthodoxy; still others attacked him for not expounding a robust Calvinism. Nearly everybody complained of his prosaic, unedifying sermons. As for the more serious charges, Noyes was branded as an Arminian, it appears, because he failed to take a clear-cut position on the central doctrines of original sin, regeneration through the supernatural influence of the divine spirit, the absolute necessity of spiritual reaffirmation in salvation and effectual calling, and justification solely through faith. Some even entertained a suspicion that he was an Arian.[21] Clap himself did not directly accuse Noyes of Arminianism, Arianism, or anything

20. Dexter, ed., *Literary Diary of Stiles,* II, 336.
21. Trumbull, *History of Connecticut,* II, 285; Fisher, *Discourse on Church of Christ,* 8.

of the like at this particular time. Apparently he did not wish
to engage in public dispute with so prominent a member of the
Corporation. In his defensive pamphlet, *Religious Constitution of
Colleges* (1754), Clap made but two indirect references to Noyes,
of which the more damaging was an oblique accusation of heresy,
stating that the college governors were bound by duty to provide
the youth with instructors of theology who could be trusted to
teach "according to the Design of the Founders." [22]

If Clap was reluctant to make a public declaration that Noyes
was an Arminian, he was perfectly willing to render candid comment on his tepid preaching. In his judgment, Noyes's discourses
were "unstudied and flat, and no ways edifying." [23] All evidence
would indicate that the criticism was just. As Henry Bamford
Parkes has observed, Noyes crops up time and time again in the
colonial history of Connecticut and always in the same role, "that
of the dullest preacher of the generation." [24] Leonard Bacon, who
served as minister of the First Church in the early nineteenth
century, recounted this bit of Clap-Noyes repartee which, as Bacon
asserts, was often spoken of by some of the senior members of the
parish. Clap once undertook to expostulate with Noyes for his
feckless preaching, whereupon he elicited this peppery reply from
the sensitive minister: "You do not know what an ignorant people
I have to preach to." To which Clap retorted: "Yes I do, and I
know that as long as you preach to them in this way, they always
will be ignorant." [25] Whether apocryphal or not, the exchange
captures the spirit of their relationship in 1753.

The establishment of separate worship came with startling sud-
denness, but it was not really an act of impulse. Actually, Clap
had contemplated this arrangement since the time of the Great
Awakening when he first began laying plans for a chair of divinity
at the college. In 1746, Philip Livingston, the wealthy New York
land baron, whose four sons had been educated at Yale, donated
to the college a sizable sum of money, which was to be used for a
chair of divinity or any other useful purpose specified by the Cor-

22. P. 11.
23. Darling, *Remarks on Clap's History of Doctrines in New England*, 46.
24. *Jonathan Edwards*, 44.
25. *Thirteen Historical Discourses*, 240n.

poration. Clap set the benefaction aside for the chair of divinity.[26] Lacking additional funds, he was unable to complete his plans at this time, and so the matter was left in abeyance.

In 1752, becoming increasingly alarmed by religious developments, he renewed efforts to establish a professorship of divinity.[27] To accumulate needed funds, he leased college lands in Litchfield County.[28] Next he considered likely candidates for the important position. After careful deliberation, he settled upon the Reverend Solomon Williams, the brother of the former rector and a close friend from Clap's ministerial days; Williams was also one of Clap's main supporters on the Corporation. Williams declined, however, because of his old age and infirmities,[29] and in the spring of 1755 Clap selected the Reverend Naphtali Daggett, Congregational minister of Smithtown, Long Island, and a Yale honor graduate (1748).[30] Daggett accepted and in late fall began his "apprenticeship" under Clap's watchful eye.[31] Daggett's appointment was still conditional upon his satisfying the Corporation.

After a four-month trial period, the young minister was found to be orthodox in spiritual matters and qualified in his academic duties. He was then installed in a ceremony that took the better part of two days to complete. The first day was spent in examination. Although he had already served four months, presumably long enough to reveal his character, Daggett was subjected to intensive questioning before the president and fellows. He was examined as to his "Principles of Religion, his Knowledge and Skill in Divinity, Cases of Conscience, Scripture History and Chronology, Antiquity, Skill in the Hebrew Tongue, and various other Qualifications for

26. Clap, *Annals of Yale,* 54; Yale Corporation Records, I, 79, Yale Univ.

27. Connecticut Archives: Colleges and Schools, 1st Ser., Pt. ii, I, 317a, Conn. State Lib.; Yale Corporation Records, I, 98-99, Yale Univ.

28. Clap, *Annals of Yale,* 60; Connecticut Archives: Colleges and Schools, 1st Ser., Pt. ii, I, 319a, Conn. State Lib.

29. Yale Corporation Records, I, 114, Yale Univ.

30. Clap to Daggett, Mar. 20, 1755, Yale MS. Daggett's biographical sketch is in Dexter, *Yale Graduates,* II, 153-56.

31. In the interim period between withdrawal and Daggett's arrival in New Haven, Clap had officiated as "Chaplain." He had conducted the regular religious exercises and provided the students with theological instruction. When Clap was "too busy and too burdened," ministerial colleagues of nearby churches conducted Sabbath services. Clap, *Annals of Yale,* 61; Yale Corporation Records, I, 105, Yale Univ.

a Professor; in all which he acquitted himself to the good Satisfaction of the Corporation." On the second day, after preaching a
sermon, he gave his full and explicit consent to all the doctrines
contained in the sanctioned catechism and confession of faith,
and to the rules of church discipline of the Saybrook Platform.
Next, he read off a full confession of faith, drawn up by his own
hand; after which he abjured the "principal Errors, prevailing in
these times," namely Arminianism, Arianism, Pelegianism, An-
tinomianism, and Enthusiasm. He was then installed into office.[32]
In this exacting manner the Livingston Chair of Divinity was
established—the first endowed chair in the history of Yale College.[33]

Two years later, Clap completed his plan of making Yale a
center of orthodoxy by organizing a college church. Against the
strong opposition of some of the fellows, he pushed his measure
through the Corporation, and the church was officially established
on June 30, 1757. A voluntary organization, its original membership consisted of the three tutors, a resident graduate, and eight
students. Daggett was its minister.[34]

Clap now seemingly had achieved his aim of sealing off the
college from "corrupt" religious influences. But it was hardly a
time for rejoicing. Quite the contrary, he found himself drawn
into the maelstrom of religious and political controversy. He was
under severe attack by the officials of the First Church, by religious
and political Old Lights, by the Anglicans, and even by some of
the fellows of the Corporation. The tides of criticism had been
rising steadily against the president from the very inception of his
office. Now, in 1757, his seventeenth year as titular head of Yale,
they began to pound with increasing force and persistency against
the dikes of orthodoxy he had thrown up around the college—and
around himself.

32. Clap, *Annals of Yale*, 67; Yale Corporation Records, I, 114-18, Yale Univ.; Clap's
Charge to Daggett at his Installment, Mar. 3, 1756, Yale MS.

33. Clap donated one acre of land for the home of the divinity professor and
contributed a liberal grant for its construction. In the presentation ceremony, Clap
made it patently clear that Daggett would find himself without a roof over his
head should he be found preaching "contrary" doctrines. Yale Corporation Records,
I, 109, 126, Yale Univ.; Clap, *Annals of Yale*, 68, 99-100.

34. Records of Church of Christ in Yale, June 30, 1757, Yale MS. The history of
this unique institution is related in detail in Ralph H. Gabriel, *Religion and
Learning at Yale, The Church of Christ in the College and University, 1757-1957*
(New Haven, 1958).

The First Church officials were among the first to voice objections to Clap's plan to convert Yale into a Congregational seminary. These objections were inspired by a combination of factors. Initially, the loss of the students represented a financial setback, for the church received fees from the college for ministering to the boys' spiritual needs. A second and equally important source of grievance was the loss of social prestige. With the withdrawal of the students, the First Church had been shorn of a substantial measure of social affluence, a majority of the Yale youth being sons of the Standing Order. These young men brought an added dignity to a church which already numbered among its membership many of the wealthiest and most socially prominent citizens of Connecticut.[35] The First Church was not disposed to give them up without a fight.

A few months after the withdrawal of the students (1753), and even before Solomon Williams had been approached on the divinity professorship, the First Church officers tried to strike a compromise with Clap. They informed him that, if he would appoint the Reverend Ebenezer Devotion as professor of divinity and permit him to preach half the time in the First Church, with the students to attend services as in the past, they in turn would pay to the college half the annual salary granted to Noyes. Expressing the will of its guiding head, the Corporation rejected this offer, but left the door open for further compromise by listing alternative conditions to which the First Church must agree before the *status quo ante* withdrawal could be re-established. There were four conditions: the governors of the Corporation reserved the right to carry on public worship within the college whenever they should deem it proper; the professor of divinity was to be given full right to use the First Church half the time; the students were to be seated in the front gallery; the professor of divinity was to be permitted to preach while the students were in attendance.[36] These proposals were rejected by the First Church fathers, whereupon negotiations reached an impasse.

The following year the church officials adopted a new course

35. Clap and his wife were in covenant with the church. New Haven First Church Records, Pt. ii, X, 91, Conn. State Lib.
36. Yale Corporation Records, I, 110-11, Yale Univ.

of strategy designed to recover the students and at the same time subvert Clap's intended plan of conducting separate worship. They issued a call to Daggett, who was still serving his "apprenticeship," to settle as a junior colleague to Noyes on a permanent basis—Daggett on occasions had delivered sermons at the First Church.[37] This was not really an improvised plan since the First Church had been attempting since 1748 to secure a second minister in order to lighten the burden of their "aged Pastor," who could no longer cope with the multiplicity of duties brought on by increased membership; nor was it unusual for the larger churches of urban New England to maintain co-pastors.[38] It was the intention of the First Church, however, to eliminate two problems at one stroke. Recognizing that Daggett was under a moral commitment of sorts to the college, the officers of the First Church applied to Clap for his release from the obligations under which he had been placed; at the same time, they offered the job to Daggett. The president, however, refused to accede to the request, and sternly warned the young minister against accepting the pastoral position. Daggett rejected the offer.[39]

Realizing that Clap was adamant, the First Church now adopted a more conciliatory attitude. In January 1756, while Daggett was still "practice preaching," as it were, the First Church made new overtures to the president, conceding every point Clap and the Corporation had outlined in the list of conditions of 1754.[40] After some consideration, Clap agreed to proceed with the "experiment," but only until commencement in September.[41] By that time it was apparent to Clap that the arrangement was not working out satisfactorily—at least not to his satisfaction. As he informed the First Church, Daggett's sharing of assignments "had not answered the

37. New Haven First Church Records, 1715-1799, I, 65-66, Conn. State Lib.; *Connecticut Gazette* (New Haven), Jan. 24, 1756; Yale Corporation Records, I, 112, Yale Univ.; Connecticut Archives: Colleges and Schools, 1st Ser., Pt. ii, I, 320a, Conn. State Lib. The Assembly voted a sum of money for Noyes's colleague.

38. Clap himself had served as a member of a three-man committee, appointed in 1749, to suggest candidates for the position and present recommendations to the parishioners. New Haven First Church Records, 1639-1812, I, 26, Conn. State Lib.

39. Jared Eliot to Ezra Stiles, Mar. 18, 1756, Yale MS.; Dexter, ed., *Stiles's Itineraries,* 597.

40. New Haven First Church Records, 1715-1799, I, 67-68, Conn. State Lib.

41. Consent of the President and Fellows of Yale College to the Petition of the Rev. Noyes, Mar. 4, 1756, Yale MS.; Yale Corporation Records, I, 119, Yale Univ.

end proposed" and had been of no advantage to the parish. He noted further that "the meetings of the students there has been attended with many disadvantages to the College." Thus the "Treaty came to an End," and separate worship was resumed.[42] All hopes for reconciliation were now shattered. Verbal brickbats again filled the air.

The sequel to the feud took place in the spring meeting of the Corporation in 1757 when Clap and his supporters charged Joseph Noyes with heresy. Noyes was specifically accused of being "unsound in the Trinity, the divinity and satisfaction of Christ, Original Sin, Election, Regeneration, and the doctrines thereon depending." During the meeting, which apparently developed into a stormy session, Clap and his supporters "partly examined" Noyes. They judged his answers to be unsatisfactory and directed him to appear for further examination at the next meeting.[43] Noyes was absent due to illness. The Corporation then ordered him to appear at a special meeting the day following commencement exercises in September.[44]

While the official charge was heresy, Noyes's obvious "misdemeanor" was his stubborn opposition to Clap and his policies. This fact was patently clear to those close to the scene. As the Reverend (and Fellow) Jared Eliot succinctly summarized the issue: "They have resolved to examine Mr. Noyes the Day after Commencement, have notified him accordingly: orthodoxy is the grand Engine of Battery." [45] Another critic perceptively noticed that Clap's attack upon Noyes had developed progressively from carping comments on his poor preaching to this final tactic: "Now comes the fatal Engine. Ring the Bells backward! The Temple, the Temple of the Lord is on Fire! The Church is in Danger!" [46]

42. Yale Corporation Records, I, 122, Yale Univ.; Clap, *The Answer of the Friend in the West, to a Letter From a Gentleman in the East, Entitled, 'The Present State of the Colony of Connecticut Considered'* (New Haven, 1755), 13-14 (hereafter cited as Clap, *Answer of the Friend in the West*). The First Church subsequently appointed Chauncey Whittelsey as co-pastor. When Whittelsey was installed, the entire Yale entourage, with the notable exceptions of Clap and Daggett, attended the ceremony. Isaac Stiles to Ezra Stiles, Mar. 22, 1758, Yale MS.
43. Yale Corporation Records, I, 129-30, Yale Univ.
44. *Ibid.*, I, 130.
45. Eliot to Stiles, July 14, 1757, Yale MS.
46. Darling, *Remarks on Clap's History of Doctrines in New England*, 46.

The initial reaction of "Father" Noyes to the announcement
that he was to be tried for heresy was that of amused restraint as
expressed in his statement: "I am too old to be catechized." [47] He
regarded the accusation as demeaning to his dignity and a smirch
upon his illustrious lineage, a lineage as honored as any in New
England. Clap's persistence in the matter, however, coupled with
the gravity of the charges against him, brought an end to levity
and galvanized the testy, sixty-nine-year-old minister into a fighting mood. Inclined to be as obstinate as Clap on occasion, he defied
the president to remove him from the Corporation on which he
had served continuously, as a trustee and fellow, since 1735, five
years before Clap entered into the rectorship. He refused either
to resign or submit himself before the Corporation for an examination. On the day appointed for his examination, he forwarded to
Clap and the Corporation a nine-point document in which he
anatomized with surgical skill the decision to try him and listed
his reasons for refusing to appear. He charged that the law upon
which Clap and his supporters had relied in ordering his examination—provision seven of the "orthodoxy act"—was "unjust," "arbitrary," "unprecedented," and "illegal"; that it was inconsistent
with the ecclesiastical constitution of Yale; that it subjected him to
suffer in his character without means of defending himself; finally,
that it had no legal basis "except in Inquisition Courts." His removal, he stated flatly, could be effected only in compliance with
the conditions in the Charter of 1745. As a parting shot, he wrote:
"I do not esteem this Corporation so important and singular, or
the Ends to be promoted by it to be so Extraordinary and peculiar
a Nature, but that these Securitys, usually given to other Cor-
porations, may be sufficient for these." [48]

The Noyes affair had unexpectedly erupted into a messy bit of
business for Clap. Apparently, the president had not anticipated
such an obdurate stand by the crusty old minister. He was now
confronted with the question either of proceeding with the impeachment, and thereby incurring greater public criticism, or of

47. *Connecticut Courant* (Hartford), Apr. 22, 1783.
48. The document is printed in Dexter, ed., *Stiles's Itineraries*, 4-5. See also Jared
Eliot to Ezra Stiles, Sept. 17, 1757, Yale MS.; Yale Corporation Records, I, 132,
Yale Univ.

dropping the issue entirely and allowing him to remain on the Corporation. The situation was not only vexing but humiliating. Ultimately, he decided upon the latter course of action. The planned examination was not held; "And it was so generally esteemed an arbitrary Proceeding," Ezra Stiles wrote in his diary, "that the Corporation dropt it; and let Mr. Noyes die in peace and a Member of the Corporation to his Death, which happened June 14, 1761 at the age of 73." [49]

Clap was, of course, roundly denounced for the attempted impeachment of Noyes. Some, likening the incident to a "Star-Chamber" procedure, vituperated against the tyrannical and "un-English" character of the trial, with the accused being brought before his accusers on a suspicion rather than a formal charge, and not being allowed to defend himself in a legally acceptable manner. In a statement significant for its Whiggish intonations, one writer expressed his indignation over Clap's arbitrariness in these strong words: "For my Part, I choose to live under a Government, whose Laws won't suffer the Judges to be arbitrary, and oppressive, tho they were disposed to be so; rather than under One whose Judges, won't practice that Oppression and Tyranny, which the Laws allow." [50] The same writer assailed the proceedings as "proper only in the Star-Chamber, and High Commission Courts of Tyrants, and in the most holy Court of Inquisition." [51]

By 1757 the president was struggling desperately in the interminable sea of religious controversy. The wave of events which had started in 1753 with the withdrawal of the students from the First Church and which had recently generated the Noyes dispute now threatened to overwhelm him. Clap was no stranger to controversy, but in the past he had enjoyed support, as in the disputes of the Great Awakening. He had felt the stings and stabs of public contumely (as in the Breck, Brainerd, and Cleaveland incidents), but he never had been subjected to such intense and persistent

---

49. Dexter, ed., *Stiles's Itineraries*, 6; *Boston News-Letter*, July 2, 1761.
50. William Hart, *A Letter to a Friend: Wherein Some Free Thoughts Are Offered on the Subject of the Reverend Mr. Noyes's Proposed Examination by the Corporation of Yale College, and Their Erecting a Church Within the Same* (New Haven, 1757), 8 (hereafter cited as Hart, *Some Free Thoughts on Noyes's Examination*).
51. *Ibid.*, 5.

criticism as now fell upon him. Ringed by enemies, he was virtually the sole target of censure.

The Old Lights were up in arms against him for the manner in which he had effected a separation from the First Church. Presenting a type of argument familiar to the president, who had invoked it repeatedly during the Great Awakening, the Old Lights contended that Clap had acted without legal sanction. "A Separation which was disorderly and sinful at First," wrote William Hart, "could never become Right by Age, nor by the mere Favour and Smiles of the Great." [52] The Old Lights argued that the college was within the jurisdictional limits of the First Ecclesiastical Society of New Haven, and the students were therefore under the legal obligation to attend First Church services. They were insistent in the belief that Clap had flagrantly violated the Saybrook Platform, that he had committed an "illegal and disorderly" act. As Hart tartly stated the proposition: "I can't at present see, that our College-Church, was erected by any better Authority, than those of our Separatists." [53]

Powerful voices of dissent against Clap's program were also sounded in the Corporation, which had approved his measures, but not unanimously. The Corporation was a house divided against itself, with at least four fellows of the ten-man board (Clap was an ex officio fellow and voted only in the event of a tie) diametrically opposed to Clap's program. When the president first submitted for approval his measure to institute separate worship, these four fellows, the "Protestors," as they were labeled by Stiles, provided stern opposition, and the issue precipitated very warm debates.[54] Their opposition became more pronounced when Clap sought approval for his "orthodoxy act," Daggett's appointment, and the establishment of the college church. Decidedly more liberal than Clap in theological belief and more secular in outlook, these "Protestors" did not share Clap's conviction that Yale's primary function was to educate Congregational ministers. And because they were Old Lights, they viewed separation as inconsistent with the Saybrook Platform. Fortunately for Clap, at least three, and

52. *Ibid.,* 20.
53. *Ibid.,* 32.
54. Darling, *Remarks on Clap's History of Doctrines in New England,* 46.

possibly four, of the fellows were in general agreement with him on religious principles and on policy. These men lit their candle from his flame. This group, of whom Noah Hobart and Solomon Williams were the most prominent, consistently voted for his measures and formed a solid core of support. By the force of his bullying personality, combined with persuasion, Clap was able to gain the additional two or three votes necessary for a majority.[55]

But the president was not at all pleased with this situation, and when vacancies occurred he carefully selected fellows who either shared his views or could be bent to his will. Notice has already been directed to his efforts to eliminate dissident fellows. An apparent opportunity occurred in 1756 when Jared Eliot, the leading agitator of the anti-Clap faction, voluntarily offered to resign. Clap, however, was placed in the paradoxical position of having to oppose his resignation. The rub was that Eliot intended to submit his resignation not to the Corporation, as was customary, but to the General Assembly, scheduled to meet in October. Eliot's obvious purpose was to provoke a legislative investigation with the idea of shattering Clap's ironclad control. But the danger was that the intrusion of the Assembly into Yale's internal affairs would result in the assertion of legislative control over the college. Clap was desirous of removing a thorn from his side, but he did not care to raise the issue of Yale's relationship to the Assembly. Neither did the fellows of the college, notably Hobart,[56] who apparently succeeded in convincing Eliot that his intended move

55. Writing on the back of a letter he had received from Jared Eliot (July 14, 1757, Yale MS.), Ezra Stiles analyzed the Corporation and its voting on the critical professor of divinity issue. As Stiles saw it, Clap could directly influence four fellows (Benjamin Lord, Anthony Stoddard, Elnathan Whitman, and Ashbel Woodbridge) and was influenced by two (his Harvard colleagues, Solomon Williams and Noah Hobart). The "Protestors" were Jared Eliot, Joseph Noyes, and Thomas Ruggles. The latter three plus William Russel were opposed to the proposal for a chair of divinity. Lord, Williams, and Hobart were in favor of it. Stoddard, Woodbridge, and Whitman remained indifferent. According to Stiles, Clap brought his influence to bear upon the latter three, insisting that orthodoxy was in peril and warning that prospective students would be drawn away by Princeton if the measure went under. (Even in the eighteenth century no self-respecting Yale man wished to have Princeton gain the upper hand.) The issue necessitated a second meeting at which Russel was absent. The vote for Daggett's appointment came at this meeting. The "Protestors" naturally protested, but to no avail.

56. Hobart to Eliot, Sept. 25, 1756, Yale MS. Hobart carried his argument to absurd lengths to dissuade Eliot. He even advanced the proposition that posterity would construe Eliot's action as a discharge rather than a voluntary act.

was not the best course of action. Eliot did not follow through on his resignation. Whatever their differences, as this incident reveals, the fellows as an aggregate were united in the belief that Yale should remain independent of legislative control. Yale had moved steadily and inexorably in the direction of autonomy since its founding.

The interposal of Fellow Hobart in the Eliot incident did not mean that Clap remained in the background during this period of flaming controversy. While he presumably played a behind-the-scenes role in Hobart's attempt to placate Eliot, and later commissioned a functionary to write pamphlets against the pestiferous Benjamin Gale, Clap was prone to assume personally the responsibility of defending his policies and private honor. For Marcus Aurelius's injunction to those in positions of authority—"Live as if on a mountain"—he had no enthusiasm. Then, too, the tradition was clearly established that the president of a colonial college was ultimately responsible for everything that affected the reputation of the school. To criticize Yale was to criticize Clap.

Conviction also was a factor in Clap's pugnaciousness. The president was fired by the certainty that his cause was righteous, that he was on "God's side." In all his acts, whether expelling students for engaging in separatist activities or abruptly separating the college from the First Church, he was animated by a scrupulous sense of duty, swerving not one degree from the lines of conduct marked out by his religious principles. Whatever the personal consequences, he was determined to maintain Yale's Congregational character. He would truckle to no man, and he refused to be intimidated by popular disfavor. He confided to a friend in 1758, when he was being scourged on all sides, that "the most virulent opposition and injurious Reflections ordinarily move me but little being fully persuaded, that [it] is the important cause of Christ, and the salvation of Precious Souls, I am engaged in." [57] At the age of sixty, he wrote in his Memoirs: "I have for above 40 Years had a steady and confirmed Hope; and upon a strickt Review I think my great steady and ultimate End and Design, has been to do and fulfil the Will of God and to promote his Glory. And my governing Principle always has been to do that which God would

57. Clap to Mrs. Williams, July 24, Pa. Hist. Soc. MS.

approve and justifie in the great Day." [58] There can be no doubt
of his conviction that he was engaged in a holy cause.

Clap's intransigence in matters of religion expressed the general
set of his personality. Endowed with a combative temper, he had a
robust appetite for controversy, and for compromise he had no
talent. To be sure, there were times when he deplored the fact
that he was a center of controversy. In July 1742, for example, at
the height of the Great Awakening, he confessed to a clerical correspondent: "I am quite Tired and Sick of all public Controversie
they are destructive to all the natural and spiritual Comforts of
Life I wish I could live a more retired life. . . . I could be more of
a master of my own time and thots and enjoy more Communion
with God." [59] Yet when pricked with criticism, he reacted immediately, and when his passions were aroused, he was not given
to forbearance.

While standing toe-to-toe against his Anglican detractors, Clap
also defended himself against the Old Lights. In 1754, he wrote
The Religious Constitution of Colleges in which he made explicit
the reasons justifying the policy of separate worship and the
establishment of a chair of divinity. He argued, in a temperate
manner, that colleges by their very nature possessed the attributes
and powers of ecclesiastical societies. They were "Religious Societies, of a Superior Nature to all others," and established for the
purpose of training youth for the ministry. It was, therefore, altogether proper for the officials of Yale to provide a Congregational
type of religious instruction. To buttress his argument, Clap piled
up the precedents afforded by European history and the legal
opinions rendered by prominent men of English jurisprudence,
particularly Sir Edward Coke. For further historical support, he
turned to other "proofs," to the preamble of the original Charter,
to the written statements of the first trustees, and to his own
Charter of 1745 and orthodoxy act. On the basis of this assorted
evidence, the president concluded that the college governors held
a legal right to shape religious policy as they saw fit. The founders,
he declared, had established Yale as a feeder for the Congregational
Church, and "the present Governors of the College; esteem them-

58. July 7, 1763.
59. Clap to the Rev. Solomon Williams, Pa. Hist. Soc. MS.

selves, bound by Law, and the more sacred Ties of Conscience, and Fidelity to their Trust, committed to them by their Predecessors; to pursue, and carry on, the pious Intention, and Design, of the Founders."

The Old Lights may have been duly impressed by Clap's powerful logic and prodigious erudition, but they were not convinced by his arguments, either as to the legality of separation or the historical relationship of Yale and Congregationalism. The Old Lights all but destroyed this latter thesis by noting that only a small proportion of Yale graduates were entering the Congregational ministry; [60] from 1740 to 1750, for example, only 71 of a total of 179 graduates became ministers, and of these 10 per cent became Anglican clergymen.[61] Similarly, the Old Lights scornfully condemned as puerile Clap's contention that colleges were of a "superior nature" to other religious societies. Old Light William Hart snarled: "What is this 'superior' Nature of Colleges, to all other religious Societies? Are they in their Nature, of superior Worth and excellence, or of superior Honour and Dignity, or of superior Power and Authority?" Hart answered in the negative on each count.[62] And Thomas Darling likewise blasted Clap's interpretation of Yale as a "ministry-factory" (as Darling crudely phrased it).

Though his arguments were torn to shreds and made to appear ludicrous by the Old Lights, the president tenaciously held to his position. When Old Light reaction became excessively severe, he hitched his horse to chaise and "toured the country," proclaiming to one and all that his religious program was working well and that the students were more orderly now than before.[63] It was, in effect, a public relations campaign calculated to elicit mass support for his program.

When a torrent of Old Light criticism swept down upon him for impeaching Noyes, he struck back with the accusation that Noyes

60. Hart, *Some Free Thoughts on Noyes's Examination*, 25.
61. A breakdown, by decades, is listed in Alpheus C. Hodges, "Yale Graduates in Western Massachusetts," New Haven Colony Hist. Soc., *Papers*, 4 (1888), 258. See also Bailey B. Burritt, "Professional Distribution of College and University Graduates," United States, Bureau of Education, *Bulletin*, No. 19 (1912), 83.
62. Hart, *Some Free Thoughts on Noyes's Examination*, 23-24.
63. Darling, *Remarks on Clap's History of Doctrines in New England*, 49-50.

was an Arminian and therefore a menace to orthodoxy. The college officials could not in good conscience permit the students to attend "another Society where Arminianism or Doctrines tending to promote Arminianism are preached; and some of the fundamental Doctrines of the Gospel are neglected and laid aside." [64] In an earlier day, Clap had forborne to level gross accusations against Noyes. Now he struck him with the charge of Arminianism, which, from the conservative point of view, was the greatest error in the current catalogue of religious heresies.

Needless to say, Clap's conduct in the period 1750-57 was inimical to his personal popularity. By his illiberal policies and personal actions, he managed to alienate a host of people in Connecticut and elsewhere, including a number of prominent religious and political leaders. In truth, he had a genius for cultivating enemies who came to resent the officious airs which made him appear to be a bulldog among spaniels. They came to suspect that he was motivated more by the desire for personal power (and pelf) than by the wish to preserve orthodoxy, that the summit of his ambition was to become the Protestant pope of Connecticut. They deprecated his self-professed ideals, and they ridiculed the theological positions he assumed in defending them. One Old Light stated that Clap's "new scheme" represented a "medley and motley mixture of errors, that no one man ever fell into." [65] Another wrote that "Mr. President has drawn up a Scheme of Religion, which I think ought to be called after his own Name, 'Clapism,' as being his own Invention, and having no Existence before it was coin'd in his own Brain." [66] And in 1765, after Robert Sandeman, the left-wing English religious leader, had toured Connecticut, Benjamin Gale, with characteristic cutting sarcasm, suggested that another edition of Clap's defense of New England doctrines be run off and Sandeman's principles be "splicd onto the *New Scheme of Religion.*" Sandeman's tenets,

---

64. Clap, Reasons Why It is Necessary That the Sacrament Should be Administered in the College, June 30, 1757, Yale MS.
65. William Hart, *A Few Remarks Upon the Ordination of the Reverend Mr. James Dana, and the Doings of the Consociation, Respecting the Same: Being a Letter, to the Author of the 'Faithful Narrative, etc.'* (New Haven, 1759), 34-35.
66. Darling, *Remarks on Clap's History of Doctrines in New England,* 30.

continued Gale, could be neatly attached to that portion of Clap's creed which held forth on the salvation of devils.[67]

Through the writings and public and private statements of such influential ministers and magistrates as Thomas Darling, Thomas Ruggles, William Hart, Jared Eliot, Benjamin Gale, and Joseph Noyes, Clap came to be represented to the general populace as a power-mad clerical tyrant. Darling, the son-in-law of Joseph Noyes, wrote: "The President's desire of Power and Grandeur is boundless. The more officers or Professors, Chaplains, Tutors, etc. he has under him, the more august will he appear." [68] Benjamin Gale, the son-in-law of Jared Eliot, further developed the "image." Gale, who dedicated himself to driving Clap from office, published a number of inflammatory pamphlets which were intended "to Convince the World that the President was an Assuming, Arbitrary, Designing Man; who under a Cloak of Zeal for Orthodoxy, design'd to govern both Church and State, and Damn all who would not worship the Beast." [69] To describe his executive superior in such an unflattering manner would have been unbecoming, if not impolitic, for Tutor Chauncey Whittelsey, but even he remarked upon Clap's uncommon officiousness and authoritarian bent. When Clap arbitrarily ordered an early commencement in 1762, an exasperated Whittelsey confided to Ezra Stiles: "I am sometimes ready to think, he only aims by new things and unusual Methods of managing to make People attend *to him,* to render himself somebody." [70] The indomitable Clap had ruled the college with the authority of an Oriental despot. But now in the 1750's there were many who, as Whittelsey sarcastically phrased it, scorned "to Dance after the old Man's Whims," who questioned his decisions, objected to his policies, and, most significantly, challenged his authority.

It was indeed an age in which questioning, objecting to, and

67. Gale to Ezra Stiles, Feb. 28, 1765, Yale MS.

68. Darling, *Remarks on Clap's History of Doctrines in New England,* 45.

69. Gale to Jared Ingersoll, Aug. 9, 1762, Franklin Dexter, ed., "Jared Ingersoll Papers," New Haven Colony Hist. Soc., *Papers,* 9 (1918), 276.

70. July 23, 1762, Yale MS. At least one New Havener who pronounced damnation upon Clap and other college officials during this period later felt a twinge of remorse. On Dec. 17, 1764, an anonymous letter appeared in the *Connecticut Courant* (Hartford) in which the writer asked forgiveness for his prior incendiary statements against Clap *et al.*

challenging authority were becoming fashionable. To the Whigs of Connecticut, who were just beginning to articulate the natural rights philosophy of Locke, Harrington, Gordon, Trenchard, *et al.*, the Yale issue came to be viewed in a wider perspective—as a microcosmical event in the eternal struggle of liberty and absolutism. It was an appropriate frame of reference. The spirit of nascent Whiggism was evident in these bristling words of Darling, directed against Clap and his subalterns:

These Things will never go down in a free State, where People are bred in, and breathe a free Air, and are formed upon Principles of Liberty; they might Answer in a Popish Country, or in Turkey, where the common People are sunk and degraded almost to the State of Brutes, by Poverty, Chains and absolute Tyranny, and have no more Sense of Liberty and Property, th[a]n so many Jack-asses: But in a free State they will be eternally ridiculed and abhorred . . . 'Tis too late in the Day for these Things; these Gentlemen should have lived 12 or 13 Hundred Years ago, or they should have been born in a Popish Country, then they would have had something to do: But as to us in this Country, we are Free-born, and have the keenest sense of Liberty.[71]

In the same vein, Henry Babcock of Newport, a future military leader in the American Revolution, wrote Darling that he had read his "excellent" pamphlet and "hope you will continue to secure the cause of Freedom and Liberty of Conscience from all Invaders of how sanctifie'd a Name soever they may be." [72] The Whigs were pointing up ideas that were soon to be sharpened to a whetted edge. Connecticut had discovered the "Royal Brute!"

A religious issue at the outset, the Yale controversy gravitated into the neighboring realm of politics; religion and politics were virtually inseparable in eighteenth-century Connecticut. The controversy provoked wide discussion throughout the colony and aroused the attention of the freemen. By 1755 it was the burning issue of the day. In the course of the dispute, weighty questions were raised relative to the nature and purpose of Yale, the relationship of the school to the General Assembly, and the extent of authority of the Corporation and President Clap; in another

71. Darling, *Remarks on Clap's History of Doctrines in New England*, 109-10.
72. Nov. 17, 1757, N.-Y. Hist. Soc. MS.

decade, the colonies and the Crown were to debate virtually the same vexing propositions in the context of imperial relations. Thus the Yale controversy was destined to be thrashed out in the political arena. The legion of anti-Clap forces viewed the prospect with keen anticipation. They realized that only through political action—only through the intervention of the General Assembly— would it be possible to dislodge Clap from his seat of absolute power.

Chapter Nine

BENJAMIN GALE BLOWS UP
A POLITICAL STORM

SINCE ministerial days in Windham, President Clap had locked horns with many formidable adversaries, but he had scarcely encountered anyone quite like Benjamin Gale [1] (Yale, 1733) of Killingworth, Connecticut. Gale's uniqueness did not stem from his polymorphous abilities—from the fact that he was a distinguished physician (one of the best in the colony), a competent scientist, and a prominent political leader. Not a few of Clap's earlier opponents had displayed like versatility and proficiency. What set Gale apart from the ordinary run of disputants were his traits of character—his volatile temperament and bulldog tenacity. He was, without a doubt, the most pertinacious adversary Clap had ever encountered. Once his teeth were sunk into an opponent nothing could shake him off.

Consumed with a passionate, uncompromising hatred for religious bigotry, especially as exemplified by the rigid Calvinists, this "singular Character," as Stiles once referred to him, was bound and determined to break the glacial grip of the clergy upon

1. On Gale, see George Groce, "Benjamin Gale," *New Eng. Qtly.*, 10 (1937), 697-16; Dexter, *Yale Graduates*, I, 477-78.

the thought and institutions of Connecticut.[2] He was, in his own
words, "a sworn Enemy to all sorts of Tyranny, civil, military and
ecclesiastical." [3] Gale had watched Clap for many years with a disapproval that had slowly mounted to the point of outrage. In his
view there resided in Connecticut no greater religious bigot, no
greater ecclesiastical tyrant, than President Clap. He was old
priest writ large.

While family affiliation possibly entered into Gale's bitter dis-
like of Clap (Gale was the son-in-law of Jared Eliot), the immediate
basis of his detestation was a clash over religious matters and a
difference of conviction as to the nature and function of the
college. Heavily influenced by the secular currents of the Enlightenment, Gale was an unmuzzled advocate of the separation of
church and state, and of the noninterference of the clergy in civil
and political affairs. As to the nature and function of the college,
he took a position diametrically opposed to that of Clap, con-
tending that it was a secular institution responsive to the public
will, and designed to train youth for all the professions. In sum,
he stressed the theme of the assimilation of the college to society.
He could find no justifiable reason for the Corporation to consist
solely of men from the "priestly Orders," or for the president to
be a Congregationalist minister. He once outlined the qualifications of a Yale president in these words of sarcasm: "the greatest
Bigot, the most Orthodox, the most obstinate Temper, . . . and
the Least Gentleman are the necessary Qualifications in order to
be pronounced fitt for the Chair and a moderate Stock of Knowledge with all the foregoing will make a finished and shining
Character." [4] There was no mistaking the model from whom these
qualifications were drawn. For the obstreperous Gale, Clap per-
sonified all that he abhorred: he was a hidebound bigot, the arche-
type of clerical absolutism; he was incessantly meddling in civil
and political affairs, seeking to impose his will upon the government. He must be destroyed. With relentless singleness of purpose,
Gale strove to accomplish the task.

2. See Ezra Stiles's characterization of Gale in Dexter, ed., *Literary Diary of
Stiles*, III, 393.
3. Quoted in Groce, "Gale," *New Eng. Qtly.*, 10 (1937), 701.
4. Dexter, ed., *Stiles's Itineraries*, 491; Gale to Stiles, Aug. 23, 1766, Yale MS.

When the Old Lights let loose their tirade upon Clap, Gale, an Old Light in political conviction,[5] joined in the general clamor; but to a greater degree than most Old Light denigrators, he was persistent, systematic, and purposeful in his criticism. The Old Lights generally railed against Clap with no other idea than to express disapproval of his policies. Gale criticized with a predetermined aim: to force his resignation or secure his dismissal through legislative action. Accordingly, Gale's criticism (at least at the outset) had a twofold purpose. Initially, it was designed to inflame public opinion against Clap. More important, perhaps, it was intended to induce the General Assembly to impose financial sanctions upon the college; that is, to suspend all further monetary assistance until the college authorities, especially Clap, would accept an investigation of the school by a select legislative committee. Gale was apparently convinced that the college could not operate without the financial assistance of the legislature. The withdrawal of the annual grant alone would force Clap to yield on the matter of legislative inquiry. And once the legislature, which was controlled by the Old Lights, was enabled to conduct an investigation, the termination of Clap's powerful hold on the college would all but be assured.

To grasp the full import of Gale's plan, it is necessary to clarify the relationship of Yale to the legislature. Although the relationship was not explicitly defined by document, it had been taken for granted since the founding of Yale that the Assembly was to serve as a sort of benevolent patron. It would provide financial support and, whenever the occasion should demand, intervene to settle serious difficulties. Accordingly, the Assembly, although not represented on the Yale governing body, provided the college with a yearly stipend of £100, assumed the expense of repairing college buildings, issued generous sums of money to help pay for the construction of new buildings and the hiring of additional tutors, and occasionally intervened to settle administrative disputes and investigate severe student disturbances. In

5. Paradoxically, Clap and Gale were political bedfellows during the Great Awakening. This fact underscores the inchoate state of politics of colonial Connecticut. John Adams's terse description of the political organization of colonial New York ("devil's own incomprehensibles") also has meaningful application for Connecticut.

the early years, the college governors did not challenge the right of the legislature to dabble in academic affairs. Since the college was dependent upon legislative financial assistance, the Yale officials were in no position to resist such intrusions even if they chose. In any case, they did not choose to resist; the Yale authorities were still imbued with "church-state" concepts. Functioning under the aegis of the established Congregational Church, Yale was widely regarded as an appendage to the Assembly: it was one arm of Connecticut's vaunted Congregational System. Therefore, the Yale governors obsequiously accepted legislative interference.

By the 1740's, however, and particularly after Clap readjusted Yale's administrative machinery in 1745, a perceptible change developed in the relationship between the Yale governing body and the Assembly. Relations became chilled. It has been noted elsewhere that even as early as the 1720's the college officials had begun to manifest displeasure over legislative intrusions. Their collective attitude became clannish. By the 1740's the displeasure of earlier years had hardened into feelings of resistance, not defiant, but nevertheless conspicuous.

It is true that the college governors, including Clap, continued to acknowledge in a mechanical, self-conscious manner that the Assembly held supreme authority over the college; but, significantly, they studiously refrained after 1745 from seeking legislative assistance in times of internal disorder. They accepted the annual subsidy and expected the Assembly to provide contingent financial aid for such items as the construction of new buildings (Connecticut Hall) and maintenance costs for other physical facilities.[6] They knew full well that the college could not survive on private resources. Yet they wished to exclude the Assembly from the management of internal affairs. In some respects, Yale's dilemma paralleled that of Connecticut's government in its relationship with the Crown.

In the early 1750's, after Clap had established separate worship,

6. The *Connecticut Records* are studded with "grants" and other monetary concessions to Yale; see vols. VIII, IX, X, XII, *passim*. See also, Connecticut Archives: Colleges and Schools, 1st Ser., Pt. ii, I, 259, 260, 273a, 318a; *ibid.*, 2d Ser., I, 41a, Conn. State Lib.

some of the Old Lights (particularly Gale) began agitating for a legislative investigation of the college. These Old Lights were still acting on the traditional assumption that the college was subject to legislative authority. Up to this time, the question of the relationship of college to Assembly had not been publicly debated. Clap, alarmed by the rising demand for a legislative inquiry, now posited the thesis that only the founders and their successors had a legal right to appoint "visitors." [7] The issue immediately became: which body was the "founding agent"—the ministers who had originally organized the college, or the General Assembly that had granted the original charter and provided generous monetary assistance? It was Clap's contention, which he based on the opinions of distinguished English jurists and the principles of English common law, that the original group of ten ministers constituted the "founding agent." [8] Clap thus directly challenged the right of the Assembly to interfere in Yale's management.

A practical man by temperament, Assemblyman Gale regarded Clap's legal arguments as pure casuistry, to say the least. His common-sense view of the matter was that since the college derived most of its income from public funds, the legislature had a legal right to supervise its affairs—an idea which continues to dominate the thinking of American politicians. In 1755 he launched his campaign to discredit Clap by publishing a polemic, *The Present State of the Colony of Connecticut Considered.* It was signed A. Z. and presented in the form of a personal letter—a conventional literary device of the period. This inflammatory treatise marked the first direct public attack upon Clap since the Great Awakening. With its appearance the Yale controversy, until now largely localized, broadened into a colony-wide political issue.

Ostensibly written as a plea for the reduction of governmental spending in the face of impending war with the French and Indians, Gale's pamphlet was really intended to persuade the General Assembly to withhold the £100 annual subsidy to the college. Gale adroitly timed its release to coincide with the regular May meeting of the Assembly when the grant was to be acted

7. Clap, *Religious Constitution of Colleges*, 1-2.
8. Clap, *Answer of the Friend in the West*, 15-16.

upon.[9] Much of the pamphlet was familiar Old Light cant. Aside from personal barbs, Gale lashed out at Clap for converting Yale into a Congregational "school of the prophets." On the important question of visitation, he challenged Clap's contention that Yale was beyond legislative reach. In Gale's view, the college was nothing more than a "Guild" or "Fraternity" that had received a license to operate from the Assembly. It therefore was subject to the authority of the Assembly.

The main feature of the pamphlet was a meticulously specific examination of the financial condition of the college. Gale stuffed his pages with facts and figures arranged to convey the impression that the college revenues were sufficiently large to cover the cost of operation without the need of Assembly aid. It was impressive arithmetic. Indeed, the pamphlet as a whole was an impressive document. In turn of phrase and twist of argument, Gale's statements were plausible enough to persuade the casual as well as the critical reader. Nothing could have been better calculated to set in motion the avalanche of public criticism. The pamphlet found willing readers in the homes and alehouses of Connecticut, and in short order became a reference source for anti-Clap dissidents throughout the colony.

Caught off-guard by Gale's pamphlet, and understandably apprehensive of its likely effect on the Assembly and on public opinion, Clap quickly published a rejoinder, *Answer of the Friend in the West;* and so began another of the seemingly endless number of virulent pamphlet battles in colonial American history.[10] Clap's general purpose was to show that Gale's pamphlet contained, in Disraeli's classic definition of the three degrees of untruthfulness, "lies, damned lies, and statistics." In the literary guise of a close friend to Gale, Clap made answer to Gale's charges point by point. He defended separation and the appointment of the divinity professor, still maintaining that Yale was a religious society occupying a peculiarly high status in the community. He again proclaimed the autonomy of the Corporation with respect to visitation: a

9. The government convened in May and Oct. of each year. The May session was held in Hartford, the Oct. meeting in New Haven; Hartford and New Haven were co-capitals.

10. The list of Gale's pamphlets can be seen in Dexter, *Yale Graduates,* I, 478-80.

founding agent was one who "first erects and endows," not one who issues a charter and provides a yearly grant of money.

While all areas of the dispute were touched upon, Clap's primary aim was to discredit Gale's thesis that Yale was in a prosperous financial condition. He lavished scorn upon Gale's computations, pointing out that he had "over-magnified and mis-represented" college accounts—"Many people will be much amused by such Computations." Connecticut, he asserted, was on a sound financial footing and could well afford the annual grant. The pamphlet concluded with an impassioned appeal for renewal of the subsidy, which was "not more to each Man, than an Half-penny Sterling, a Pint of Cyder, or one quarter of a Pound of Tobacco, per annum."

An accomplished controversialist, Clap fell back upon traditional smear techniques in an effort to discredit his adversary. Thus he linked Gale with the Arminian movement, and more specifically with John Taylor (1694-1761) of Norwich, England, a chief secular saint of the Enlightenment, whose work *The Scripture Doctrine of Original Sin Proposed to a Free and Candid Examination* had been instrumental in weakening one of the main pillars of the Calvinist theological structure. If Clap was to be represented as a colonial counterpart of the pope, it was altogether proper (so Clap apparently reasoned) that Gale should be projected as a nonbeliever who was seeking to raze long-standing Christian institutions and promote infidelity. Clap thereby placed God by his side in the trench of orthodoxy and Gale at the opposite end of the battle field with the heretics. The president issued this chilling admonition: "If orthodoxy be right, Dear Sir, you will be found to fight against God."

Even before Clap's pamphlet could reach the inns of Connecticut, the Assembly voted to suspend the grant, citing as justification the high expenditures of the war against the French.[11] Whether

---

11. Making no mention of Gale, Clap, in his *Annals of Yale* (p. 52), attributed the suspension of the grant to the war and the attendant drain on Connecticut's financial resources. That Connecticut was not in serious financial trouble, as Clap himself had asserted in his answer to Gale, is evidenced by the research of Charles M. Andrews and Lawrence H. Gipson. Compare Andrews, *Our Earliest Colonial Settlements* ... (N. Y., 1933), 128; Gipson, "Taxation in Connecticut 1750-1775," Conn. Tercentenary Com., *Publications*, No. 10 (1933).

Clap's work would have halted this action is questionable. It is also dubious, for that matter, whether Gale's pamphlet, persuasive as it was, was the chief determinant of the Assembly's action.[12] Probably a more important factor was the dominance of the Assembly by Old Lights. Although not completely limited in viewpoint, nor infused with the same religious zeal that inspired the Old Lights of the Great Awakening, this group still acknowledged the authority of the Saybrook Platform. On this basis, they were obdurately opposed to Clap's program of separate worship, judging it to be illegal as well as a menace to social and religious stability. By refusing to act on the grant, the Old Lights were merely registering, in a most effective manner, their disapproval of Clap's policies.[13] By so doing, they served notice to Clap that he was *persona non grata* in the Old Light movement.

Shortly after the suspension of the grant, the president underwent what the puzzled Chauncey Whittelsey described as a "transmutation."[14] He severed longstanding ties with the Old Lights and transferred his allegiance to the political New Lights— as of 1755, he acquired the sobriquet "New Light Pope."[15] It was a startling reversal. To his contemporaries, it was incomprehensible that he could now break political bread with a group against whom he had fought tooth and nail less than a decade earlier.[16]

The general astonishment aroused by Clap's about-face under-

12. Convinced that Gale was the culprit singly responsible for the Assembly's action, Fellow Noah Hobart, probably in complicity with Clap, flayed him with a vicious satiric blast. *A Congratulatory Letter From a Gentleman in the West, to His Friend in the East; Upon the Success of His Letter, Entituled, 'The Present State of the Colony of Connecticut Considered'* (New Haven, 1755).

13. Ezra Stiles also came to this conclusion. The Yale Library has a copy of the Oct. 18, 1755, issue of the *Connecticut Gazette* (New Haven) that has some perceptive marginal comments by Stiles. The paper lists the representatives returned in the General Assembly. Stiles noted that the New Lights represented one-third of the representatives, and he added that the Old Lights withdrew the annual grant under the pretext of war expenses but actually because Clap had set up separate worship.

14. "But what shall we say of that transmutation he underwent from 1754 to 1757?" Dexter, ed., *Stiles' Itineraries*, 461n.

15. *Ibid.*, 492.

16. Note the reaction of Darling, *Some Remarks on Clap's History of Doctrines in New England,* 50-51.

scores his importance as a political figure. Indeed, the president took a keen and active interest in politics, both on the local and the colony level. He was in frequent contact with the Assembly on matters relating to Yale; in a real sense, Clap functioned as a one-man lobby for the college. It had been largely due to his persuasive efforts that the Assembly had taken such an active financial interest in Yale, and his personal influence had also been instrumental in securing legislative approval of the revolutionary Charter of 1745. But his dealings with the Assembly often went beyond academic business. A man of "natural Despotism and high notions of Dominion," he could scarcely abstain from trying to influence the course of public affairs, at least in matters of religion. In this sense, he was an anachronism, for he expected to wield the authority of a seventeenth-century cleric. During the Great Awakening, he had become deeply involved in politics, acquiring the reputation of a main pillar of the Old Light party. It was because of his affiliation with the Old Lights that many, including some among his own inner circle, were confounded by his sudden apostasy.

Actually, Clap's reversal was a reasonable course of action. That he was out of favor with the Old Lights there could be no doubt, and it was the first time in his presidential career that he was alienated from the dominant political party of the colony. He was now a political outcast, a discredited Old Light without influence and without friends in the government who would support him in his program. This latter condition made the situation grave, for Clap realized that it would be exceedingly difficult, perhaps impossible, to operate the college without financial assistance from the Assembly. As for securing the money by sanctioning a legislative investigation—this was out of the question, since it would undoubtedly result in the destruction of separate worship, and might possibly bring about a reduction of his personal authority by legislative decree, or even his outright dismissal. Of course, additional funds could be secured for the college by raising tuition fees, but this move was inexpedient because it would more than likely produce a storm of parental reaction. Already there was grumbling over the rising cost of education at Yale. Moreover, an increase in tuition might conceivably lead to a drop in enrollment, as prospective students would enter other colleges where rates were lower. Yale already competed with other schools, most notably Princeton (then known as the College of New Jersey), in attracting students.[17]

Mere expediency dictated Clap's switch in political alliance. As a New Light, he was assured of substantial legislative support. The New Light party, although still a minority, was gaining strength in the legislature, particularly in the power-wielding lower house. There was a strong possibility that it might wrest control from the Old Lights in the very near future, in which case Clap would again be in a commanding position to request financial aid for Yale.

A second factor to consider in analyzing Clap's decision is the change in the character of the New Lights that had occurred by the middle of the century.[18] Significant changes in political alignment had taken place since the revival period when the first coherent political parties appeared. The original parties were based almost wholly on religious issues. Social and economic factors had entered in, to be sure, but they were by and large subordinate. With the abatement of the Awakening, however, religious issues were devaluated, and other issues, particularly of an economic nature, assumed major importance. The titles of the parties remained, but the parties themselves spoke a new dialogue. Whereas separatism, enthusiasm, itineracy, and the like had been key issues, the Susquehannah Land Company now became a determining factor in political alignments.[19]

On religious matters, too, the parties had shifted. The Old Lights, although still largely representative of the Standing Order, were no longer considered the party of staunch orthodoxy. Many active members, especially the leaders, were pronounced latitudi-

17. Beverly McAnear, "The Selection of an Alma Mater by Pre-Revolutionary Students," *Pennsylvania Magazine of History and Biography,* 73 (1949), 429-40.
18. There is no single exhaustive study of the political developments in pre-Revolutionary Connecticut. The most useful secondary sources are: Edmund S. and Helen M. Morgan, *The Stamp Act Crisis, Prologue to Revolution* (Chapel Hill, 1953), 224-25; Zeichner, *Connecticut's Years of Controversy,* 25-27; Edith Bailey, *Influences Toward Radicalism in Connecticut, 1754-1755,* Smith College *Studies in History,* 5 (1920), 226-30.
19. Julian Boyd, "The Susquehannah Company: Connecticut's Experiment in Expansion." Conn. Tercentenary Com., *Publications,* No. 34 (1935).

narians. The change in religious outlook is best exemplified by Benjamin Gale, a prototypal Old Light of the 1750's, just as Clap had been a prototypal Old Light during the years of the Awakening. Gale was a member of the Standing Order and conservative in social philosophy, but on the other hand he was a Universalist in religious conviction and a dedicated opponent of clericalism.

The New Lights of the 1750's, likewise, were no longer the party of militant revivalism. Many of them, if they had one eye focused on heaven, fixed the other on their pocketbooks—an ambivalence revealed in the membership of the Susquehannah Company, which was largely composed of New Lights. The party still adhered to the religious doctrines of the Awakening, however, and secular interests were counterbalanced by a pietistic element which gave to the political movement as a whole a fervently moralistic tone. But New Light political doctrine had now become leavened with the conservative religious principles of the "new divinity"—the reconstituted Calvinism of Edwards, Samuel Hopkins, and Joseph Bellamy. With such a religious system Clap had no reason for dissent, although he never bothered to analyze it carefully and examine the full implications of its key doctrines; to the other aspects of the movement Clap could well be indifferent. Politics concerned him only so far as religious issues were at stake. The Dana dispute, of which more later, is a case in point.[20] With respect to such raging, colony-wide issues as the Susquehannah land controversy and, later, the Stamp Act crisis, he remained an interested but passive bystander. The position of the New Lights on purely secular issues would be of little consequence to him.

If Benjamin Gale was pleased by Clap's secession from the Old Lights, he was under no illusion that Clap proposed to surrender his authority. It was apparent to Gale in 1755 that Clap was stubbornly intent upon operating the college without the support of the legislature. But Gale was not one to abandon the contest. With the persistence of an Ahab, he tracked his opponent with single-minded dedication. For the next eight years, an unbroken stream of abuse flowed from his mouth and pen, the acerbic nature of which can be readily gathered from a summary examination of the

20. Discussed below, pp. 215-19.

pamphlets he published.[21] Exercising no restraint, Gale tore at the
vitals of Clap's personal character and administrative policies.
His charges were scurrilous and all-pervasive, ranging from malad-
ministration to corruption and embezzlement of funds by Clap
and other college officials. He placed special stress upon Clap's
harsh disciplinary system, particularly multiple fines upon individuals. The president's "arbitrary and oppressive Exactions" had
been outlandishly high from the outset, Gale wrote in one of his
philippics, but lately they had been still further increased to compensate for the loss of revenues resulting from the withdrawal of
the annual grant. He sarcastically observed that it would have been
better had the Assembly voted to continue the grant since Clap
"seems determined to have the Money, by Hook or by Crook." [22]

And did fines deter wrongdoing? Did they induce virtuous
habits? Not in the least, was Gale's ready answer. He pointed to
the repeated student riots which had rocked the college; "Tumults
and Insurrections" were becoming commonplace. Fines, wrote
Gale, hardened the students against all correction, corrupted the
morals of youth and taught them to hate their governors; they also
filled the pockets of these same governors. In the universal manner
of critics who have never been engaged in disciplining a troop of
young Hotspurs, he suggested that more humane methods be
employed, that Clap and the tutors substitute moral suasion for
force and compulsion, that they exercise "a wise mixture of
Authority and Love, and fatherly Tenderness and Compassion." [23]

A second point which Gale emphasized was the denial to stu-

21. Three are especially noteworthy: Gale, *A Letter to a Member of the Lower
House of the Assembly of the Colony of Connecticut: Shewing, That the Taxes of
Yale College Are Stated Higher Than Necessary to Defray the Annual Expences of
That School; by Which a Very Considerable Addition Is Made to the College
Treasury Annually. With Some General Observations on the Laws and Government
of That Society. By a Lover of Truth, and His Country* (New Haven, 1759) (here-
after cited as Gale, *Letter to a Member of the Lower House*); Gale, *A Calm and
Full Vindication of a Letter, Wrote to a Member of the Lower House of Assembly ...
Being a Full Answer to a Letter ... With Some Further Remarks on the Laws and
Government of That Society* (New Haven, 1759) (hereafter cited as Gale, *Calm and
Full Vindication*); Gale, *A Few Brief Remarks on Mr. Graham's Answer; and on
His Vindication of Mr. President Clap* (New Haven, 1760) (hereafter cited as Gale,
Few Brief Remarks on Mr. Graham's Answer).

22. Gale, *Letter to a Member of the Lower House*, 2-3, 10; Gale, *Calm and Full
Vindication*, 26.

23. Gale, *Letter to a Member of the Lower House*, 11-14.

dents of any right to appeal faculty and Corporation judgments to higher authority. He cited specific cases in which, as he alleged, students had been fined "unmercifully" and "expelled without remedy," and denied the right of seeing copies of their judgments. Arguing in a "rights of Englishmen" context, at this time a most fashionable frame of reference for disputation, he asserted that an English subject possessed the right to see written transcripts of all judicial proceedings against himself so that he could have an opportunity to determine if he had been "illegally used." In Gale's view, Clap's position was that of a ruthless autocrat, an *imperium in imperio*. Such concentration of power was a "monstrous Absurdity in Politicks, and the surest Foundation in the World, for a tyrannical administration." [24]

Gale also devoted considerable space in his pamphlets to his secular interpretation of the nature and function of Yale. Time and again, he stated that the purpose of Yale was simply to educate youth and promote useful knowledge. He forcefully stressed the point in these words: "For my part, I consider the college as a school that every man hath an interest in, and ought to be concern'd for; which, under proper regulation, may be a seminary for training up youth in learning, and virtuous, and generous principles; and which under a bad management, may have a dangerous influence upon the whole community, and diffuse arbitrary principles, bigotry and corruption all over the land." [25] Gale proposed that the General Assembly—"who are the proper visitors of the college"—should appoint a committee to reform and correct the abuses and irregularities that had developed. Should this corrective action not take place, he warned, Yale would be rendered "infamous and contemptible in the Eyes of all Mankind." [26]

To allow these strictures to go unanswered was unthinkable to Clap, but for undetermined reasons he did not wish to grapple with Gale in an unrestrained pamphlet battle. He therefore made a close friend, the Reverend John Graham of Woodbury, Connecticut, the instrument of his redemption, although Clap remained the power behind the pen. Graham, a zealous sycophant,

24. *Ibid.*, 16-17; Gale, *Calm and Full Vindication*, 28-29.
25. Gale, *Calm and Full Vindication*, 31.
26. *Ibid.*, 32; Gale, *Letter to a Member of the Lower House*, 20.

was an excellent choice for the job. Of "choleric, warm and haughty Temper," [27] he was a master of hyperbole and as relentless as his adversary from Killingworth.

Primarily defensive in character, Graham's pamphlets were designed to answer allegations and refute accusations. They supplied "authentic" facts and figures to counter Gale's claim that the college treasury was bulging with funds. They unequivocally denied his charges that the students were fined exorbitantly and refused liberty of appeal; that Clap wielded dictatorial powers and was dipping his fingers into school funds for private gain; that the students were in a state of anarchy, and that their riots constituted something little short of a blood bath. All Graham's arguments had one point: Gale's assertions were "false and scandalous stories, gross misrepresentations, and bitter invectives."

In keeping with the adage that the most effective defense is a strong offense, Graham returned insult for insult with Gale and matched his accusations with countercharges. Thus he accused Gale of deliberately falsifying his accounts of the financial condition of the college—his figures were "a scurrilous Calumny." [28] Against the charge that the students were running into riot, Graham furiously asserted that Gale and "mischievous men" were goading the boys into disorder to embarrass the administration.[29] Graham also played hard on the imputation that Clap frequently had emphasized, that Gale was attempting to subvert orthodoxy and introduce Arminianism. For six years, Graham stated, the

27. The last page of the Yale Library's copy of Graham's *A Letter to a Member of the House of Representatives of the Colony of Connecticut, in Vindication of Yale College Against the False Aspersions and Scandalous Misrepresentations Contain'd in a Late Anonymous Pamphlet, Intituled, 'A Letter to a Member of the Lower House'* (New London, 1759) (hereafter cited as Graham, *Letter to a Member of the House of Representatives*) contains a hand-written biographical sketch. It states that Graham was an emigrant from Ireland who settled in the Congregational ministry in Woodbury, Connecticut; that he became a "flaming New Light" during the Awakening; that he offered his pen in the defense of Clap with the idea of being appointed a fellow of the Corporation. The sketch is of undetermined authorship. Franklin Dexter (*Yale Graduates*, II, 565) writes that Graham was a Scotsman who received an honorary M.A. from Yale in 1737 and later became Clap's protégé. Another pertinent Graham pamphlet is: *An Answer to Mr. Gale's Pamphlet: Entituled, 'A Calm and Full Vindication, etc.' Relating to Yale College* (New Haven, 1759) (hereafter cited as Graham, *Answer to Mr. Gale's Pamphlet*).

28. Graham, *Letter to a Member of the House of Representatives*, 7.

29. *Ibid.*, 16; Graham, *Answer to Mr. Gale's Pamphlet*, 22.

firebrand from Killingworth had been trying to crush orthodoxy by spreading false rumors, writing inflammatory pamphlets, influencing members of the legislature, and calling for investigations of Yale. Rather than investigate the college, declared Graham, the legislature should appoint a committee "to sift into the Principles and Designs of this ever-lasting Scribbler, and Accomplices." Graham was convinced that they would discover a "Design form'd, and a Plot laid, to subvert the Doctrines and Principles of our eccleseastical Constitution, and to overturn the College, which under God, is the best Means of training up Young Men, for the Support and Defense of it." [30] And so the argument went from page to page, yielding more heat than light. If the pamphlets of both men proved anything, it was that eighteenth-century gentlemen usually forgot their manners when they rushed into public print.

Graham's pamphlets had no effect upon Gale. Already well supplied with exploitable issues against Clap, he was given more forensic ammunition by another incident. In 1759-60, a group of New Haven New Lights participated in some political skulduggery that had as its object the capturing of the upper house and governorship. In effect, it was an attempt to secure complete control of Connecticut's central government. The attempt to execute a "mighty Change in Government" stemmed from a religious controversy, the Dana dispute, which had erupted in Wallingford, Connecticut, in 1758.[31]

In many ways the Dana issue was a replica of the Breck incident. While the dramatis personae were new, the general plot and even the course of action were strikingly similar to those of the Springfield contention some thirty years before. In the early summer of 1758, Joseph Dana, a Harvard ministerial candidate (B.A., 1753) [32] with a known reputation as a religious liberal, arrived in Wallingford and began to preach in that town's First Church with the hope of being chosen to fill the vacant pulpit. His preaching being

30. Graham, *Letter to a Member of the House of Representatives*, 17-18.
31. For detailed discussions of the Dana dispute, see Charles H. S. Davis, *History of Wallingford, Connecticut* (Meriden, Conn., 1870), chap. 9; Trumbull, *History of Connecticut*, II, 408-49; Warham Williams to Stephen Williams, Jan. 3, 1759, Pa. Hist. Soc. MS. Trumbull's account is studded with pertinent documents.
32. See Harris Elwood Starr in *DAB* s.v. "Dana, James."

judged satisfactory by a majority of the parishioners, Dana was invited to settle. Meanwhile, a minority of the society, representing the conservative membership, expressed disapproval of Dana because of his pronounced Arminian tendencies. Fearful that Arminian doctrines "would be destructive to the souls of men," this group sought to interrogate Dana in order to delve deeper into his theological position. Dana, however, refused to submit to such an examination, whereupon the minority party appealed to the New Haven Consociation to exert its influence to prevent the forthcoming ordination—Wallingford was a member of the Consociation. Thus began a religious controversy that threw the "whole Colony into a Flame." [33] The antagonistic Wallingford factions, as a contemporary put it, went at it "hammer and tongs." [34] The clergy and general populace of the colony kept abreast of the "high dispute" [35] via the cartload of pamphlets that the issue precipitated.

On October 10, 1758—a "memorable day" in Connecticut's ecclesiastical history [36]—at the request of the New Haven Consociation, a general meeting was held in Wallingford for the purpose of breaking the deadlock and restoring harmony in the parish. Present at the meeting were the members of the New Haven Consociation, representatives from the feuding major and minor parties of the First Church, and the Dana ordaining council, the latter comprised of eight ministers from New Haven County and one from Hingham, Massachusetts.[37] Two days of heated and fruitless discussion followed, capped finally by the majority party's issuing a declaration denying the jurisdiction of the Consociation

33. O'Callaghan, ed., *N.-Y. Col. Docs.*, VII, 396-97.

34. Chauncey Whittelsey to Ezra Stiles, Sept. 25, 1759, Yale MS.

35. Francis Alison of the College of Philadelphia made these comments in a letter to Ezra Stiles: "I am heartily grieved for the contentions and divisions that are like to prevail in Connecticut [Wallingford]; I highly esteem that church, and people, and had almost determined to make it the retreat of my old age; but am vexed that they bite and devour one another. Nothing can be more fatal to their piety, morals, or liberty; they will be swallowed up by the Episcopal Church, who envy their prosperity, and will avail themselves of these divisions." Dexter, ed., *Stiles's Itineraries*, 424. For the Anglican viewpoint, see Hawks and Perry, eds., *Documentary History of Episcopal Church*, II, 4-5.

36. In the opinion of Leonard Bacon, *Thirteen Historical Discourses*, 268. The dispute is discussed on pp. 268-73.

37. Joseph Noyes, now one of Clap's most implacable foes, was a member of the ordaining council. The council is listed in Trumbull, *History of Connecticut*, II, 411.

and calling for the immediate ordination of Dana. Along with the declaration, the eight ministers who belonged to the New Haven Association of Ministers and who were serving on the ordaining council announced their severance from the Consociation and made ready to ordain Dana.[38] This group also affirmed that the Consociation lacked authority to interfere in the internal affairs of the First Church. The Consociation replied by issuing a stern interdict against the majority party and ordaining council, advising them to bypass Dana and select a minister bearing its stamp of approval. On October 12, in open defiance of the Consociation, the First Church ordained Dana.

The climax of the dispute was reached in the following year (June 1759) when a joint council of delegates representing the New Haven Consociation and the Consociation of the southern district of Hartford County issued a declaration censuring the pro-Dana group for not adhering to the Saybrook Platform; judging them guilty of "scandalous contempt"; and placing them in a state of non-communion with the established churches of the county, thereby excluding them from all organized religious affairs. Furthermore, the joint council acknowledged the minority party as the legally established church for the town.

It should be readily observable that the fundamental issue of the Dana dispute was identical with that of the Breck controversy: could a church choose and ordain its ministers without yielding to the authority of a consociation? In broader terms, what was the relation of a church to the consociation? The majority party, like the Breck adherents, took the "strict Congregational" or Cambridge Platform viewpoint. Final authority and decision-making power on matters concerned with church government resided with the congregation, and the consociation could only serve in an advisory capacity. The minority party, on the other hand, holding to a Presbyterian system of polity, appealed to the authority of the Saybrook Platform, which conferred upon the consociation overriding powers in the selection of ministers and the settlement of internal disputes within churches.

Although evidence directly implicating Clap in the Wallingford

38. Three of the rebel council members subsequently underwent a change of heart and dropped out of the proceedings.

dispute is scanty, there can be little doubt that he was an active, behind-the-scenes participant. While he did not take part in the civil war of belles-lettres that broke out, he apparently aided in formulating the strategy for the New Haven Consocation in its fight to block the ordination. Gale wrote in one of his pamphlets that the "Great Man" [Clap] sent a letter to the Consocation convened in Wallingford in which he outlined that body's course of action in its future dealings with the majority party; this act afforded Gale "convincing proof of an undue thirst of power and dominion." [39] The very fact that Gale's assertion was not denied by Clap (or Graham) in a public statement strengthens its credibility. Moreover, Clap and Noah Hobart were the controlling powers in the Consocation, which makes the president's implication all the more probable.

In addition to charging the religious atmosphere of New Haven County and arousing widespread interest among the general public of the colony, the Wallingford controversy also had a number of political ramifications. The General Assembly spent considerable time during its two sessions in 1759 reviewing the dispute and the issues resulting from it.[40] Finally, in the October session, the lower house, now controlled by New Lights, adopted a memorial creating the minority party as an autonomous society. Further, it freed the minority party from all financial obligations to the church under Dana's ministry, and granted them liberty to convene and worship at any place they saw fit to choose.[41] This act, however, was vetoed both by the upper house, controlled by the Old Lights, and by Governor Fitch, also an Old Light. The issue then reached an impasse. It was at this point that political New Lights from New Haven, angered by the action of the Old Lights, concocted their scheme to effect a "mighty Change in Government," and throw the rascals out. Their plan was to defeat, in the forthcoming general election of 1759, Governor Fitch and the Old Light councilors

39. Gale, *Letter to a Member of the Lower House,* 21-22.

40. O'Callaghan, ed., *N.-Y. Col. Docs.,* VII, 396-97, 439; William Samuel Johnson to Jared Ingersoll, Sept. 10, 1759, printed in Eben E. Beardsley, *Life and Times of William Samuel Johnson, L.L.D., First Senator in Congress from Connecticut and President of Columbia College* (N. Y., 1876), 17-18.

41. Trumbull and Hoadly, eds., *Conn. Recs.,* XI, 344.

who had sided with the pro-Dana group.[42] Since public officials in Connecticut were normally elected by the voters on the basis of seniority in office and held positions virtually for life, this plan had the elements of a revolutionary conspiracy.

The New Light coup was intimately related to the elective process by which the councilors were chosen. Twice yearly, in April and September, the freemen of Connecticut met in their respective towns to appoint two delegates to the lower house, which convened in May and October. In the September meetings, in addition to selecting two assemblymen, each town nominated twenty men, residing anywhere in the colony, as candidates for higher office in the government. The lists sent in by the towns were reviewed by the Assembly in the October session. The twenty men chosen by the greatest number of towns were declared candidates for the spring election, when the councilors and other high elective officers were voted upon. When the freemen again assembled in April, they chose from these twenty men the governor, deputy-governor, treasurer, secretary, and twelve councilors. The Assembly, in its May meeting, counted the ballots and announced the winners.[43]

After the annual October session of the Assembly, it was customary for James Parker, the New Haven printer, to publish and circulate at governmental expense a list of the twenty nominees for the spring election. In 1759, however, Parker died, and the official list was not published. Unidentified New Lights from New Haven then drew up hand-written lists, egregiously omitting the names of the pro-Dana supporters and substituting men known to be friendly to the minority party. Emissaries were then dispatched to towns throughout the colony to distribute the lists and spread reports "to the Prejudice of the Gvr. etc. and to stir up the Disaffected."

But New Light efforts to bring about an "innovation in the state" were unsuccessful. As Chauncey Whittelsey informed Ezra Stiles, the emissaries "had been using their Influence in almost

42. The immediate target was the group of Old Light councilors; the gubernatorial candidates were not selected in Connecticut until just prior to the spring election.
43. The elective process is discussed in Lawrence H. Gipson, *The British Empire Before the American Revolution* (Caldwell, Idaho, 1936), III, 84.

every Place; but their Scheme was rather despised than approved of by the Body and better part of the People." [44] Lacking support in more heavily populated southwestern Connecticut, a solid Old Light district owing to its large Anglican element, the New Lights were unable to capture a majority in the council. They sustained a stinging, and more humiliating, defeat when the freemen of Wallingford and New Haven spurned their advice and selected Old Lights to represent them in the forthcoming session of the Assembly.[45]

As New Light machinations were brought to public attention, the Gale element naturally designated Clap as the chief instigator. Some extremists even circulated the rumor that Clap had forged letters warning against the spread of Arminianism, claiming they had been sent to him from people in all sections of Connecticut—even Gale discounted this accusation, calling it an "idle tale." [46] But Gale was thoroughly convinced that Clap was an accessory to the plot to unseat the governor and Old Light councilors, and he said so publicly.[47]

Through the medium of Graham, the "pretender" who had assumed the role of an Achates, Clap emphatically denied complicity. Indeed, he steadfastly maintained that he cared not a whit about political affairs, insisting that he neither had seen nor consulted with anyone on a nomination list within "two or three years"; [48] to which latter assertion Gale caustically retorted, "very few men of any character who have liv'd fifty years, can say so." [49] Clap nevertheless insisted that he could recall but one instance when, while in a tavern, a man offered to show him a nomination list, but he refused to look at it.

The president's claims of disinterest and protestations of noncomplicity in the events of the day were weakened, if not irreparably shattered, by Gale, who ("villainously," according to Graham) intercepted a letter to Clap from Graham containing a

44. Sept. 25, 1759, Yale MS.; the scheme is also recounted in Gale, *Calm and Full Vindication*, 25.
45. Whittelsey to Stiles, Sept. 25, 1759, Yale MS.
46. Gale, *Few Brief Remarks on Mr. Graham's Answer*, 4.
47. *Ibid.*
48. *Connecticut Gazette* (New Haven), Oct. 6, 1759.
49. Gale, *Few Brief Remarks on Mr. Graham's Answer*, 6.

political article destined for the *Connecticut Gazette*. For Gale both documents constituted a veritable bonanza, and he was quick to share his good fortune. He promptly published a pamphlet, in which the letter and Graham's article, which he succinctly characterized as a "piece of scandal, infamous railing, and party-wickedness," were included.[50] Veiled in the anonymity of a classical figure, "Philalethos," and directed to the freemen of the colony, Graham's work threshed out old stubble in the process of urging the election of men who would preserve the religious heritage of the colony and uphold the established ecclesiastical constitution. Conversely, it warned against the election of "irreligious politicians" who had "brot in anarchy" by supporting Dana, attacking Clap and the college, and inveighing against orthodoxy. It was a most damaging piece of evidence against Clap. It lent color to Gale's charge that he was an unscrupulous cleric.

Quite naturally, Graham was furious at the interception and publication of his writings. His pride of authorship was also piqued, since the pamphlet had not as yet been "lick'd into shape." In an attempt to extricate Clap from the political pit into which he had been suddenly cast, Graham assumed full responsibility for the political squib. As for directing it to Clap, he explained that this was done merely for correction, minor alteration, and editorial comment—in effect, proofreading.[51] It was not convincing prose. Graham's explanation put a strain upon credulity, for Clap was hardly the type to perform the function of a proofreader. Thus, Graham dug the pit of Clap's implication even deeper.

Whatever Clap's actual role in the political plot of 1759-60 (and it never has been fully determined), the general public, as well as some prominent men in Connecticut and Massachusetts who were not closely connected with Gale, were inclined to believe that he was "privy to the scheme." Charles Chauncy gave expression to the general sense when, in alluding to Clap's activities in the Dana dispute and electioneering coup, he wrote that the president tried, "under the influence of bigottry, and tyranny, to crush some gentle-

50. *Ibid.*, 7-11.
51. Graham, *A Few Remarks on the Remarker Shewing That Gale's Inferences From the Contents of a Letter, Villainously Intercepted and Broke Open, Are Entirely Groundless and Injurious* (New Haven, 1760) (hereafter cited as Graham, *A Few Remarks on the Remarker*).

men of more worth than himself; but I believe, and have always thot, that, in the end, he will suffer more than any of those, he might intend to demolish. I wish him a better turn of mind; but suspect he is incurable in his thirst for lawless power and undeserved honor." [52] Others delivered like studied insults.

By 1760, calls for visitation and the curbing of Clap's power were reverberating throughout Connecticut. Indeed, organized attempts at visitation had already been made.

While demands for visitation had been broached as early as 1753, the first positive action came in 1757, one year before the Dana controversy developed. In May of 1757 Fellows Jared Eliot and Benjamin Ruggles petitioned the Assembly to inquire into Yale's government. The petition directed attention to the constitutional limitations placed upon the Corporation by the Charter of 1745. This document explicitly stated that the laws of Yale could not be "repugnant to the Laws of England, nor the laws of this Colony"; and the legislature was given the right of review over Corporation acts. The memorialists contended that such acts as establishing separate worship, a professor of divinity, and the college church represented a "daring affront to the Legislative Power of this Colony, and such a glaring Evidence of an undue Aim at exorbitant Power, as loudly calls for the timely check of the Legislature." They called for a legislative review of these acts. Should they be found illegal, the legislature was to "interpose and correct" the situation. Submitted jointly with the memorial was a letter in which Eliot and Ruggles sharply protested Clap's dictatorial management.[53] The memorial and protest were laid aside to be considered at the October session. Both, however, were ignored when the session was held.

In May 1759, Assemblyman Gale took up the baton from his father-in-law and introduced a motion calling for visitation. A bitter debate ensued. When the motion was put to the vote, according to Graham, less than one-fourth of the representatives

52. Dexter, ed., *Stiles's Itineraries*, 441.
53. Connecticut Archives: Colleges and Schools, 1st Ser., Pt. ii, I, 338a, 339a, Conn. State Lib.; Memorial to the General Assembly, Yale MS.; Eliot to Stiles, July 26, 1758, Yale MS.

were in favor of visitation. Undeterred by this setback, Gale promptly drew up a formal letter calling for visitation and presented it to both houses of the legislature. Again, he struck a hard wall of resistance. No action was taken.[54]

In October 1761, the Assembly received another memorial urging visitation. Signed by two ministers and one layman, all of whom had sons attending Yale, this memorial concentrated on the issue of student unrest, and particularly on Clap's inability to preserve order. It pointed out that for the "last half year little or no study has been done, the students have had their minds embroiled with Enmity and Turbulent Spirit; and have spent much of their Time in caballing against President and Tutors." The memorialists additionally expressed parental indignation against Clap's harsh methods of discipline, claiming, much as Gale had done, that his severe discipline (especially fines) had produced "resentments" which had driven the students into "high Violence against the President and Tutors." Again echoing Gale, they charged that the college officials exercised discretionary powers, particularly Clap, who had become the "Sole Law." [55] Once more, the Assembly voted to lay the memorial aside.

Two years later, in May 1763, the Assembly received still another memorial. This petition contained a full-dress summary of the charges that had been directed against Clap during the preceding eight years. It listed five recommendations for resolving the controversy. The General Assembly should review Corporation acts; maintain a close check on the financial accounts of the college; restrain Clap from levying excessive fines; grant to the students a right of appeal to the governor and council; and appoint visitors to investigate Yale. Attached to the memorial was a rider signed by five prominent clergymen. Admitting that they were not completely informed about college affairs, they went on to say that the facts at hand provided strong evidence that Yale was in a "Deplorable State." They strongly urged the Assembly to act upon the memorial.[56]

54. Graham, *A Few Remarks on the Remarker*, 3.
55. Connecticut Archives: Colleges and Schools, 1st Ser., Pt. ii, I, 340a, Conn. State Lib.; Eliot to Stiles, Aug. 2, 176[0], Yale MS.
56. Connecticut Archives: Colleges and Schools, 1st Ser., Pt. ii, II, 66, 67, Conn. State Lib.

Perhaps of greater significance than the memorial itself were its sponsors. Not one of the three clergymen and six laymen who affixed their signatures was from New Haven. Not one was considered an active participant in the controversy. All were men of recognized prestige. Moreover, three of the laymen and one of the clergy were former students of Clap. A second clergyman was the son of a former trustee. Of the five clergymen who signed the rider, two were former students and a third, Stephen White, was Clap's successor at Windham. A fourth signer, the Reverend Ebenezer Devotion, had received the honor of having Clap preach at his ordination.[57] The preponderance of clergymen and ex-students of Clap lent a special significance to the document. Moreover, because these men came from scattered parts of Connecticut, the memorial reflected a ground swell of public opinion.

The breaking point had been reached. The dispute had raged continuously for nearly a decade, increasing in intensity and scurrility with each passing year. The public was clamoring for legislative action, and the fires of discontent were still being stoked. In the Election Sermon of 1763 (May 12),[58] the Reverend Stephen White concluded his hortatory disquisition on the interdependence of civil and divine rule with a list of issues to which the government should direct its attention. The Yale problem was included. White bluntly called for an "Inspection into the State and Circumstances" of Yale. "And I would humbly Suggest," White added, in addressing his large and distinguished audience, "whether it be not the Duty of the Legislature, in this Day, when there are so many Complaints about the College, so much Discontent among its Members, and such a general Dissatisfaction in the Government concerning it, to enquire into the Reasons of it."

The Assembly, now controlled by New Lights,[59] could no longer turn its back on the matter. It agreed to consider the memorial,

---

57. The analysis can be seen in Dexter, *Yale Graduates,* II, 777-81.

58. The election sermons cited in this work are housed in the Connecticut State Library.

59. There is a division of opinion among secondary authorities as to when the New Light party gained control of the Assembly. A contemporary, William Samuel Johnson, wrote in Jan. 1763 that the New Lights were "nearly the ruling part of the government owing to their superior attention to civil affairs and close union among themselves in politics." Schneider, eds., *Writings of Johnson,* III, 266.

and accordingly directed a communication to Clap ordering him to appear in Hartford to answer the specified charges.[60]

Clap's inveterate enemies and mere critics were naturally delighted by the Assembly's decision. Many of them traveled to Hartford in gleeful anticipation of seeing at first hand Clap receive his comeuppance. This was their moment of triumph. As Benjamin Trumbull observed: "Gentlemen from different parts repaired to Hartford, to hear the pleadings. That class of people, who had been so long and so strongly opposed to the college, flattered themselves with the pleasing prospect of bringing the college to their feet, and of amply reaping the fruit of their past labors." [61] To increase the possibility of success, the memorialists hired Jared Ingersoll and William Samuel Johnson, who were, in Trumbull's opinion, "the two most learned and famous attornies, at that day, in the colony," to present their charges.[62] Both were former students of Clap, and Ingersoll was even related to the president by marriage; if anything, family affiliation seems to have accentuated, rather than diminished, the enmity between religious disputants in the colonial period.

With the State House creaking under the weight of numbers, and in an atmosphere electric with emotion and excitement, the hearing commenced. The memorialists' charges were formally presented by Ingersoll and Johnson. Then the short, thickset figure of Clap moved to the front of the room, now cloaked with a solemn stillness. The president stood motionless for a brief moment, his piercing eyes sweeping over the huge, unfriendly audience, his hands arranging his stiff-papered notes. This was the climax of his career. This was Armageddon! He was aware that more was at stake than his position. Whether Yale would remain orthodox or fall to the Gale element, fall to the forces of irreligion, would be decided on this day.

He began, speaking in his usually restrained, conversational manner, without gesture, without flourish. He opened with some

60. Connecticut Archives: Colleges and Schools, 1st Ser., Pt. ii, II, 67b, Conn. State Lib.

61. Trumbull, *History of Connecticut*, II, 275.

62. *Ibid.*, II, 275. On Ingersoll, see Gipson, *Jared Ingersoll*. Johnson's legal career is treated in Groce, *William Samuel Johnson*, chap. 2.

general remarks on the memorial and its signers. The memorial itself he characterized as a tissue of "misrepresentations" and "untrue allegations." He suspected that the document was not actually the work of its signers but had been instigated by others. To give strength to his suspicion, he called attention to one portion of the memorial in which it was stated by the memorialists that they had been "advised and informed" of affairs at Yale. With these opening remarks, there was no mistaking that Clap was accusing Gale and his associates of instigating the memorial and of having influenced prominent men in the colony to present it to the Assembly.

Getting down to the business at hand, he proceeded to examine the crucial question of the founding of Yale. Upon the resolution of this question hung not only the fate of the college, relative to legislative control, but possibly his own position as president. The case of the memorialists was constructed on the premise that the General Assembly was the rightful and legal founder of the college and thereby could appoint "visitors" to look into its affairs. The destruction of this premise was Clap's primary objective. He entered into a detailed, highly technical legal disquisition calculated to prove that the original ministers, who later became the first trustees, were the legal founders of the college. It was precisely the same argument he had set forth in 1754 in his *Religious Constitution of Colleges,* only now his exposition was stated in more complete form—that is, in greater detail—and was characterized by a far greater display of erudition. He enveloped the issue in a fog of legalism.

That the Assembly, in its legislative capacity, held supreme authority over the college, he readily acknowledged. But by English common law, he went on, the legislature was not to be considered as the founder of the college. Making repeated references to Coke's *Reports,* Raymond's *Reports,* Wood's *Institutes,* and other less prominent legal texts, he developed his argument with consummate skill to show that the first trustees, who were nominated by the ministers with the general consent of the people and who became a society of quasi-corporation a "Year or two" before they had a charter, were the legal and rightful founders.

The act of founding, as distinct from "purpose and Intention" of founding, he continued, occurred "above a Year" before the issuance of the Charter by the Assembly, when the ten ministers brought "a large Number of Books principally out of their own Libraries and in formal Manner gave and laid them down together as the Beginning or Foundation of the Library for the College." Again he drew upon the opinions of the English legal galaxy to establish the fact that a founding agent was one who made the first donation, not one who issued a charter that gave legal being to a corporation. Arguing from this position, Clap averred that the Assembly, despite its generous financial aid through the years, did not hold a legal sanction either to appoint "visitors" or investigate the college; these rights were reserved to the heirs or successors of those who had made the "First Donation." [63]

Having disposed of this crucial legal issue, Clap spent the remainder of his time denying and refuting less serious accusations. The charge that he acted in an arbitrary manner he swiftly dismissed as a "very gross Mistake and Misrepresentation." As for certain college laws being inconsistent with, and an infringement of, the "natural rights of Englishmen," he replied that by common law universities held discretionary powers in the management of their internal affairs; again, he cited volume and page. He denied imposing "double fines" upon students for failing to attend religious meetings—"a mere Fiction of Fancy and Imagination"; defended his "College Laws" from the charge that they were too comprehensive and contained too many "trifling laws"; and steadfastly maintained that only through vigorous execution of laws was it possible to maintain order at the college.

The seriousness of the problem of student disorders constrained Clap to enlarge upon the issue. He emphatically denied the accusation that the spirit of the college youth had been "broken" and

63. As a result of some painstaking research by Franklin Dexter, Clap's account of the founding of Yale has been discredited. Dexter's judgment is that Clap consciously presented an "embellished story" to bolster his case. This topic is carefully treated in Dexter, "The Founding of Yale College," New Haven Colony Hist. Soc., *Papers,* 3 (1882), 1-31; Charles H. Smith, "The Founding of Yale College," New Haven Colony Hist. Soc., *Papers,* 7 (1908), 34-64; compare with Clap, *Annals of Yale,* 2-11.

their morale "shattered." These reports were grossly exaggerated. Only a few students were recalcitrant, he said, and it was these few who provoked the others into mischief. Taking the offensive, he repeated the charge that he had frequently directed at Gale, that the youth were being undermined and led into seditious acts by "designing Men," who instilled in them disorderly ideas and prejudiced them against their rightful governors. He then clinched his point by producing the confession of one boy who admitted being advised by townspeople "to run into Riots, Rebellions and Disorders, to bring a Scandal upon the College," with the ultimate object being the overthrow of Clap and the seating of a more "lenient" president.

As to the charge that the college governors extracted funds from the students for various items not directly related to the educational process, Clap readily conceded that the students were obliged to contribute funds for one—and only one—such item: for the maintenance of a certain "necessary house" known as "Joseph." Continuing in this facetious vein, Clap stated that the "house" frequently became "rotton" or was overturned, whereupon it was necessary to construct a new one. On this basis, he impishly asserted, he entertained serious doubts as to whether his forcing the students to contribute to this fund could be construed as an infringement of the "rights of Englishmen," as had been charged.

Clap discarded levity as he took up the accusation that orthodoxy was not being preserved at the college. This was no joking matter. It was a well-known fact, he stated, that the president and fellows showed "proper Care and Zeal" for the preservation of orthodoxy. Indeed, so severe was their program that "some Gentlemen"—and the reference was obviously directly at Gale and company—had taken offense and were endeavoring to obstruct the college government and undermine the "flourishing State" of the college.

In concluding his defense, Clap affirmed that the college "never was in a better state" so far as student discipline was concerned; despite reports to the contrary, the disorderly students were under the control of the authorities. In his final remarks, Clap appealed to the Assembly to take action against those who were inciting the students to riot and spreading false rumors against the college government.[64]

To the great dismay of Clap's opponents, the General Assembly, after short deliberation, refused to act on the memorial. Benjamin Trumbull, who in all likelihood attended the hearing,[65] reported: "The memorialists, and their whole party, were greatly disappointed and chagrined, and the president got much honour by the defence which he made of the college. He appeared to be a man of extensive knowledge and real greatness. In points of law, especially as they respected colleges, he appeared to be superior to all the lawyers, so that his antagonists acknowledged that he knew more, and was wiser than all of them." [66] And Clap, in his *Annals of Yale,* recorded the action of the Assembly in these cryptic—and somewhat smug—words: "When these Arguments were considered by the Honorable the General Assembly, but very few appeared to be of the Opinion, that the Assembly were the *Founders* of the College; and so they acted nothing upon the Memorial. And it is generally supposed that this Question will never be publickly moved again." [67] Clap's supposition proved to be correct. Although the Old Lights persistently reminded the Assembly that, as stated by the Reverend Edward Dorr in the Election Sermon of 1765, "You are the Fathers, you are the Founders of that Society," the Assembly stood pat.

The question arises: was it Clap's prodigious legal erudition and cogent reasoning that persuaded the Assembly to ignore the memorial of 1763? More than likely, the answer is in the negative. That Clap's cause was considerably strengthened by his scholarly presentation must be granted. He exhibited an amazing grasp of legal detail. From the legal standpoint, his argument was "masterly," as Justice Joseph Story has described it.[68] But possibly

64. Answer of President and Fellows of Yale College to the Memorial of Mr. Edward Dorr and Others Preferred to the General Assembly at Hartford, May 1763, Connecticut Archives: Colleges and Schools, 1st Ser., Pt. ii, II, 71, Conn. State Lib.; Answer to the Assembly, Yale MS. See also Clap's summary account in *Annals of Yale,* 69-76.

65. Professor Dexter was of this belief. *Yale Graduates,* II, 780.

66. Trumbull, *History of Connecticut,* II, 279.

67. Pp. 76-77.

68. Charles H. Smith, "Early Struggles in American Education," *Conn. Mag.,* 8 (1903-4), 183-84. It is significant to note that a legal argument similar to that

an even greater element in Clap's victory was the control of the Assembly by his political allies. While this fact may tarnish the dramatic luster of Clap's defense, it is too obvious to be ignored. The New Lights, as a party, were committed to the support of Clap and his program. Only political exigency could have dictated such an unpopular decision.

To the president, it doubtless mattered little why he had won. From every point of view, this was his greatest moment. He was at the very peak of his power. He had scotched visitation and, in so doing, eliminated the threat of his deposal through legislative action. These were the paramount considerations. In a more personal sense, he had withstood the malignant opposition of arch-opponent Benjamin Gale. The latter had played his trump card and gone down to ignominious defeat. With the New Lights solidly in control of the Assembly and with the experience of 1763 serving as a stark reminder, it was unlikely that Gale would make another attempt to unseat him through political means. And he never did.

Undoubtedly flushed with triumph, the president, now fifty-nine-years-old and in his twenty-third year as head of Yale, returned to New Haven to resume his regal station. Having won a climactic battle in staving off the Old Light challenge and consolidating his own position, he might have anticipated an era of administrative calm. Yet, he discovered that the struggle had not abated; it was being renewed on another front—in the form of student disorders on a scale which the college had never known. Indeed, by 1763 it was written in the sands of time that the end was drawing near for the battle-weary Puritan. With a sense of fatigue, Clap himself must have begun to entertain harrowing doubts about his continued association with the college. The irony of the situation was that, having bearded his enemies at Hartford and thwarted the consuming ambition of Benjamin Gale, he had returned to the college only to be confronted by a rebellious student body whose collective aim paralleled Gale's ambition. But the

---

developed by Clap was presented in the celebrated Dartmouth College case of 1819, although the Yale precedent was not cited.

students used other methods. What Gale and company had failed to effect by political action, the young Christian gentlemen of Yale proposed to achieve by violence.[69]

69. This is not to suggest that Gale *et al.* were not involved in the rebellious activities of the students. There seems to be validity to Clap's repeated assertion that the Gale faction constantly urged the students to perpetrate acts of violence so as to discredit the administration and pave the way for his dismissal. The proof to this charge is admittedly hard to come by.

Chapter Ten

THE STUDENTS "SKIN OLD
TOM CLAP'S HIDE"

MODERN critics have indicted Clap on a number of counts, but no one as yet has dared to suggest that he mollycoddled his students or permitted them to indulge their every whim. That Clap did not direct a country club is an indisputable fact. Guided by a clearly defined philosophy of education, he worked diligently to prepare youth for service in church and state, and—an even greater destiny—for "celestial Felicity." His administration functioned on the traditional theory that the chief aims of higher education were to discipline the mind and inculcate moral notions. The energies of youth were to be channeled for the most part into intellectual activities. Furthermore, the academic experience was conceived to be an all-absorbing process, conducted with monastic rigor.[1]

To the twentieth-century observer, collegiate life at Yale during Clap's administration, and earlier, is noteworthy for two conspicuous features. Initially, it was based upon the system of *in loco parentis,* with the college authorities exercising the disciplinary

1. On undergraduate life at Yale during the eighteenth century, see Alexander Cowie, "Educational Problems at Yale College in the Eighteenth Century," Conn. Tercentenary Com., *Publications,* No. 55 (1936); Franklin Dexter, "Student Life at Yale in the Early Days of Connecticut Hall," New Haven Colony Hist. Soc., *Papers,* 7 (1908), 288-97.

functions of the parent while the boy was entrusted to their care. Secondly, and closely allied to this, Clap's regime resembled nothing so much as a benevolent despotism. While in residence, the students came under his watchful supervision. Their social, religious, and educational activities were closely regulated, their personal conduct sedulously scrutinized within and without the classroom. Students seldom had an opportunity to indulge themselves in the luxury of privacy. The authority of the college extended to all phases of a student's life. One lad, for example, a great-uncle of Oliver Wendell Holmes, was fined for traveling on the Sabbath, a violation of "Divine and Civil Law," and, doubly damning, "with a Burden or Pack behind him." [2] When a scholar walked through the streets of New Haven, the eagle eye of college authority was even more firmly fixed upon him. By college law, he was required to wear, in addition to hat and coat, an academic gown, making him all the more conspicuous. The unrelenting vigilance of the college officials is best revealed by an incident that took place in 1762. Finding collegiate life unendurable and yearning for a more adventurous experience, one lad packed his few belongings and secretly boarded a ship bound for the West Indies. But the ever-alert Clap somehow learned of his plans and snatched him from the vessel before it set sail.[3] Assuredly, there were many among the student body who nursed the ambition to flee.

Governed by the time-honored Puritan belief that Satan reigned supreme in the minds of the idle, and adhering to the hard-and-fast schedule in effect since the founding of Yale, Clap saw to it that the students had a minimum of leisure time to spend in mischief. The daily living pattern of the student was reduced to rigid rule and system, with a fixed time set for rising, eating, recreation, and study. The student began the academic day "intra Horam Sextam et Solis Ortum." Awakened by the college bell, he hastily dressed and dashed off to morning prayers, which, according to student

2. Records of the Judgments and Acts of the President and Tutors of Yale College, 3 vols., I, 3, Yale MS. (hereafter cited as Faculty Judgments). Holmes journeyed from Wallingford to New Haven, a distance of about ten miles. His fine was waived after he made a public confession.

3. A lazy scholar and perennial troublemaker, the boy was subsequently dismissed after examination revealed that he was not up to the standards of an incoming freshman. *Ibid.*, II, 89-91.

opinion of the nineteenth century, were held "sometime during the night, generally toward morning." Following this spiritual "uplift," he began his daily academic routine.[4] Aside from the time allotted for three meals, an afternoon "bever"—the eighteenth-century equivalent of the modern "coffee break"—a recreation period in the early afternoon, and evening prayers, the student spent the bulk of the day in recitations and study. College law required him to be in his chamber diligently applying himself to his studies by nine o'clock in the evening in the spring and summer months, and by seven o'clock in the late fall and winter months, when night closed in early on the New Haven community. To assure compliance with this law, Clap and the tutors, more usually the latter, conducted a daily chamber check. The task of maintaining a close vigil over the boys was simplified somewhat by the tutors' residence within the college hall; from the vantage point of their chambers they could easily keep their spirited charges under surveillance. There were, on the other hand, definite disadvantages to this housing arrangement. In some ways, it was like residing in the crater of an active volcano.

The time for retirement was not specified by law, but in view of the grueling daily schedule, the early rising hour, and the hovering presence of the wardens of the house, it would be reasonable to assume that the generality of the students snuffed out candles before midnight and with bleary, burning eyes turned from Minerva to the blessings of bed. For on the following morning the weary grind began again. As Trumbull lamented:

> In the same round condem'd each day,
> To study, read, recite and pray. . . .[5]

Routine also followed the students into the commons. The most distinctive feature of the food served at Yale, aside from its skimpiness, was its monotonous uniformity. It was fare without benefit of dietetics. Students during Clap's time would have understood the motivational impulse that inspired a Yale youth of a later

---

4. Insight into the daily routine, with emphasis upon academic activity, is provided by an extract from a student diary of 1762, printed in William Kingsley, ed., *Yale College, a Sketch of Its History, With Notices of Its Several Departments, Instructors and Benefactors, Together With Some Account of Student Life and Amusements, by Various Authors* (N. Y., 1879), I, 444-46.

5. *Poetical Works*, II, 15.

period to write in the margin of a library book: "Sottmeet and mustard for Dinner and for Dinner 1800 times over." [6] Gathered together in the college hall, the boys were confronted with provender designed primarily to alleviate hunger pangs and solidly fill the stomach cavity, and only incidentally to propitiate the taste. Not only the daily bill of fare but its individual components were meticulously prescribed by college law.[7] The morning repast consisted of a pint of beer and a hunk of bread in amounts barely sufficient to sustain life—in making a loaf of bread, the cook was directed not to use more than one pound of dough. The noon meal, or dinner, supposedly the highlight of the daily menu, was far more substantial than morning "bever" but hardly a culinary work of art. The menu called for another loaf of bread, one quart of beer, and, as the *pièce de résistance*, two and one-half pounds of either beef, veal, or mutton; these items were to be divided among four boys, the quarterly division making a so-called "mess." For the sake of variety, and because of its availability and cheapness, one and three-fourths pounds of salt pork were substituted for the aforementioned meats about twice a week during the summer months. Following a late afternoon "sizing" of more bread and beer came the evening meal, which featured the usual loaf of bread, plus two quarts of milk, the bounty again to be divided on a quarterly basis. In the event milk was not available, what purported to be an ample serving of pie was provided. By law, each pie was to contain one and three-fourths pounds of dough, onefourth pounds of hog's fat, two ounces of sugar, and one-half peck of apples. From contemporary comment, it appears that the "pye" also contained a generous portion of bone, gristle, and fat; and the most eminent quality of its crust was a leathery consistency. In general, such was the daily diet. Occasionally, there was a slight modification with the inclusion of cheeses and puddings. Many

6. For this and subsequent references to marginalia (with one exception), I am gratefully indebted to Mrs. Edmund S. Morgan of New Haven, who has scanned the margins of many of the books in the "Library of 1742."

7. Yale Corporation Records, I, 69 Yale Univ.; Dexter, ed., *Documentary History of Yale*, 351. During most of Clap's administration, the students ate breakfast in their chambers, after picking it up at the buttery. The noon meal was always served in commons. Although the records are hazy on the point, dinner, too, was apparently served in the commons.

of the students paid their tuition fees with provisions, the bulk of which eventually found its way into the commons.

The commons was managed (or mismanaged, as the students often thought) by a steward, who was usually selected on the basis of business acumen rather than culinary imagination. Under the severe handicap of operating on a niggardly budget, the steward was hard pressed to set either a bountiful or attractive table; in any case, tradition was against pampering scholars. As indicated above, the meals were decidedly unbalanced, with a pronounced leaning toward starchy foods, which were miserably prepared and unappetizing. Students could rent cellar lockers in which they could store nonperishable snacks. Parched and hungry boys could also find relief at the buttery, which served as an appendage to commons and offered for sale such delicacies as fresh fruits, chocolate, and sugar loaves.

It is universally acknowledged that students, while only intermittently interested in providing nourishment for their minds, are always concerned for the gratification of their stomachs, and for this reason the commons became a central nursery of grievance during Clap's administration. The stewards themselves were frequently the object of student pranks, some of malicious intent. The prosaic character of the food provoked numerous "bread and butter" riots, of which the more serious culminated in the smashing of dishware, the pitching of food about the college hall and out the windows, and the manhandling of tutors, who had the unenviable, and oftentimes hazardous, duty of enforcing discipline during the meals.[8] The lines of the mock-heroic "Rebelliad," commemorating a furious and famous food-slinging battle between Harvard freshmen and sophomores, spoke a story common to Yale as well:

8. One case is offered as an illustration. In Jan. 1765, in the course of a meal, a student took some pieces of cheese from his plate and recklessly hurled them across the room. For this "indecent Action and Waste of the Cheese," he was severely reprimanded by the tutor in attendance. When the tutor rose to leave, the same youth "violently threw a hard Piece of Cheese" which winged past the tutor's head and crashed against the door. Rushed before Clap and ordered to explain his actions, the boy responded that his aim had been errant, that his target was actually a student named Hunn. Hunn was called for and testified that he had a seat "at the opposite Part of the Hall." The thrower of cheese "offered nothing further in Extenuation of his Crimes." Faculty Judgments, III, 50, Yale MS.

> ... Nathan threw a piece of bread,
> And hit Abijah on the head.
> The wrathful Freshman, in a trice,
> Sent back another bigger slice;
> Which, being butter'd pretty well,
> Made greasy work where'er it fell.
> And thus arose a fearful battle;
> The coffee-cups and saucers rattle;
> The bread-bowls fly at woful rate,
> And break many a learned pate. . . .[9]

In later years some of the Yale students came to the conclusion that a more satisfactory way of sustaining life was to eat in local taverns rather than in the commons. They therefore began the practice of selling their food rations to those who were still of a mind to eat in the college hall.[10]

While "bread and butter" riots were commonplace, the most serious incident developed as a consequence of eating, rather than throwing, the viands. After the morning meal on April 14, 1764, eighty-two of the ninety-two students boarding at college (plus two tutors and a cook) were seized with "violent Vomitings, great Thirst, Weakness in the Extremities and some with Spasms, and other Symptoms of Poison." Through the application of "Emetics, Oleaginous and mucilagonous Draughts," medicinal preparations designed to induce vomiting, the retching students were restored to health, although many remained pale and "weak in their joynts and affected in their Eyes" for some time afterwards.

The incident caused great excitement and consternation not only in the college community and New Haven but throughout the colony as well. Influenced by the strong (if not irrational) anti-French sentiment that pervaded the New England colonies in the period of the French and Indian War, many in Connecticut were convinced that the "poyson plot" had been perpetrated by some French Acadians who recently had become residents in New Haven. The president, however, knew otherwise. After conducting an extensive investigation of the "disaster," he attributed the inci-

9. Quoted in Morison, *Three Centuries of Harvard*, 208-9.
10. As is to be expected, Clap was favorably disposed to the college fare. "This Provision is generally agreable, so that the Tutors always, the President frequently, the Fellows, and many other Gentlemen, occasionally are entertained with it." *Annals of Yale*, 85.

dent to "either some accident, or some strong physic, and not [to]
any mortal poyson, put into the Victuals with a Design to bring
a Slur upon the provisions made in the Hall." Certain students,
continued Clap's report, had sworn under oath "that some of the
Scholars manifested a pleasure what befell the Commons as hoping
that it might be a means of getting rid of them, and one of them
went to one of the Cooks on the Lords day and offered her a
Dollar if she would poison or Physic the Commons again, provided she would let him know the time, and added that if it was
done once more there would be an end of Commons." So as to
allay the fears of the alarmed citizenry, Clap ordered that, in the
future, none of the kitchen staff could be of French extraction.
Further, he directed that only approved persons could set foot
in the areas where food was being prepared.[11]

Despite the grueling daily schedule, student life was not entirely
a dull, humorless existence. Clap permitted the youths to engage
in such non-academic and pleasurable activities as "Gunning,"
fishing, sailing (provided they did not stay out longer "than from
one Tide to the next"), recreational walks, and inter-class snowball
fights.[12] By such means the boys were able to dissipate at least a
portion of their pent-up energies and break the tedium of daily
routine. Fagging, or hazing, was yet another means by which the
students, except for freshmen, could work the devil out of their
systems. Clap was a firm supporter of hazing, and he lent to the
custom the massive weight of his office.[13] He publicly admonished
one stout freshman, who burst out with the expletive "Damn 'em"
after a group of sophomores ordered him to be quiet.[14] He suspended another freshman because the boy showed his heels to a
group of sophomores who were abusing him; the boy left the
room stating "I sware I will not stay here any longer." [15]

11. Investigation of Alleged Poisoning in Commons, Yale MS.; John Ballantine
Diary, Apr. 20, 1764, typewritten copy in American Antiquarian Society. Ballantine
was convinced that the French were involved in a "horrid attempt" to kill off the
student body.
12. Inter-class snowball fights began near the mid-century. They were declared
illegal by President Stiles in 1786 because of the frequent blood-letting. (Apparently
the boys began reinforcing the snow with rocks.) *Yale Univ. Lib. Gazette,* 3 (1928), 43.
13. Clap, *Annals of Yale,* 42-43.
14. Faculty Judgments, I, 32, Yale MS.
15. *Ibid.,* I, 7.

If Clap was concerned with the social benefits of extracurricular activities, the students were more intent upon indulging puckish instincts. Because they were looking for fun, and because they were full of sap and bounce, the boys engaged in many activities not bearing the stamp of administrative approval. Actually, a great gap existed between the theory and reality of student life; between what Clap wished it to be and what the boys made it to be. The Judgments of the President and Faculty, and the Corporation Records, graphically point up that Trumbull was not at all exaggerating when he wrote:

> There vice shall lavish all her charms,
> And rapture fold us in her arms,
> Riot shall court the frolic soul,
> And swearing crown the sparkling bowl;
> While wit shall sport with vast applause,
> And scorn the feeble tie of laws:
> Our midnight joys no rule shall bound,
> While games and dalliance revel round.[16]

Breaking free from the "feeble tie of laws," as well as from the binding fetters of monotonous academic routine, the scholars engaged in a wide variety of surreptitious mischief. They went canoeing and sailing without bothering to secure presidential sanction (at times, they stole the canoes), amused themselves by playing cards and dice, bloodied each other in fist fights, tore the plaster from the walls of the college hall and the casings from the windows, and carved their initials on doors, chairs, desks, shingles, and lead sashes. Each year brought forth a few enterprising lads, usually upperclassmen, who recognized the money-making potentialities of the lottery. The lotteries usually featured old textbooks as prizes; like modern church bazaars, they were utilized to dispose of unwanted articles. A less sophisticated form of misdemeanor was the periodic raids which the boys made under cover of darkness, breaking into cellar lockers and bearing away precious food and drink. The usual targets of these nocturnal forays were lockers belonging to tutors, since these repositories were almost certain to contain a sizable cache of wine, beer, and hard cider. In July 1761, to cite one example, some students raided a tutor's

16. *Poetical Works*, II, 37-38.

locker and hauled away twelve bottles of cider. A few days later, they repeated the raid and stole eighteen.[17] At another time, four students broke open a tutor's locker, smashed a barrel of cider, and made off with two bottles of wine. They were ultimately apprehended and found guilty of stealing the wine and "Damnyfying the Cellar." [18] Aside from the certainty of procuring viands of higher quality in a tutor's locker, students often expressed their animosity for a particular tutor in this fashion.

Raiding the rooms of fellow denizens of the college hall for chocolate, sugar loafs, and other edible tidbits was another customary practice, but one not always performed in jest. Some of the boys who became extremely proficient with "Pick-Locks" were obviously intent upon thievery. The records also mention a few individuals who accumulated a "large bunch of keys" and then proceeded to rifle the chambers with professional thoroughness. One wayward lad had the unfortunate experience of having a key stick in a lock at a most inopportune moment—as a group of boys suddenly entered the corridor. Finding it expedient to leave the scene on the run, he lost his entire ring.[19] Whether inspired by prankish instinct or by a more sinister motive, students occasionally broke into the monitor's quarters and stole the financial statements and the attendance records. Such thievery produced a massive investigation, with all students having to account for their whereabouts at the time of the incident. In virtually every case the guilty parties were apprehended.

Oftentimes, a few scalawags, feeling the knife-edge of starvation, would band together for a nocturnal sortie upon a neighboring farm for chickens or other edible fowl. The pungent aroma of roasting hen, prepared by the raiders in their rooms, sometimes seeped through the locked doors and reached the sensitive noses of Clap and the tutors who strolled periodically through the corridors during the evening hours sniffing the air for trouble.

Without question, however, the most frequent unlawful offense was the ringing of the college bell. The bellrope held a singular fascination for the boys. They seemed to have a compulsive urge to

17. Faculty Judgments, II, 48-49, Yale MS.
18. *Ibid.*, II, 19-28.
19. *Ibid.*, III, 4.

give it a tug. The frequency of this violation, more than the noise, nearly drove Clap mad. On one occasion in 1755, he became so incensed with the students because of a pre-dawn clangor that he administered an inordinately severe penalty to a junior caught red-handed in the act. One hundred students, virtually the entire student body, signed a petition calling for a softening of the penalty. Clap reprimanded the petitioners and levied fines. Enraged by this, the boys overturned his privy and committed numerous other pranks, whereupon the president departed for Hartford "to give them time to cool." With his return two weeks later, the bell began to ring again.[20]

If the ringing of the bell diminished the sleeping time of the tutors, it was really the least of their problems as far as relations with the students were concerned. Badgering—or "plaguing"—the tutors was a popular student pastime. Some of the traditional inanities included locking the tutors in their rooms, smoking the poor fellows out of their rooms, smashing their windows, and keeping them awake nights by screaming and whistling outside and by rolling large stones down the stairs of the college hall (the tutors' chambers were located near the staircase). It was a chief responsibility of the tutors to maintain discipline within the college hall during the evenings—no easy feat even by daylight.[21]

Closely linked with student indiscretions, especially those of a more violent nature, was the problem of drinking (the problem was Clap's, of course). The Faculty Judgments afford ample evidence of the fact that lounging in tap rooms was a common practice, especially after 1750. Assembled in the forbidden paradise, the boys frequently presented plays, or "bad frolicks," as Clap called them, some of which required elaborate costumes and the impersonation of females. Quite often, especially in the later years, the brazen scholars brought the tavern to the college, staging boisterous bacchanalian orgies within their chambers. In this connection, a particular speciality of the students was homemade wine

20. Schneider, eds., *Writings of Johnson,* I, 214; Nathan Williams to his father, Mar. 4, 1755, Pa. Hist. Soc. MS. The student punished by Clap stated in his defense that he grabbed the bell rope in order to keep from plunging down the stairwell. He lost his balance as he stepped back to permit some seniors to pass by.

21. For two classic examples of the problems tutors experienced in controlling the youth, see Faculty Judgments, I, 7-13; II, 32-35, Yale MS.

punch. The "College Laws" stipulated a monetary reward to any student reporting a violation of liquor regulations. It would appear from available records, however, that such a reward was never granted during Clap's administration.

The most violent and most protracted disorders occurred during commencements. At such times, the suppressed emotions of youth were released with unprecedented abandon and all the excesses, particularly drinking, were intensified many-fold; for an entire week, a carnival air prevailed in New Haven. The uninhibited funmaking of the evening hours was in sharp contrast to formal daytime exercises. The historian of Harvard has designated the period of the colonial commencement as the "puritan midsummer's holiday." [22] But this is an understatement; in terms of whisky-letting, indulgence of all sorts, and general hell-raising, the event was perhaps nearer in spirit to a modern Mardi Gras. Even before Clap became affiliated with Yale, the tradition of unrestrained drinking and riotous revelry during commencement had become firmly established. Everyone joined in the festivities, including the "Rabble" of the town. The following admonitory ditty by William Brattle, while referring to Harvard commencements, could be justly applied to Yale:

> Commencement's come, but (friendly) I advize
> All sorts of Rabble now their Homes to prize,
> For if to it they come, so Blind they'll bee,
> That Really no Body will see.[23]

The rabble could have replied in defense that they wished only to emulate their betters—especially the young gentlemen of Yale. For, in their efforts to quench a seemingly unquenchable thirst, the students, particularly the graduating seniors, consumed a staggering quantity of alcoholic beverages, from strong cider to powerful domestic and foreign rums. Sailors, longshoremen, nondescript wharf-rats, and town ne'er-do-wells, substantially fortified by drink and in search of excitement, often invited themselves to the festivities and participated in such customary commencement capers as firing cannons, smashing the windows of the college dor-

22. Morison, *Harvard in Seventeenth Century*, II, 465.
23. Col. Soc. of Mass., *Publications*, 18 (1917), 335.

mitory (the candles placed in each window for decorative purposes offered an inviting target), starting bonfires, setting off firecrackers, indulging in noisy processions, tearing down the college fence, overturning and burning outhouses, and "tingling" the college bell in the early hours of the morning. But the alliance of "town and gown," like an entente cordiale, was never of a lengthy duration. The sharp social cleavage between the two groups was too wide even for spirits to bridge. Protracted contact engendered mutual antagonisms. Antagonisms provoked name-calling. Name-calling precipitated bloody brawls. It was indeed an unusual commencement that did not feature at least one pitched battle or produce at least one first-class riot. As a plain fact, commencement was incomplete without a clash between "town and gown." [24]

While not inclined to the use of flagellation, President Clap was nonetheless a severe disciplinarian, perhaps without peer among college administrators of colonial America. It was with good reason that he earned the reputation among the students as a "Tirant and a sovraign," as one boy doodled in the margin of a book. A second bit of pugnacious marginalia points up the same unflattering fact. After reading Laurence Echard's discussion of Nero in *Ecclesiastical History,* a student inscribed this sentiment: "omnis Homo Thomas Clap of our Town arbitrariousest person."

Teeming with admonitions, fines, rustications, and expulsions, the faculty records testify to Clap's watchfulness. These judgments, it is to be noted, were rendered by him with the "advice" of the tutors. In actuality, he was the main, if not the sole, dispenser of discipline; the tutors merely presented the evidence. As noted earlier in the discussion of Clap's theory of discipline, the penalties were arranged on a graduated basis, and were commensurate with the seriousness of the crime. Less serious offenses, such as profanity, called for admonitions and fines. In one instance, a student was fined a small sum for shouting "Damn the Window" when the

24. Bad blood always existed between "town and gown" as indicated by the many incidents cited in the records. In 1753, for example, Clap fined a student for threatening to shoot a townie with whom he had had an "affray." The boy, with loaded pistol in hand, was apprehended while searching out his victim (Faculty Judgments, I, 24, Yale MS.). On another occasion, a group of town fathers overpowered, and delivered to Clap, a student who clubbed some local boys because they had been "saucy" to him (*Ibid.,* II, 74-75).

window crashed down upon his fingers.[25] At another time, a boy, while being publicly admonished for committing a minor violation, said "damn it" when the judgment was read off, and he "spake so loud as to be heard by some that sat near him." Profanity under these circumstances was a more serious offense: this particular boy was suspended.[26] The records do not clarify whether the punishment was inflicted for uttering the expletive or because of its audibility.

Clap was particularly severe in his punishment of those convicted of stealing and of damaging or destroying college property. If a student was judged guilty of stealing an article, he was required to reimburse the victim with a monetary sum three times in excess of the article's original price. If money was stolen, expulsion automatically followed. Flagrant contempt for the college officials also resulted in expulsion, as did the "heinous Sin" of fornication, noted but once in the records during Clap's tenure.

Bellringing was unquestionably Clap's greatest single disciplinary problem. He racked his brain for its solution. (The thought of removing the bell apparently never entered his mind.) He ran the gamut of mild punishments, from assorted fines to designating the offenders "official" bellringers, with the expectation, perhaps, that they would ring the obsession out of their systems. His methods proved unsuccessful. The "pernicious Practice" persisted. He finally abandoned mildness in the 1750's and began boxing the ears of those "catched in the act." [27] Such detection was not easy, as darkness was the great ally of the bellringers. The records relate many exhaustive and amusing investigations in which Clap and the tutors sought to establish the identity of sneaky culprits who had given the bellrope a violent jerk and then fled pell-mell through the corridors of the college hall to their rooms. The inductive process was never used with greater effectiveness, not even by the peerless Holmes himself.

Since the threat of having their ears rapped was no deterrent, Clap was forced to preventive, rather than disciplinary, measures.

25. *Ibid.,* I, 37.
26. *Ibid.,* I, 5.
27. The students protested vigorously when Clap began the policy of cuffing their ears. They charged that he was violating college law which stipulated a fine for the offense. *Ibid.,* I, 55-56.

At one time he directed the butler, who had the official responsibility to ring the bell, to fasten the bellrope in the belfry and place a lock on the door. The students, however, were not to be denied. They climbed into the belfry from the roof of the college hall, unfastened the door, broke the lock, and took up where they had left off.[28] On another occasion, when a siege of bellringing developed, Clap had the butler cut the rope, whereupon the ingenious students tied a string to the shortened rope and continued their "outragious and riotous Conduct."[29] Clap never solved the problem.

The president also engaged in many administrative maneuvers to checkmate drinking among the students. At different times, he explicitly forbade them to frequent taverns; limited the amount of alcoholic beverages to be dispensed by the butler; restricted the students in their wine purchases; refused to allow boys to board in taverns unless their parents were the owners of these establishments; terminated the practice of serving beer with the evening meal; appointed one tavern keeper who was bound by a rigid set of regulations to act as official dispenser of alcoholic products to undergraduates; implored, and sometimes directly ordered, tavern keepers not to serve intoxicants to the boys without a written statement signed either by himself or by the tutors;[30] in 1763, he even threatened court action against any tavern keeper within a three-mile radius of the college who catered to students.[31] Despite all his efforts, the president was remarkably unsuccessful in curbing student drinking. Only the Stamp Act crisis, it would seem,

28. *Ibid.*, II, 33-34. Clap convicted two boys accused of this offense. He boxed the ears of one. The second lad then ran out of the room and away from college, paying no heed to Clap's sharp command to return.

29. Clap's decision to cut the rope was prompted by the fact that a riot was going on at the time. When the tutors, then in town, heard of the trouble at college they hastened to the scene. They were met at the gate of the college by "guards" who yelled some threatening remarks. The tutors "thought it not prudent, under these hostile and riotous Appearances to venture among them but went and inform'd the Sherief." *Ibid.*, I, 80-83.

30. It was a common practice for the students to forge these statements. Likewise, when the boys did receive permission to purchase wine, rum, or brandy, they frequently increased the allotment.

31. In 1764, Clap demanded of one keeper, who dealt in "strong" literature as well, that he provide him with an account of his dealings with the students. The man sent word back that "the President had no right to know his Tradings with the Scholars in strong Drink." *Ibid.*, III, 48.

could effect such a reform; in 1764, at the suggestion of a tutor, the zealously patriotic students voluntarily agreed not to drink any "foreign spirituous Liquors any more." [32] On this score alone, Clap may have joyfully welcomed the political crisis. Yet, even in this case, the era of self-imposed restraint was short-lived.

The president likewise tried various stratagems to prevent riotous celebrations and drunken revelry at commencements. Some years he followed a Harvard precedent of holding commencement as a private ceremony, restricting it to members of the college community and local ministers and magistrates. On such occasions he incurred the wrath of those members of the Standing Order who lived outside New Haven. These men eagerly looked forward to the event since it provided an all-too-rare opportunity for renewing old friendships, for exchanging news, gossip, and bawdy stories, and for emptying bottles. Another technique Clap commonly employed was to withhold the announcement of the commencement date until just before the event. By this means, he hoped to reduce the time to lay up alcoholic supplies, and "keep the Rabble from coming." Some years he canceled the public feast traditionally held on the day following commencement. As with his efforts to stop the students from excessive drinking, however, all his attempts to reduce commencement to a sober academic exercise were a failure. Whether private or public, whether announced beforehand or just prior to the actual ceremony, with or without the traditional feast, commencement remained a week-long saturnalia, punctuated by bellringing, cannon-firing, and "town and gown" fighting.

Had student disorders been limited to those mentioned, including the turbulent commencement demonstrations, the problem of discipline at Yale could not have been considered acute. Until the 1750's, student misdemeanors at Yale were on a par with those committed by boys in the other colonial colleges and in the English universities. It is true that Yale experienced extraordinarily serious disturbances during the Great Awakening. As noted elsewhere, finding that the youth had gotten out of hand, Clap

32. Anson Stokes, *Memorials of Eminent Yale Men, A Biographical Study of Student Life and University Influences During the Eighteenth and Nineteenth Centuries*, 2 vols. (New Haven, 1914), II, 176.

closed the school in the spring of 1742 before the authorized date of termination. But things returned to normalcy by fall. Clap secured a firm hold over the boys, and during the next decade a general tranquillity pervaded the college.

This tranquillity, marred only by the tumultuous commencement disturbances, lasted until the mid-1750's, when the president became entangled in the thorny religious controversies cited earlier. After 1755, the students began to manifest a growing rebelliousness, to strain against the leashes of Clap's fiat, and to question his disciplinary methods. "Old Tom Clap," one pensive student wrote in the margin of a book, "you are quite wrong in your form of government." [33] A distinct change in the character of student disturbances was discernible. Rather than reflecting youthful ebullience, demonstrations began to assume the form of protests against the administration, and they were explicitly directed at Clap, for "old Tom Clap" was the administration.

It is not possible to pinpoint just when the change in mood occurred, but the critical date would appear to be 1756. In this year the boys began the practice of posting "defamatory Libels" near the college and in the yard itself. Such actions infuriated Clap and prompted him to issue directives suggestive of a police regimen. Students who found the letters were ordered to destroy them on the spot and not to divulge their contents to anyone. If one revealed the contents, he would be punished "as much as if he appeared to be the Author of it." [34] In this same year, there also occurred the first manifestation of mass disapproval of Clap. While a Corporation meeting was in progress, a number of boys staged a "generall remarkable Riot." The youthful insurgents detonated a homemade bomb and paraded through the college grounds, "screaming and shouting with the utmost Vociferation." A gentleman in attendance rightly surmised that the raucous scene was to be attributed to Clap's "confounded arbitrary Government." [35] This outburst was but one of a number of spontaneous riots (or,

33. This bit of marginalia was discovered by the sharp-eyed Yale librarian, the late Andrew Keogh. "The Yale Library of 1742," Lydenberg and Keogh, eds., *William Warner Bishop, a Tribute,* 83.
34. Faculty Judgments, I, 47, Yale MS. Clap's new method of dealing with bell-ringers (boxing their ears) may have provoked these incidents.
35. Dexter, ed., *Stiles's Itineraries,* 597.

in the vernacular of the authorities, "great Rout Riot and Disorder") that shook the college in the period of 1755-60. As noticed earlier, Clap came under heavy fire from his critics, Gale in particular, because of the student unrest and his inability to prevent disorder. By inflicting swift and severe punishment, Clap was able to break the riots and restore order. Until 1760, at least, his *auctoritas* was a powerful weapon of restraint. Few students could summon the courage to challenge it openly. To be in the presidential presence was still to be in awe. Nevertheless, the unrest was symptomatic of a growing and irrepressible opposition to his regime among the students at Yale.

The gulf between president and students gradually widened. With each passing year, discipline crumbled, slowly, almost imperceptibly. Evading prayers and classes became more widespread, frequenting taverns more popular, thumbing the nose at Clap's authority more open. The educational process continued, to be sure, but the current of revolt grew progressively stronger. By 1760, it was evident that it was only a matter of time before the students would rebel.

The first uprising occurred during the Commencement of 1760. When the Corporation met in July to lay plans for the affair, Clap strongly urged that the ceremony should be a private affair held at the completion of examinations near the end of the month. He was overruled, however, by the fellows,[36] who were apparently responsive to the strong public demand for a commencement with all the traditional trappings.[37] The Yale governing body did endorse Clap's proposals to regulate the liquor traffic. Each senior was to submit to the Corporation an estimate of the amount of wine he intended to purchase and his planned expenditure for the item, and on commencement day to declare under oath that he had not exceeded his estimate. Moreover, all who obtained degrees were to proceed immediately to their homes rather than remain in

36. Jared Eliot to Ezra Stiles, July 30, 1760, Yale MS.

37. Another factor may have played some part in the Corporation's decision. The gentry's attendance at commencements that were held prematurely had a disruptive effect on Connecticut's economy. In 1762, after Clap's will had prevailed on the issue of an early commencement, John Hubbard wrote to Stiles: "Nothing looked to me more mean than to see a Number of Gentlemen of good Sense so tamely noosed by the President, their Country all the while cursing them for interrupting the Joys of Harvest." Dexter, ed., *Stiles's Itineraries*, 507.

New Haven spending their time in "Idleness and Frolicking." [38]

Clap's difficulties began even before commencement got under-way, and at first they had nothing to do with liquor. A few days before the scheduled academic exercises, and for reasons unknown, he became "disgusted" with the ranking member of the senior class. By tradition, this boy was to deliver the salutatory oration. Clap now appointed the student ranked second in the class stand-ing to deliver the address. He refused. The president then went down the entire list extending the offer. All refused. Incensed by their insubordination, he ordered that the degrees be granted after the examination and that the public ceremonies be canceled. The seniors promptly sent a memorial to the Corporation, re-questing that body to countermand Clap's order. Much to the president's displeasure, the Corporation acquiesced in the stu-dents' request. At the same time, it enacted a measure limiting each senior to two gallons of wine; those found guilty of violating the act were to forfeit their degrees.

The limitation on wine was a blow, but one which the seniors knew ways of circumventing. The evening before commencement, while making a routine check of the buildings and yard, Clap came upon a "small cagg of rum" in one of the entryways. All circumstances pointed to the fact that it had been dropped in haste. He placed it in the care of the butler. Shortly after, two seniors laid claim to it and carted it off to their chambers. The president now swung into action. He questioned the transgressors and, when they could only plead "custom" for their act of purchasing the rum, he denied them their degrees. On the next day, a three-man delegation of seniors met with Clap and the Corporation and argued against the decision. They speciously pointed out that the new law applied only to wine. Moreover, they affirmed, as had the principal offenders, that an old law prohibiting the drinking of rum was void by reason of the fact that it had been neither ob-served nor enforced in the past ("custom"). The seniors' admission of guilt was one matter. But their assertion that the law they had violated had passed into limbo because of a lack of enforcement reflected unfavorably upon the Yale governing body. This group

38. Yale Corporation Records, I, 141, Yale Univ.

rewarded the spunky seniors by refusing to grant their degrees. Later in the morning, all but five of the senior class approached the Corporation and admitted having purchased rum without first receiving a permit. All were denied degrees.

What had originated as broad farce now assumed the character of a small-scale rebellion against the administration. The Corporation announced that degrees would be awarded only if the guilty seniors submitted a confession. By late afternoon, under the persuasive urging of parents and prominent magistrates and ministers, who were chafing with impatience, the rebellious scholars were ready to concede. With reluctance, they drew up and signed a confession and presented it to the Corporation. Clap insisted that the paper be read in the meetinghouse of New Haven, the largest auditorium in town, rather than in the college hall, "which occasioned some demurrer." The "humble confession," which replaced the salutatory oration, opened the commencement exercises. The president introduced the confession in "his unpolite manner." [39] It was clearly Clap's victory, but a hollow one, as time was to prove.

He was soon to be made aware of a general and progressive degeneration of discipline. In the three or four years following the commencement dispute of 1760, the classes continued to meet and prayers were performed as usual, but it was education at a three-quarter pace. There was an appreciable increase in absences from recitations and prayers. A memorandum on July 26, 1763,[40] bears witness to the fact. From June 4 to July 26:

	absent	tardy
Cushman	16	3
Whiting	16	10
Buckley	27	3
Woodruff	11	7
Williams	35	12

39. *Ibid.*, I, 143-44; Chauncey Whittelsey to Ezra Stiles, Sept. 15, 1760, Yale MS. The freshmen also contributed to the febrile excitement of commencement eve. Ostensibly in celebration of the end of their period of bondage, they marched through the college yard making a "violent and scandalous" noise, led by a boy brandishing a "naked sword." They also beat the fence with "clubs and staves." Yale Corporation Records, I, 145, Yale Univ.

40. Faculty Judgments, III, 12, Yale MS.

The students were becoming more unruly in their classroom behavior. The tutors constantly complained of "levity, whispering and inattention." During study periods, many of the boys were not to be found in their chambers grubbing away at their books. Instead, they whiled away the time in "idleness, loud talk and laughter," or committed "many secret acts of wickedness."

With increasing regularity, the youth began staging parties and dances in houses in New Haven. On weekends many left New Haven altogether and traveled to nearby towns where they set up camp in a tavern and indulged in wine, women, and song. From the records, it would seem that Milford was to Clap's generation what New York City is to the Yale youth of today. The more legalistic-minded *bon vivants* who were hell-bent for pleasure frequently requested Clap's permission to leave for these weekend carousals, offering the excuse that they had pressing business commitments. Others simply drifted out of New Haven without bothering to secure presidential sanction. In one instance, a group of blithe spirits assumed that they had been granted permission when the president had said "the Word *go*" after hearing their request. Upon their return to college, the boys learned, assuredly without surprise, that they had read too much into the verb. As Clap informed the boys, "it is an universal Practice for the Pres^dt when he has said all to any Scholar which he intends at that Time to conclud with telling him he may go." [41]

In this same three-year span the tempo of violence increased. The sight of students stripped to the waist, handkerchiefs pulled high over their noses, and with clubs, stones, or pistol in hand, was all too common. Violence was fast becoming the prevailing condition. "It seems to be still times with our new Lights," Jared Eliot wrote to Stiles in 1761, "but not at College where there has been a tumult. the Desk pulled down, the Bellcase broken and the bell ringing in the night. Mr. Boardman the Tutor beaten with clubbs." [42] On September 8, 1761, a mixed group of towns-

41. *Ibid.*, III, 54-55.
42. May 25, 1761, Yale MS. Although it may not have provided any great comfort to his bruised body, the tutor derived perhaps a measure of spiritual succor from a vote of confidence placed in him by the Corporation. Yale Corporation Records, I, 147, Yale Univ. Clap made the usual intensive investigation but failed to uncover the assailants. Eliot to Stiles, July 28, 1761, Yale MS.

people and students, with collars turned high, congregated near the college and "hallooed and shouted," fired "Great Guns" and pistols, broke down "about Seven or Eight Rods" of the college fence, and threw stones and clubs at the college hall, smashing forty or fifty squares of glass, mostly in the tutors' chambers. During a lull in the assault, a student emerged from the building and informed the raiders that Clap and the tutors were not inside but could be found at the president's home, located across the street. One of the rioters, obviously chagrined by this news, then yelled, *"Damn it* let us go and give it to them there." And give it to them they did, by smashing Clap's windows.[43]

What particularly disturbed Clap in this period, perhaps even more than having stones crash through his windows, was the growing contempt manifested against his authority. It was evidenced in a great many ways. In July of 1761, the president and two fellows went to investigate a "great noise" emanating from a chamber. Demanding entrance, they received, instead, this threatening and irreverent retort: "You have no business here; if you come, you come at your peril. The man that enters dies." Clap and his companions knew better than to force the issue. They retreated to the counsel room and drew up stiff penalties against the impudent boys *in absentia*.[44] Similarly, there was a symbolic significance in the antics of one Tertius White who "stood up and profanely mimicked the President" at prayers.[45]

At another time, Clap popped in on a student soiree which was being held in a town house. The boys, flushed with wine, quickly extinguished the candles and fire (they could not so quickly extinguish the fire within), and made "loud Noises in Contempt." Clap ordered them to disperse. In open defiance of the presidential edict, most of them remained in the house for an additional hour.[46] On November 20, 1762, to cite another instance, the president re-

43. Faculty Judgments, II, 62-65, Yale MS. Clap later published a letter in the *Connecticut Gazette* (New Haven), Sept. 12, 1761, in which he asserted that the mob was composed of townspeople with "some few strangers." He and the tutors passed through the assemblage but did not detect one student. Those wearing gowns he branded as impostors.

44. Yale Corporation Records, I, 147, 150, Yale Univ. Two of the boys were denied a second degree and two were expelled.

45. Faculty Judgments, III, 27, Yale MS.

46. *Ibid.*, II, 93-94.

ceived some "contemptuous Papers," and later learned that one brazen youth had spoken the unsettling comment, "if any are expelled, I will be one that will skin old Tom Clap's Hide." [47]

The most serious large-scale clash between Clap and the students, during the period 1761-64, took place in November 1762. Once again, Clap was pitted against the senior class. The disturbance stemmed from the refusal of the seniors to comply with a new policy of examination introduced by Clap. Under his revised system, he and the tutors were empowered to examine a senior at any given time in the course of the academic year. Previously, only one annual examination had been held, in July. The seniors informed the president that they would not comply with the new policy unless it was approved by the Corporation. The contents of the letter were sufficient to provoke Clap's anger, but his sense of outrage was further increased by the way in which the boys had affixed their signatures "round the letter . . . in an odd and ludicrous manner."

The seniors had issued a direct challenge, and Clap was disposed to accept it. He convened the class in the library and ordered four boys to turn to a certain page of a text and prepare for examination. With deliberate effrontery they refused. Sensing the futility of proceeding further, Clap dismissed the class. He then proceeded to take disciplinary action against those guilty of this "great contempt" of authority. A hasty inquiry revealed the identity of two seniors who had organized class opposition and drawn up the letter of protest. On the following morning, after devotions, Clap read off his judgment against these and other suspected leaders of the "Rebellion." Two were suspended and three minor ringleaders were to be publicly admonished. Hearing the judgment, the two boys who had been suspended rose from their seats, put on their hats, and trooped out of the room, all the while lustily calling out to their classmates and others to "follow on my brave Boys."

With a degree of accord that must have been shocking to Clap, over one-half of the student body followed. They stormed out of

47. *Ibid.*, II, 94. The students also began to assert themselves in oratory. Declamations began to take on a pointed tone. The theme of one declamation in 1765 was that "Tumults and Commotions" would cease if rulers were kind and benevolent. The student cited Caesar Augustus as a model ruler. Yale MS.

the room and "made a great hallooing in the Yard in contempt and defiance and then went down to the waterside in a kind of triumph." Two hours later, after having paraded through the dusty streets of town, they returned to the college and further displayed their sulphurous contempt for Clap by playing a football game (a form of present-day soccer) on the green during the regular study period. This act compounded their insolence, since football was banned as a form of recreation. Later in the day, they dispatched an ultimatum to the president: they would not observe any further "college orders" until the two suspended seniors were restored to the class standing and the new policy of examination was abandoned. Clap refused to consider these demands.

The students, locked in a pledge of mutual loyalty, stood firm. They remained away from college the greater part of a week. The gravity of the crisis necessitated an emergency meeting of the Corporation—an intervention of Jovian dimensions. Siding with Clap, the fellows sternly ordered the boys to put an end to the nonsense and make a full confession of their misdeeds. At the same time, they exiled four ringleaders of the revolt to country parsonages ("rustication"). Two boys were expelled outright. This swift and decisive action broke the backbone of student resistance. Their youthful bravado shattered for the moment, the delinquent saints returned to college—and resumed the plotting of ingenious mischief.[48]

The final two years of Clap's administration, beginning in the fall of 1764, were a period of incessant turmoil and rampant rebellion. "Probably there has never been a time in the experience of Yale," Professor Dexter has correctly written of these two years, "when antagonism between the authorities and the students had been so ingeniously and assiduously cultivated." [49] It was then that Clap, in a final desperate effort to restore order, began stringent enforcement of an earlier law, which ordered the tutors to search the chambers, studies, and lockers of the students three times daily for "strong drink" and "lascivious books"; Clap himself made a

48. Yale Corporation Records, I, 159-61, Yale Univ.; Dexter, ed., *Literary Diary of Stiles*, III, 232.

49. Dexter, "On Some Social Distinctions at Harvard and Yale Before the Revolution," Amer. Antiq. Soc., *Proceedings*, New Ser., 9 (1893), 45.

thorough inspection once a week.[50] "Lascivious books" was a reference to the Earl of Rochester's *Poems,* a work "greatly tending to debauch the Minds of Youth," in the opinion of the college officials. The students, it seems, had a keen appetite for Rochester's salacious offerings.

As a climax to the school year 1764-65, in which infractions of discipline reached singular proportions, a small group of townspeople and students made an assault upon Clap's home on commencement eve. On this particular evening, the president was consulting with four fellows on the details of commencement. In the nearby tavern of Christopher Kilby, the malcontents were conversing on less serious matters over a bottle of wine. As the midnight hour approached and blood became warmer, a member of the party proposed that they "go and raise a dust at Colledge," a perfectly natural suggestion under the circumstances. To this proposal all were in congenial agreement. A second member then voiced the corollary to the proposition, that they should first proceed to Clap's home and offer a "blessing" to the president. The corollary had a stronger appeal. It was not necessary to put the question to a vote or to define the euphemism "blessing." With wine glasses in hand, the revelers left the tavern and noisily set out in the direction of Clap's home. Arriving there, they tore down a gate and peppered the house with stones and cattle horns, all the while "swearing and shouting." Their mission accomplished, they moved swiftly, although unsteadily, into the safety of darkness —but only for a moment. Regrouping, the young bucks ruminated over the assault. It was ultimately concluded that the venture just completed was definitely not of a professional order. Was not a gate still operable? Were there not unshattered windows in the house? They retraced their steps to proffer a second "blessing." The lone workable gate was pulled from its hinges and smashed, and the remaining window panes were shattered. The tipsy marauders were obviously aware that their missiles were "to the great Peril of the Life and Limbs" of Clap and other occupants of the house. What they probably did not realize at the moment was that Clap had been slightly wounded by flying glass in the course of the two assaults. After completing the second lively

50. Yale Corporation Records, I, 165, 167, Yale Univ.

fusillade, the raiders left the scene. The original plan—to "raise a dust" at college—was abandoned. A few of the students returned to the college hall and consumed more wine before stumbling off to bed.[51]

On the following morning, Clap, by way of a Corporation judg-ment, fired off a stern warning to the New Haven civil authorities. If precautionary measures were not taken in the future "to sup-press the disorders that are frequently committed at Commence-ment and protect the President and Fellows from being insulted," he would order that future commencements be held in some other town.[52] The prospect of losing the annual commencement busi-ness spurred the town officials into action. In late August eight culprits were arrested and tried. Clap was a chief witness for the prosecution. The accused pleaded guilty and received stiff fines.[53]

The three students involved in the "very wicked Riot" were hauled before the college authorities and presented with a second dosage of punishment. The youth judged responsible for Clap's injury was expelled; this arrant rascal had worn his academic duties lightly since his entrance as a freshman and had been mov-ing steadily towards Avernus. A second offender was farmed out to a neighboring minister for one year of spiritual seasoning. The third participant, whose father was not only a respected minister but a Corporation member to boot, was directed to read a public confession. This lenient penalty was prompted by the boy's action of testifying for the prosecution, an action not likely to endear him to his fellow students.

In the early months of 1766 the spirit of rebellion reached a riotous climax.[54] The contumacious students now gave up all pre-tense of serving Minerva. In mid-February, spearheaded by the seniors, they made an organized attempt to oust Clap from office. They drew up a petition listing "grievances and intolerancies,"

51. Faculty Judgments, III, 55, Yale MS.; Kenneth Scott, "A 'Dust' at Yale and a 'Blessing' for President Clap," Conn. Hist. Soc., *Bulletin*, 23 (1958), 46-49.

52. Yale Corporation Records, I, 170, Yale Univ.

53. Records of the Superior Court, New Haven Session, 1763-1765, XV, Aug. 27, 1765, Conn. State Lib.

54. For detailed accounts of the rebellious events of this period, see Journal of a Scholar's Conduct, entries for Feb. through Apr., Yale MS.; Yale Corporation Records, I, 174-75, Yale Univ.; "Extracts From Diary of Joseph B. Wadsworth," *College Courant*, 3 (1868), 132.

explicitly charging Clap with refusing to grant appeals of his disciplinary judgments to the Corporation, with keeping them in ignorance of disciplinary measures, and with imposing ex post facto penalties. For good measure, they asserted that he was in his dotage. All but a handful subscribed to the petition, the seniors intimidating the freshmen into signing.[55] To be on the safe side, they selected the student son of a fellow [56] to deliver the document to the members of the Corporation.

When the students realized that the Corporation planned no action on their memorial, as shown by its failure to convene in emergency session, they abandoned legal tactics. As of March, as one student tersely phrased it, "all study broke up"—the college, too, for that matter! The failure of the Corporation to act released all the Furies of disorder on the campus. The students went on a rampage. With triumphant finality, the angry young men of Yale rang the bells at will; broke down the "clock-case"; smashed doors and windows of the college halls (the tally for March 31 alone numbered "80 squares" of glass—the grand total was over "400 squares"); tore up the garret floor and tossed the boards upon bonfires spontaneously set in the yard; smashed benches, fences, and furniture; stole psalm books from the chapel (not for spiritual purposes); posted abusively "Satyrical" letters in conspicuous places in the yard; infrequently attended prayers and classes; and refused to pay their bills to the monitor. They also launched a reign of terror against the new brace of tutors who had replaced the Sandeman-tinged instructors sacked by Clap in 1765. After smashing their windows, the boys threatened them with a fearful fate should they remain at college. For these young instructors, survival took precedence over dignity; they hastily packed their belongings and rode out of New Haven. Having removed these agents of restraint, the seditious students reigned supreme within the college. Anarchy prevailed!

The engine of discipline had come to a grinding halt. It reflected the complete breakdown of Clap's disciplinary mechanism that a group of boys was called before the president for being

55. Dexter, ed., *Stiles's Itineraries*, 455; Journal of a Scholar's Conduct, Yale MS.; *Diary of David McClure, Doctor of Divinity, 1748-1820*, notes by Franklin B. Dexter (N. Y., 1899), 9.
56. George Beckwith, appointed to the Corporation in 1763.

absent "64 Times from Prayers this [Quarter], but we was none of us fined." [57] The fact that not a single entry was recorded in the Faculty Judgments for the school year 1765-66 would indicate that Clap knew that he was powerless. His mountain of authority had been leveled.

The Corporation, belatedly recognizing the gravity of the situation, and fearful that the students would reduce the college buildings to a heap of rubble, met in emergency session in April, some two weeks before the regular spring vacation. The malcontent students were called in and permitted to express the grievances outlined in their petition of February. As was to be expected, the governing body found their arguments unconvincing. For the record, it attributed the miseries of Yale to the "Spirit of the Times and the Influence of others," that is, to the Stamp Act crisis and to the Benjamin Gale element. Since the school was without tutors, the fellows voted to terminate teaching until after the vacation period. The students were to return to their homes.[58]

This procedure accomplished nothing. When the college reopened in May, "the good old Lady [Yale] seemed just to breath[e], but ready to expire," as ex-tutor Chauncey Whittelsey so poignantly phrased it.[59] A mere forty, representing but one-third of the student body, returned to New Haven. Furthermore, the college was still without tutors, Clap having been unsuccessful in his efforts to hire replacements for those who had left in April. For ten harried days during the vacation period, he had traveled through adjacent towns seeking out qualified instructors. But the unpleasant, if not terrifying, thought of coping with "Wild Fire not easily controlled and governed," as Ezra Stiles later aptly described the youth of Yale in ruminating over whether he should become president,[60] apparently deterred anyone whom Clap approached. It was now an acknowledged fact that a tutorial position at Yale had little to recommend it. The spectacle of a college

57. "Extracts From Diary of Joseph B. Wadsworth," *College Courant*, 3 (1868); see the entry for Mar. 28.

58. Yale Corporation Records, I, 173, Yale Univ.

59. Whittelsey to Stiles, July 9, 1766, Yale MS. Whittelsey further lamented, "I am almost ready to weep; Alma Mater is truly in a deplorable Situation, and I fear will be ruined." The letter is printed in Dexter, ed., *Stiles's Itineraries*, 589.

60. Dexter, ed., *Literary Diary of Stiles*, II, 209.

functioning without a teaching staff prompted James Dana of Wallingford, who was no friend to Clap, to comment wryly: "Tis indeed somewhat droll, that there should be a college invested with a President and divinity professor, but no instructors." [61]

With Clap and Daggett supervising the instruction of what few class meetings were held, the school remained in session through May and June. But it had become increasingly evident that the future of the college was in jeopardy should Clap stubbornly persist in his intention to remain in office. Dissolution appeared imminent. Dana gave perfect expression to the public mood of Connecticut when he wrote, with painful clarity, that Clap must "be controul'd, or greatly alter his phylosophic (rather unphylosophic) government, or be discharg'd, or college is ruin'd." [62] It was no idle prophecy.

Ruefully and reluctantly, Clap recognized the truth. He knew he was beaten. Such tribulation, such battering, the college could endure no longer, nor could he personally sustain the campaign of violence. His only proper course was to surrender. When the Corporation assembled in another emergency session on July 1, the sixty-three-year-old president, a defeated, pathetic figure, shorn of his characteristic haughtiness, tendered his resignation. Stating that he was "somewhat tired and fatigued" by the "Care, Business and Labour" of his office, that his health was not as "firm" as formerly, and that he was "entring upon or approaching towards the Decays of Nature," he asked to be relieved of his duties.[63] Understandably, he made no mention of the prevailing disorder. Doubtless out of compassion, the Corporation refused to accept his resignation, but tactfully urged him to continue "as long as Divine Providence would permit, at least till the next Commencement." Clap responded to the cue, agreeing to finish out the school year. That his administration would conclude on a peaceful note was all but assured by the Corporation's action of sending the three lower classes to their homes; the seniors were to remain in New Haven and pursue their studies in private.[64]

61. Dexter, ed., *Stiles's Itineraries,* 456.
62. *Ibid.*
63. *Connecticut Courant* (Hartford), July 21, 1766; *Connecticut Gazette* (New Haven), July 12, 1766; Yale Corporation Records, I, 174, Yale Univ.
64. *Ibid.,* I, 174-76.

In September 1766, Clap terminated his long and turbulent academic career by presiding over the commencement exercises. The high point of the ceremony was not the disputations, as in past years, but Clap's "pertinent and pathetic" Latin address, which followed the conferring of degrees and closed the day's program. In content, the address was disappointingly conventional; in tone, characteristically bland. It followed form to the letter. The president began by reaffirming the medieval principle of the function of higher education, that colleges were erected for the purpose of enlarging the "noble Faculty" of reason, "especially that the human Mind may have the clearest Conceptions and most sublime Ideas of the divine Nature, and be fitted and prepared for celestial Felicity." Continuing, he indulged in some back-slapping, recounting the many visible signs of improvement at Yale during his administration, "its Increase in Edifices, Instructors and Students, and in almost every kind of useful and polite Literature; especially that it has for a long Time annually produced so many shining Lights in the Ch[urc]h, and firm Pillars in the Civil State." Next followed his reasons for requesting retirement. He had "always been involved in more Care, Business and Labor, than is proper for one Man, or usual with other Presidents; which Labor for the good of College I have, with the greatest Pleasure and Chearfulness, gone thro' for almost Twenty seven years." Now the infirmities of age had set in. He was desirous of the "Sweets of Retirement and a private Life." Of honor, he had had enough; of burden, "by far too much." He had labored long to promote the welfare of his society, "especially that the Minds of Young Men might be replenished with the Principles of true Religion." He prayerfully hoped that the religious foundation of Yale would be "preserved safe and pure to the latest Posterity," and he earnestly beseeched the school authorities never to turn aside from the "Way of Orthodoxy; and that you never chuse a President or Fellow, who is lukewarm or indifferent to the Principles of Religion, thro' whose Indulgence or Want of Care, any Corruption may steal into this sacred Fountain, and thence into the Churches." It was evident that a few embers of passion still glowed in the burned-out heart of the battle-weary president. Whatever the turn of events, his convictions on the historical nature of Yale and its purpose as an institution of higher learning remained as solid as Savin Rock.

Clap concluded on a profoundly nostalgic note, bidding "Farewel, my Reverend Brethren: Adieu, ye Lights of the church—and all of you who have been educated in this Seat of Learning. Shine more and more in Chh. and State. Lastly, I bid you one and all farewell. May you be happy to all Eternity." [65] It was one of the more poignant moments in the history of colonial Connecticut. As reported in the *Connecticut Courant,* the address, "for its peculiar Elegance and Dignity, merited and obtained the Attention and Approbation of the learned and judicious Audience; who could not but be much affected with the parting Speech of one who they knew had been very greatly instrumental in promoting the Noble Cause of Religion and Learning, and whose superior Understanding and knowledge had very much exalted the Honour and Reputation of the Academy over which he presided."

The address completed, a remarkable epoch in the history of Yale College came to an end. For the students, it was a time for high celebration. Zeus had been toppled. That night, the seniors danced in the "State House." [66]

Freed from the burdens of office, Clap busied himself with his many scientific projects, and with a study he had contemplated for many years, for which he had been collecting materials: a history of Connecticut.[67] But his life was nearly at an end. He was destined not long to outlive his presidency, as if his office and his mission had sustained him beyond his span of years. Failing health forced him to curtail his intellectual pursuits; in August (before commencement) he had traveled to Stafford Springs, Connecticut, and bathed in the famous mineral waters of that spa. In late December, he was taken with fever and confined to bed. Confronted with the awesome fact of death, he remained stoically composed,

65. *Connecticut Courant* (Hartford), Sept. 22, 1766; the address is also printed in Dexter, ed., *Stiles's Itineraries,* 61-62.

66. "Extracts From Diary of Joseph B. Wadsworth," *Yale Alumni Weekly* (June 17, 1896), entry for Sept. 10.

67. "Roger Wolcott's Memoir Relating to Connecticut," Conn. Hist. Soc., *Collections,* 3 (1895), 325-36; Clap, A Plan or Heads of a History of the Colony of Connecticut, Yale MS. Some in Connecticut thought that Clap aspired for a seat in the upper house. Dexter, ed., *Stiles's Itineraries,* 510-11.

firm in his faith. As he had stood erect before his mortal enemies, so, too, did he face without fear the ineluctable enemy of life. In the spirit of the Anglican Laud, who, with his head resting on the block, calmly spoke out, "Lord, I am coming as fast as I can," Clap looked forward to his demise with a sense of supreme optimism and serene assurance of salvation. Naphtali Daggett described the last hours of the venerable Puritan:

When he apprehended death probably near, he sensibly expressed an entire Resignation to the Will of God, and a firm unshaken hope of his good estate. And when it was observed to him, that he was looked upon to be very dangerously sick, he made a little exception to the propriety of the expression: that the situation could not be properly called 'dangerous,' in which he was so advanced so near to the end of all his toils and labours, and so nigh to the Haven of eternal rest. He was perfectly calm and composed, and reconciled to dying.—The King of Terrours could not daunt him, or shake the Foundation of his hope.—He gave the natural symptoms of pretty strong pains in body, thro' the night preceeding his dissolution; and soon after the natural Sun had risen upon our Hemisphere, this bright Luminary in our Church, and Republic of Literature, who had much resembled the Sun in the Steadiness of his Course, and in diffusing the Light of Knowledge around him was extinguish'd by having his eyes closed in the slumbers of sleep: without a groan or struggle he fell asleep.[68]

Contemporary accounts suggest that the physical cause of death was a pulmonary disorder. Some, however, shared the opinion of a student, who believed that Clap's demise had been hastened "by the mortification of a resignation and by relinquishing the regular and uniform habits which he had pursued through the long period of his presidency." [69]

68. *Faithful Serving of God*, 35-36. Clap died on Jan. 7, 1767.
69. *Diary of David McClure,* notes by Dexter, 9.

Chapter Eleven

THE OBSOLESCENCE
OF "CLAPISM"

$\mathbf{I}$F Thomas Clap could see present-day Yale, he would be horrified by the changes wrought by time. More than likely, he would prefer to return at once to his grave and sleep on in peaceful anonymity, away from the appalling din and carbon-monoxide-laden atmosphere of the modern campus.

In truth, the modern university bears little resemblance, physical or otherwise, to the colonial college. The campus of Clap's time, which snuggled along the west side of the New Haven Green, has been enlarged at least fifty-fold, and could in fact be neatly tucked into a "coffin corner" of the ponderously massive Yale Bowl. The severe simplicity and simple dignity of Yale College, Connecticut Hall, and the chapel have given way to a babel of architectural design, from the austere Gothic of the Memorial Quadrangle to the modernistic, functional style of the art gallery. (Some sardonic local residents maintain that Yale blends beautifully with the architectural chaos of the nearby business center.) The instructional staff of four has soared to the astronomical figure of 1,800.[1] The student body, including graduate students, no longer consists predominantly of male members of the Congregational social

1. This figure was provided by Stephen Kezerian, director of the Yale University News Bureau, in May 1959.

elite. Diverse in religious affiliation, it includes Catholics, Methodists, Baptists, Quakers, Jews, Moslems, and Hindus; it even includes women! The curriculum has been expanded and atomized, altered beyond recognition. The once fearsome "College Laws" and the "Freshman Laws" have long since been consigned to limbo. Incoming freshmen are now informed by a University publication that "a Yale education is above all an exercise in freedom. There are few rules, and they are flexible." [2] Aside from the few scraps of memorabilia that have been preserved, the sole visible links with the college of Clap's time are the shell of Connecticut Hall and the exhibition Library of 1742 in the Sterling Memorial Library.

Yet, Clap's shadow is still cast on the modern university. The most bitter denigrators of the Puritans would admit that the intellectual and spiritual strength of Yale runs deep into its Puritan past. "A university," wrote Charles Seymour, a recent president of Yale, "acquires life through the lives of its members and, as in the case of all human institutions and probably more than in most, the character of its vitality depends upon past generations." And Yale's Puritan past is inseparable from the character and principles of Thomas Clap. One thinks of Emerson's well-known aphorism, "the institution is the lengthened shadow of one man."

Viewed in the perspective of Yale's colonial history, Clap's era stands out as the school's most decisively constructive period, as its Periclean Age. Under his dynamic, if despotic, leadership, a primitive school was transformed into a leading intellectual center of the New World. Clap was a chief architect of what has become one of the world's great centers of learning. As Professor Dexter has indicated, he served as the vital link between James Pierpont, the "true founder" of the college, and Timothy Dwight (the elder), the "far-sighted projector and herald of the expanded university." [3] To dismiss Clap as an irascible reactionary, as is often done, without acknowledging his significant accomplishments as an academic administrator, is improper. Yale did not develop out of a colonial

2. "An Introduction to Yale," Yale University *Bulletin*, Ser. 53, No. 18 (1957), 7.
3. Dexter, "Clap and Writings," New Haven Colony Hist. Soc., *Papers*, 5 (1894), 270.

vacuum as some accounts would have us believe.[4] Although student violence and religious illiberalism marred his administration, Clap personally forged a new Yale, gave the college a new sense of direction, and set the stage for the subsequent achievements of Stiles, Dwight, and Day. Unfortunately, the positive aspects of his presidency have been submerged in the criticism of his reactionary religious policies.

Unquestionably he was reactionary in religious matters. Despite concessions to Anglicans, Clap tried to maintain the college as a narrow sectarian agency. During his tenure of office, Yale stood against the tide of secularization and nonsectarianism in American higher education. In the face of rising anthropocentric and mechanistic credos, Yale continued to affirm the moral nature of society and the Messianic vision of human destiny. The curriculum was strongly oriented toward religion, which infused all subjects and was regarded as the focus of the educative process. While progressive Harvard gave way to change and moved steadily toward Unitarianism, Transcendentalism, and New Education (the elective system), Yale refused to join the "restless pursuit of novelty," preferring religious orthodoxy and the classical liberal arts curriculum. It would be too much to say that Clap imposed this conservative outlook upon the college. As Professor Roland Bainton observes, Yale was conservative "before she was born." [5] But Clap can be credited with fortifying and helping to sustain the tradition. For at least a century after him, Yale cleaved to religious orthodoxy.

Dedication to religious conformity reflected a general conservatism in social philosophy that is also a part of Yale's tradition. As Professor George Pierson, a loyal son of old Eli, observes, Yale has always preferred "discipline to free thinking, organization to originality . . . customs to books." [6] Compared with Harvard, there is no disputing Samuel Eliot Morison's statement that from the first Yale was "more cautious and less adventurous than her ancient

4. A classic example of this interpretation is Charles E. Cunningham, *Timothy Dwight, 1752-1817, a Biography* (N. Y., 1942). A close second is Moses Coit Tyler, *Three Men of Letters* (N. Y., 1895).

5. *Yale and the Ministry,* 1.

6. Pierson, *Yale College, an Educational History, 1871-1921* (New Haven, 1952), 5.

rival." [7] In 1892, Harvard's George Santayana, a most perspicacious observer, visited the New Haven school and later made this comparison: "Yale is in many respects what Harvard used to be. It has maintained the traditions of a New England college more faithfully. Anyone visiting the two colleges would think Yale by far the older institution. The past of America makes itself felt there in many subtle ways: there is a kind of colonial self-reliance, and simplicity of aim, a touch of non-conformist separation from the great ideas and movements of the world." [8] Since Santayana's time, Yale has undergone many changes which have brought the university into the forefront of American institutions of learning. It has succumbed to the movement of the times. Yet there remains a touch of that deference to authority and tradition which became Yale's custom under the inflexible rule of Thomas Clap.

Beyond college walls or even the boundaries of the colony, Clap exerted an influence upon American development that has not hitherto been recognized. It is linked with the mere fact that some seven hundred and fifty young men took B.A. degrees during his administration. Many of them became figures of weight and influence in the Revolutionary and Constitutional periods. Selecting at random, one could cite such men of high talents as William Samuel Johnson, Pelatiah Webster, Silas Deane, Manasseh Cutler, Oliver Wolcott, Lewis Morris, Lyman Hall, John Morin Scott, Samuel Seabury, and William Smith. Of course, not all Yale graduates achieved national prominence. The greater number remained in the towns and hamlets of New England (and elsewhere), performing less dramatic, but essential, professional services. A breakdown of the occupations of some 700 graduates in the period 1741-65 shows that 280 entered the ministry; 75 became lawyers; 79 became medical practitioners; 15 became educators; and 24 followed political careers.[9] Yale's graduates were important figures on the local and national scene.

The inevitable question arises: What, if any, was the influence of

7. *Three Centuries of Harvard,* 50.
8. Santayana, "A Glimpse of Yale," *Harvard Monthly,* 15 (1892), 94; quoted in Pierson, *Yale College, an Educational History, 1871-1921,* 7.
9. Burritt, "Professional Distribution of College and University Graduates," U. S. Bureau of Education, *Bulletin,* No. 19, 83.

President Clap on these men of Yale? The historian should be the first to acknowledge that the causes and conditions that unite to form the ethical and intellectual character of a human being are many, diverse, and imperceptibly subtle in their workings. Yet, if their schooling had any effect upon Yale's students, they could hardly have escaped Clap's influence. Within the college, he was a massive personality, a monolithic power, a Leviathan; he dominated the intellectual life not only of the academic community but of the colony as well. Clap carried the college with him. Tutors came and went with predictable regularity, generally remaining for a period of three to four years. Clap was at his post for over a quarter of a century! Little wonder that, in his generation, his name became synonymous with Yale and that he came to regard the college as his personal possession. In the spirit of Louis XIV, Clap would have been fully justified in proclaiming, "Le collège, c'est moi!"

In his joint capacity of disciplinarian and teacher, he exercised a direct influence, planting at every turn his religious and social beliefs, his moral and social conservatism, into the pliable minds of youth. No student who graduated escaped Clap's own course in moral philosophy, which was broad in sweep and flexible in content, and admirably adapted to propagate whatever information or judgments Clap wished to transmit. The record suggests that the president communicated an abundance of both. "Clapism," as Chauncey Whittelsey once characterized the content of a set of commencement theses,[10] apparently made an indelible impression upon the minds of many students. Injected into the men sent forth from Yale, Clap's Puritan religious and social values sifted down through the strata of colonial society. Thus Clap helped to form the spiritual life of America and to shape the character of American civilization.

To the student of intellectual history, Clap is of special interest. His idea-system harmoniously combined the mutually antagonistic elements of Christian supernaturalism and the scientific rationalism of the Enlightenment. In this aspect, he exhibits the steady transformation of seventeenth-century Puritanism into nineteenth-

10. Dexter, ed., *Stiles's Itineraries*, 585.

century Unitarianism.[11] By his acceptance of science and the values implicit in the scientific traditions of the "new philosophy," he demonstrated his intellectual kinship with the Enlightenment. In scientific thought, he was a child of the new age, as progressive and as up-to-date as Franklin, Jefferson, or any other colonial of rationalistic, humanistic bent.

But the religious instinct remained at the center of his personality. Thus he insisted with Olympian intransigence upon the retention of a moribund theological system. If the type of Puritanism he espoused deviated sharply in some areas from that championed by his forefathers, its fundamental doctrinal substance was still drawn from the Calvinistic fount, was still suffused with the dogma of human depravity and the misery of mortal life. In embracing these doctrines, Clap was looking backwards. New Englanders were less deeply absorbed in those problems of eternal destiny which had been the staple of existence for their fathers. Such propositions no longer squared with common experiences. They had lost their former sense of immediacy, and no longer offered a sense of direction and a meaningful relevance to human life. Failing to maintain a social sanction, they dropped from their position of primacy in New England religious life.

Some Puritan clerics recognized the dissymmetry of idea and condition and moved freely with the flow of religious rationalism —but not so in the case of Clap. He remained an apostle of philosophical gloom. This was the "fatal flaw." Resolutely attached to ancestral religious institutions, inherently suspicious of innovation, unalterably convinced that rationalism would sweep his venerated way of life into the rapids of irreligion and social anarchy, the president doggedly stood fast on the solid deck of old values. With concentrated passion, he fought for the preservation of the "tried and true." It was inevitable that this last member of the Puritan old guard would be engulfed by the tide of change. In failing to recognize that New England had moved into a new

11. This is not to suggest that the Puritan movement as a whole metamorphosed into Unitarianism. I refer only to the segment that exalted reason and the rational approach to religion as opposed to evangelical fervor. Charles Chauncy, Jonathan Mayhew, and Ebenezer Gay were the chief lights of the movement. Interestingly, Clap was closely akin to them in general intellectual orientation, but he was far more conservative in ecclesiastical matters.

dimension of religious experience, in refusing to adjust his religious ideology to the new value patterns of the Enlightenment, he laid the basis for his eventual downfall. In short, he became obsolete.

If intellectual myopia was the underlying cause of his fall from power, the rebellious student body was the direct cause. In the final analysis, it was the raised arm of student violence that toppled Clap. The question logically follows: Why was his administration plagued with such extraordinarily severe student turmoil? While the disruptive events of the Stamp Act crisis and the prodding efforts of Benjamin Gale and confreres undeniably helped to stir up the passion of rebellion among the youth, a more fundamental provocation for disorder was Clap's antiquated disciplinary method. Heir of a medieval tradition of authoritarianism, he ruled by force and compulsion. He was sadly lacking in comprehension of the psychology of youth. He had no vital sympathy for youth, showed no compassion for the weaknesses of immaturity, made little concession to human frailty. Furthermore, he failed to see that it is sometimes necessary and expedient to wear the velvet glove over the iron hand of authority. Following the educational traditions of the past, he insisted upon treating "boys as being men." [12] He refused to see any differences in temperament between a lad of fifteen and a sage of fifty. Through experience he ruefully learned that his theory of discipline was antiquated; he also learned that boys of fourteen to seventeen years of age, although fuzzy-cheeked, were equally as capable as men of upending constituted authority by violent means.

One may well believe that Clap regarded his repudiation by the students as the bitterest pill of all. To their educational well-being, to their personal service, he had dedicated the greater part of his professional career and lavished his prodigious energies. The religious programs and personal deeds which had earned for him the enmity of the general public—as well as the historical reputation of chief denominational tyrant of colonial Connecticut—were designed for their benefit. He considered no sacrifice too great when the spiritual and educational welfare of the students was at

12. Quoted in William B. Sprague, *Annals of the American Pulpit* (N. Y., 1859), I, 349.

issue. He gave his best to them. The students reciprocated with brickbats, cattle horns, and the clenched fist. With a few isolated exceptions,[13] they applauded his deposal, feeling no remorse for the spiritual agony it presumably occasioned in their former head. The lad who scribbled in the margin of a book, "Tomme Clap you Fool do not think that I mind your Finis," expressed the general sentiment of the student body. And these few words best express the personal tragedy of Thomas Clap.

13. David McClure, who had been intimidated into signing the petition calling for Clap's ouster, was one who felt remorseful. He wrote in later years: "For myself, I was afterwards sorry, for he had been *particularly* attentive to my Class and to me and one another, in particular, as he condescended to attend to us to hear an *extra* recitation about 3 evenings in the week at his own house." *Diary of David McClure,* notes by Dexter, 9.

BIBLIOGRAPHICAL NOTE

"Go east, young man" was the first directive I received upon undertaking the study of Thomas Clap at the University of Washington. The logical place to initiate research on a Yale figure is the Sterling Memorial Library, Yale University, where are to be found many of the basic source materials upon which this study rests. The single most important source is the collection of Clap manuscripts, which include such items as his Memoirs, an assortment of administrative documents, memoranda, personal correspondence, sermon note books, and manuscript copies of published writings. The major limitation of this material is the scarcity of private correspondence. A plentiful supply of materials exists relative to the history of Yale during his term of office, and such official papers and published pamphlets are extremely useful; they enable us to trace his career and to portray his character as it emerges in action. But they do not afford the revealing insights of personal communication, for lack of which the inner life of Thomas Clap seems destined to remain unrevealed.

Aside from the Clap Papers, the Yale Library has a considerable body of contemporary manuscripts. The Ezra Stiles Papers, for example, are an invaluable source, for they contain correspondence between Stiles and virtually every prominent figure associated directly or indirectly with the college during Clap's administration. The Yale Library also has these vital resources: excellent runs of the two most important colonial newspapers in Connecticut, the *Connecticut Courant* (Hartford) and the *Connecticut Gazette* (New Haven); commencement sheets and master's *quaestiones;* student commonplace books and assorted manuscripts; the printed pamphlets of Benjamin Gale, John Graham, Thomas Darling, William Hart, *et al.,* which bear upon the religious controversies of the period; Clap's pamphlets, and the manuscript and printed copies of his *Annals of Yale;* the records of the Judgments and Acts of the President and Tutors of Yale College; standard secondary accounts of Yale, New Haven, and Connecticut; and the remarkable collection of rare books in the exhibition Library of 1742. Another indispensable source is the Yale Corporation Records, a typescript of which is readily available at the office of the Secretary of the University.

The Connecticut State Library in Hartford also contains some pertinent materials. The well-organized archival records pertaining to colonial Connecticut ecclesiastical affairs and the General Assembly's relationship with Yale College are a rich source and a delight to the researcher. The State Library has excellent newspaper resources plus an additional item of great value: an index to the *Connecticut Courant.* Other materials to be found there include the original records of the Windham First Church and the New Haven First Church, the probate record of Clap's estate, Connecticut election sermons, and an outstanding collection of Connecticut county histories.

A number of other depositories have papers relative to the field of this study, but the material is rather fragmentary. The Harvard Archives has Tutor Henry Flynt's sermons, President John Leverett's Diary and a few other items, but one searches in vain for documents pertaining to Clap's collegiate career. Scattered among the many other libraries in Boston is a smattering of Clap manuscripts and allied materials, but it is not of sufficient quality or quantity to excite the researcher. In the Essex Institute Library at Salem there are some helpful John Cleaveland documents and a manuscript on science written by Manasseh Cutler while he was a student under Clap. Among the Eleazar Wheelock Papers at Dartmouth College, there are some revealing letters relating to

Yale during the Great Awakening. The New-York Historical Society has some of the Clap-Johnson correspondence which revolves around the Anglican question at Yale. The Historical Society of Pennsylvania has, in its incomparable Gratz Collection, a handful of important Clap letters. The Library of Congress houses Jared Ingersoll's lengthy manuscript recounting the effect of the Great Awakening upon Connecticut.

Depositories in Great Britain are likewise conspicuously lacking in sizable bodies of Clap papers, notwithstanding the fact that he corresponded with British scientists. The Royal Society in London has a few of Clap's scientific communications, and the Royal Society of Arts Library and the Congregational Library, also in London, own additional pieces of correspondence. While the Library for the Society for the Propagation of the Gospel in Foreign Parts has no Clap documents, as such, it does have a considerable amount of valuable primary materials in the form of reports drawn up by S.P.G. missionaries of the New Haven area. These reports are filled with allusions to Clap, and, at times, they make direct mention of him.

Any sizable library will have most, if not all, of the secondary works that were essential for this study. Among serials, the *Papers* of the New Haven Colony Historical Society (New Haven, 1865-1918), the *Collections* of the Connecticut Historical Society (Hartford, 1860-1932), the *Connecticut Magazine,* and the *Publications* of the Tercentenary Commission of Connecticut are studded with vital information, whether in the form of documents or articles. Of secondary value are the *Collections* (Boston, 1792——) and *Proceedings* (Boston, 1879——) of the Massachusetts Historical Society and the *Publications* of the Colonial Society of Massachusetts (Boston, 1895——). A number of articles and documents in the *William and Mary Quarterly* (3d Ser., Williamsburg, Va., 1944——) and the *Proceedings* of the American Antiquarian Society (Worcester, Mass., 1843——) bear upon this study, either directly or indirectly.

A list of pertinent secondary works would resemble a guide to the historical literature of the period. I shall therefore cite only key works. On Puritanism, there are Perry Miller's numerous books; a highly recommended single volume is Edmund S. Morgan's *The*

Puritan Family (Boston, 1956). There are four other monographs
on religious developments worthy of mention: Edwin Gaustad,
The Great Awakening in New England (N. Y., 1957); Conrad
Wright, *The Beginnings of Unitarianism in America* (Boston,
1955); Herbert Morais, *Deism in Eighteenth Century America*
(N. Y., 1960); Roland N. Stromberg, *Religious Liberalism in
Eighteenth-Century England* (London, 1954).

While books on colonial science are not plentiful, there are a
few helpful works: Brooke Hindle, *The Pursuit of Science in
Revolutionary America, 1735-1789* (Chapel Hill, 1956); I. Bernard
Cohen, *Some Early Tools of American Science . . .* (Cambridge,
Mass., 1950); Whitfield J. Bell, Jr., *Early American Science: Needs
and Opportunities for Study* (Williamsburg, Va., 1955); Louis
McKeehan, *Yale Science, The First Hundred Years, 1701-1801*
(N. Y., 1947); Theodore Hornberger, *Scientific Thought in Ameri-
can Colleges, 1638-1800* (Austin, Texas, 1945). Bell's study is
especially significant because of its excellent bibliographical data.

Most of the colonial colleges have had their histories recounted
in comprehensive fashion. I have used the standard histories of
King's College, the College of Philadelphia, and the College of
New Jersey. Although many have written of Harvard's illustrious
history, Samuel E. Morison's works are pre-eminent. His *Three
Centuries of Harvard, 1636-1936* (Cambridge, Mass., 1937) and his
two-volume *Harvard College in the Seventeenth Century* (Cambridge, Mass., 1937) provide a partial explanation for his designation as *the* "historian of Harvard." Unfortunately, there is no
equivalent study of Yale. Edwin Oviatt's *The Beginnings of Yale,
1701-1726* (New Haven, 1916) is rich in detail but reverential in
tone, limited in scope, and littered with stylistic defects. Ebenezer
Baldwin's *Annals of Yale College . . .* (2d ed., New Haven, 1838),
is distinctly second-rate.

I should like to call special attention to the writings of Clifford K. Shipton and Franklin B. Dexter. Shipton's *Biographical
Sketches of Those Who Have Attended Harvard College . . .*
(Cambridge, Mass., 1933——), which is a continuation of John
L. Sibley's pioneer effort, is an impressive body of scholarship and
was of inestimable value for this study. It is truly a *vade mecum*
of New England intellectual history. Dexter's six-volume *Bio-*

graphical Sketches of the Graduates of Yale College ... (N. Y., 1885-1912) does not have the analytical depth of Shipton's volumes but is still an essential reference tool; throughout the course of this study, it stood close at hand, especially Volumes I and II. Of almost equal value were Dexter's two editorial works on the Ezra Stiles Papers: *Extracts From the Itineraries and Other Miscellanies of Ezra Stiles* (New Haven, 1916) and *The Literary Diary of Ezra Stiles,* 3 vols. (N. Y., 1901). Nor should one slight Dexter's articles in historical journals. For Yale's early history, Dexter's writings are as close an approximation as Yale has to those of Harvard's Morison.

This Book

was composed by Van Rees Book Composition Company
and printed by Van Rees Press, New York.
The text type is 11 point Baskerville, leaded 2 points.
Binding was by Van Rees Book Binding Corporation.
The designer was Richard Stinely.